Nicholas Tims

with Herbert Puchta and Jeff Stranks

English in Mind

* Teacher's Book 3

CAMBRIDGE
UNIVERSITY PRESS

CAMBRIDGE UNIVERSITY PRESS
Cambridge, New York, Melbourne, Madrid, Cape Town, Singapore,
São Paulo, Delhi, Dubai, Tokyo

Cambridge University Press
The Edinburgh Building, Cambridge CB2 8RU, UK

www.cambridge.org
Information on this title: www.cambridge.org/9780521750660

First published 2005
5th printing 2009

Printed in the United Kingdom at the University Press, Cambridge

A catalogue record for this publication is available from the British Library

ISBN 978-0-521-75066-0 Teacher's Book
ISBN 978-0-521-75064-6 Student's Book
ISBN 978-0-521-75065-3 Workbook with CD (audio) / CD-ROM (Windows, Mac)
ISBN 978-0-521-75067-7 Teacher's Resource Pack
ISBN 978-0-521-75068-4 Class cassettes
ISBN 978-0-521-54506-8 Class CDs (audio)

Contents

Teacher's notes and keys

Unit	Grammar	Vocabulary	Pronunciation
Module 1 — People and animals			
1 Best of British	Present simple/continuous review. Present perfect simple review.	Giving statistics & making generalisations. Making new friends.	Schwa /ə/ in prepositions & articles.
2 Ways of talking	Past simple vs. present perfect simple.	Body language. *say* & *tell*. Phrasal verbs with *up*. Everyday English.	Sentence stress: rhythm questions.
3 A true friend	Past simple/continuous review. Time conjunctions. Past simple vs. past perfect simple.	Friends & enemies.	Linking sounds.
4 A working life	Present perfect simple/ continuous review. *had better / should / ought to*	Jobs & work.	/ɔː/ (sh*or*t).
Module 1 Check your progress			
5 Travel	Future review.	Travel. Movement.	/gənə/ (*going to*).
6 Live forever!	Future predictions. First conditional review, *if & unless*. Time conjunctions.	Verbs with prepositions. Phrasal verbs with *into*. Everyday English.	Weak & strong forms of prepositions.
7 Campaigning for survival	Present/Past passive review. Present perfect & future passive. Causative *have*.	*make* & *do*.	Stress pattern in *have something done*.
8 Reality TV	*make, let, be allowed to*. Modal verbs of obligation, prohibition & permission.	Television. Extreme adjectives & modifiers. Collocations with *on*.	/aʊ/ (all*ow*ed).
Module 2 Check your progress			
9 Good and evil	Verbs + gerunds/infinitives. Verbs with gerund & infinitive.	Noun suffixes. Belonging to a group.	Stress in nouns, adjectiv & verbs.
10 Getting into trouble	Second conditional review. First conditional vs. second conditional. *wish / if only* + past simple.	Crime. Phrasal verbs with *down*. Everyday English.	*I wish ... & if only ...*
11 Two sides to every story	Linkers of contrast. Modal verbs for deduction in the present.	Problems.	/əʊ/ (th*ough*).
12 Mysterious places	Indirect questions. Modal verbs for deduction in the past.	Phrasal verbs. Expressions with *be* + preposition.	*have* in *must have / might have / can't have couldn't have*.
Module 3 Check your progress			
13 Love	Reported statements review. Reported questions review. Reporting verbs.	Appearance. Personality. Relationships.	Intonation in reported questions.
14 Anger	Third conditional review. *wish / if only* + past perfect simple. *should / shouldn't have done*.	Anger. Everyday English.	*should / shouldn't have*
15 Fear	Defining & non-defining relative clauses. Articles.	Adjectives with prefixes. Phrasal verbs with *sit*.	Pausing in non-defining relative clauses.
16 Happiness	*be used to* + gerund vs. *used to* + infinitive. Grammar of phrasal verbs.	*feel*. Expressions with prepositions.	Stress in phrasal verbs.
Module 4 Check your progress			

Module 1 — People and animals

Module 2 — Survival

Module 3 — Right and wrong

Module 4 — Emotions

Projects ● Pronunciation ● Speaking: additional material ● Irregular verbs and phonetic chart ● Wordlist

Speaking & functions	Listening	Reading	Writing
How you spend your money. Presenting statistics. Describing recently completed or unfinished actions. Cultural influences.	Statistics about teenagers in Britain. Interviews with foreign visitors in Britain.	Quiz about British teenagers. Interview with a foreign student. Culture: Cultural Influences.	Report about the lifestyle of your family and friends.
Problems of being deaf. Talking about recently completed actions. Body language. Exchanging information.	Information on communicating with deaf people. Interview about body language.	Sharing silence. Story: Meeting up again.	Describing a friendship.
Telling a story. Talking about friendship. Discussion: a love story.	Ghost story.	Ghost story. Questionnaire: Are you a loyal friend? Fiction: Staying Together.	Rewriting a short story about a relationship.
Your future job. Describing recently completed / unfinished actions. A job interview.	Dialogue about a dream job. A job interview. Song: So You Want to Be a Rock 'n' Roll Star.	Future Jobs.	Job application letter.
Sailing alone. Space tourism. Talking about travel. Solo journeys.	Interview with Ellen MacArthur.	Britain's Solo Sailor. Space Tourists. Culture: Going it Alone.	Email about a trip.
Micro-chips in your brain. Discussing causes of stress.	Interviews about the secrets of long life.	Intelligent Machines. Story: Ben calls Caroline.	A composition about life in the future.
Organisations which help tribal people. Talking about life in the future. Crime stories.	Speeches about town development.	Tribes in Danger. Fiction: But Was it Murder?	Letter to a newspaper about plans to build a new hotel.
Reality TV. Talking about rules in your home.	Interview about reality TV. Song: Somebody's Watching Me.	Reality TV.	Magazine article about a new TV show.
Computer games. Exchanging information. Graffiti.	Dialogue about a computer game.	Introductions of classic novels. Culture: The Writing's on the Wall.	Discursive composition: advantages & disadvantages.
Discussing getting into trouble. Describing hypothetical situations. Discussing crime. Things you wish could be different.	Dialogue about doing something wrong. Interviews about teenage crime.	Questionnaire: Are You Really Honest? Story: A problem for Matt.	Formal letter of opinion.
Discussing the making of the film The Beach. Discussing conspiracy theories. Hypnotism.	Radio programme about the first moon landing.	The making of the film The Beach. Fiction: The Real Aunt Molly.	Discursive composition: giving your opinion.
Mysterious places. Indirect questions. Speculating about Seahenge.	Interview about Seahenge. Song: The Curse of the Mummy's Tomb.	No One Knows Why They're There.	Narrative: setting a scene.
Giving & receiving presents. Describing someone. Weddings in your country.	Description of the film The English Patient.	The Gift of the Magi. Culture: Wedding Ceremonies.	Description of a person.
Something you regret doing. Talking about things that make you angry.	Dialogues about getting angry.	Regrets.com. Story: Working things out.	Narrative.
Discussing scary films. A ghost story.	Description of the film The Blair Witch Project.	The Fear in All of Us. Fiction: The Lady in White.	Film review.
The 'flow' of happiness. Talking about your idea of happiness.	Dialogues about being happy. Song: Thank You.	The 'Flow' of Happiness.	Poem.

Introduction

'If you can teach teenagers, you can teach anyone.' Michael Grinder

Teaching teenagers is an interesting and challenging task. A group of adolescents can be highly motivated, cooperative and fun to teach on one day, and the next day the whole group or individual students might turn out to be truly 'difficult' – the teacher might, for example, be faced with discipline problems, disruptive or provocative behaviour, a lack of motivation, or unwillingness on the students' part to do homework assigned to them.

The roots of these problems frequently lie in the fact that adolescents are going through a period of significant change in their lives. The key challenge in the transition period between being a child and becoming an adult is the adolescent's struggle for identity – a process that requires the development of a distinct sense of who they are. A consequence of this process is that adolescents can feel threatened, and at the same time experience overwhelming emotions. They frequently try to compensate for the perceived threats with extremely rude behaviour, and try to 'hide' their emotions behind a wall of extreme outward conformity. The more individual students manage to look, talk, act and behave like the other members of their peer group, the less threatened and insecure they feel.

Insights into the causes underlying the problems might help us to understand better the complex situation our students are in. However, such insights do not automatically lead to more success in teaching. We need to react to the challenges in a professional way.[1] This includes the need to:

* select content and organise the students' learning according to their psychological needs;
* create a positive learning atmosphere;
* cater for differences in students' learning styles and intelligences, and facilitate the development of our students' study skills.

English in Mind has been written taking all these points into account. They have significantly influenced the choice of texts, artwork and design, the structure of the units, the typology of exercises, and the means by which students' study skills are facilitated and extended.

The importance of the content for success

There are a number of reasons why the choice of the right content has a crucial influence over success or failure in the teaching of adolescents. Teachers frequently observe that teenagers are reluctant to 'talk about themselves'. This has to do with the adolescents' need for psychological security. Consequently, the 'further away' from their own world the content of the teaching is, the more motivating and stimulating it will be for the students. The preference for psychologically remote content goes hand in hand with a fascination with extremes and realistic details. Furthermore, students love identifying with heroes and heroines, because these idols are perceived to embody the qualities needed in order to survive in a threatening world: qualities such as courage, genius, creativity and love. In the foreign language class, students can become fascinated with stories about heroes and heroines to which they can ascribe such qualities. *English in Mind* treats students as young adults, offering them a range of interesting topics and a balance between educational value and teenage interest and fun.

As Kieran Egan[2] stresses, learning in the adolescent classroom can be successfully organised by starting with something far from the students' experience, but also connected to it by some quality with which they can associate. This process of starting far from the students makes it easier for them to become interested in the topic, and also enables the teacher finally to relate the content to the students' own world.

A positive learning atmosphere

The creation of a positive learning atmosphere largely depends on the rapport between teacher and students, and the one which students have among themselves. It requires the teacher to be a genuine, empathetic listener, and to have a number of other psychological skills. *English in Mind* supports the teacher's task of creating positive learning experiences through: clear tasks; a large number of carefully designed exercises; regular opportunities for the students to check their own work; and a learning process designed to guarantee that the students will learn to express themselves both in speaking and in writing.

Learning styles and multiple intelligences

There is significant evidence that students will be better motivated, and learn more successfully, if differences in learning styles and intelligences are taken into account in the teaching–learning process.[3] The development of a number of activities in *English in Mind* has been

---

[1] An excellent analysis of teenage development and consequences for our teaching in general can be found in Kieran Egan: *Romantic Understanding*, Routledge and Kegan Paul, New York and London, 1990. This book has had a significant influence on the thinking behind *English in Mind*, and the development of the concept of the course.

[2] Ibid.

[3] See for example Eric Jensen: *Brain-Based Learning and Teaching*, Turning Point Publishing, Del Mar, CA, USA, 1995, on learning styles. An overview of the theory of multiple intelligences can be found in Howard Gardner: *Multiple Intelligences: The Theory in Practice*, Basic Books, New York, 1993.

influenced by such insights, and students find frequent study tips that show them how they can better utilise their own resources.[4]

The methodology used in *English in Mind*

Skills: *English in Mind* uses a communicative, multi-skills approach to develop the students' foreign language abilities in an interesting and motivational way. A wide range of interesting text types is used to present authentic use of language, including magazine and newspaper clippings, interviews, narratives, songs and engaging photo stories.

Grammar: *English in Mind* is based on a strong grammatical syllabus and takes into account students' mixed abilities by dealing with grammar in a carefully graded way, and offering additional teaching support (see below).

Vocabulary: *English in Mind* offers a systematic vocabulary syllabus, including important lexical chunks for conversation.

Culture: *English in Mind* gives students insights into a number of important cross-cultural and intercultural themes. Significant cultural features of English-speaking countries are presented, and students are involved in actively reflecting on the similarities and differences between other cultures and their own.

Consolidation: Four 'Check your progress' revision units per level will give teachers a clear picture of their students' progress and make students aware of what they have learned. Each revision unit is also accompanied by a project which gives students the opportunity to use new language in a less controlled context and allows for learner independence.

Teacher support: *English in Mind* is clearly structured and easy to teach. The Teacher's Book offers step-by-step lesson notes, background information on content, culture and language, additional teaching ideas, the tapescripts and answers. The accompanying Teacher's Resource Pack contains photocopiable materials for further practice and extra lessons, taking into consideration the needs of mixed-ability groups by providing extra material for fast finishers or students who need more support, as well as formal tests.

Student support: *English in Mind* offers systematic support to students through: Skills tips; classroom language; guidance in units to help with the development of classroom discourse and the students' writing; a wordlist including phonetic transcriptions; list of irregular verbs and phonetics (at the back of the Student's Book); and a Grammar reference (at the back of the Workbook).

English in Mind: components

Each level of the *English in Mind* series contains the following components:

- Student's Book
- Class Audio CDs or Class Cassettes
- Workbook with accompanying Audio CD / CD-ROM
- Teacher's Book
- Teacher's Resource Pack
- Website resources

The Student's Book

Modular structure: The *English in Mind* Student's Books are organised on a modular basis – each contains four modules of four units per module. The modules have broad themes and are organised as follows: a) a two-page module opener; b) four units of six pages each; c) a two-page Check your progress section.

Module openers are two pages which allow teachers to 'set the scene' for their students, concerning both the informational content and the language content of what is to come in the module itself. This helps both to motivate the students and to provide the important 'signposting' which allows them to see where their learning is going next. The pages contain: a) a visual task in which students match topics to a selection of photographs taken from the coming units; b) a list of skills learning objectives for the module; c) a short matching task which previews the main grammar content of the coming module; and d) a simple vocabulary task, again previewing the coming content.

The **units** have the following basic structure, although with occasional minor variations depending on the flow of an individual unit:

- an opening **reading** text
- a **grammar** page, often including pronunciation
- two pages of **vocabulary** and **skills** work
- either a **Culture in mind** text, a **photo story**, a **Fiction in mind** text or a **song** followed by **writing skills** work.

The **reading** texts aim to engage and motivate the students with interesting and relevant content, and to provide contextualised examples of target grammar and lexis. The texts have 'lead-in' tasks and are followed by comprehension tasks of various kinds. All the opening texts are also recorded on the Class Audio CD/Cassette, which allows teachers to follow the initial reading with a 'read and listen' phase, giving the students the invaluable opportunity of connecting the written word with the spoken version, which is especially useful for auditory learners. Alternatively, with stronger classes, teachers may decide to do one of the exercises as a listening task, with books closed.

---

[4] See Marion Williams and Robert L. Burden: *Psychology for Language Teachers*, Cambridge University Press, 1997 (pp. 143–162), on how the learner deals with the process of learning.

Grammar follows the initial reading. The emphasis is on active involvement in the learning process. Examples from the texts are isolated and used as a basis for tasks which focus on both concept and form of the target grammar area. Students are encouraged to find other examples and work out rules for themselves. Occasionally there are also Look boxes, which highlight an important connected issue concerning the grammar area; for example, in Unit 3, work on the present perfect has a Look box reminding students that *know* is not normally used in the continuous form. This is followed by a number of graded exercises, both receptive and productive, which allow students to begin to employ the target language in different contexts and to produce realistic language. Next, there is usually a speaking activity, aiming at further personalisation of the language.

Each unit has at least one **Vocabulary** section, with specific word-fields. Again, examples from the initial text are focused on, and a lexical set is developed, with exercises for students to put the vocabulary into use. Vocabulary is frequently recycled in later texts in the unit (e.g. photo stories or Culture in mind texts), and also in later units.

Pronunciation is included in every unit. There are exercises on common phoneme problems such as /əʊ/ in *though*, as well as aspects of stress (within words, and across sentences) and elision.

Language skills are present in every unit. There is always at least one **listening skills** activity, with listening texts of various genres; at least one (but usually several) **speaking skills** activity for fluency development; **reading skills** are taught through the opening texts and also later texts in some units, as well as the Culture in mind and Fiction in mind sections. There is always a **writing skills** task, at the end of each unit.

The final two pages of each unit have either a **Culture in mind** text, a **photo story**, a **Fiction in mind** text or a **song**. The **Culture in mind** texts are reading texts which provide further reading practice, and an opportunity for students to develop their knowledge and understanding of the world at large and in particular the English-speaking world. They include a wide variety of stimulating topics, for example, the influence of other cultures in Britain, graffiti and hip-hop culture and weddings in different British cultures. The **photo stories** are conversations between teenagers in everyday situations, allowing students to read and listen for interest and also to experience the use of common everyday language expressions. These **Everyday English** expressions are worked on in exercises following the dialogue. The **Fiction in mind** texts are extracts from the Cambridge Readers series which provide further reading practice. The text is also recorded on the Workbook CD/CDRom for extra listening practice.

The final activity in each unit is a **writing skills** task. These are an opportunity for students to further their control of language and to experiment in the production of texts in a variety of genres (e.g. letters, emails, postcards).

There are model texts for the students to aid their own writing, and exercises providing guidance in terms of content and organisation. Through the completion of the writing tasks, students, if they wish, can also build up a bank of materials, or 'portfolio', during their period of learning: this can be very useful to them as the source of a sense of clear progress and as a means of self-assessment. A 'portfolio' of work can also be shown to other people (exam bodies, parents, even future employers) as evidence of achievement in language learning. Many of the writing tasks also provide useful and relevant practice for examinations such as Cambridge ESOL PET or Trinity Integrated Skills Examinations.

When a module of four units closes, the module ends with a two-page **Check your progress** section. Here the teacher will find exercises in the Grammar and Vocabulary that were presented in the module. The purpose of these (as opposed to the more formal tests offered in the Teacher's Resource Pack) is for teachers and students alike to check quickly the learning and progress made during the module just covered; they can be done in class or at home. Every exercise has a marking scheme, and students can use the marks they gain to do some simple self-assessment of their progress (a light 'task' is offered for this).

Beyond the modules and units themselves, *English in Mind* offers at the end of the Student's Book a further set of materials for teachers and students. These consist of:

- **Projects**: activities (one per module) which students can do in pairs or groups (or even individually if desired), for students to put the language they have so far learned into practical and enjoyable use. They are especially useful for mixed-ability classes as they allow students to work at their own pace. The projects produced could also be part of the 'portfolio' of material mentioned earlier.
- An **irregular verb list** for students to refer to when they need.
- A listing of **phonetic symbols**, again for student reference.
- A **wordlist** with the core lexis of the Student's Book, with phonetic transcriptions. This is organised by unit, and within each unit heading there are the major word-fields, divided into parts of speech (verbs, nouns, adjectives, etc.). The wordlists are a feature that teachers can use in classrooms, for example, to develop students' reference skills or to indicate ways in which they themselves might organise vocabulary notebooks, and by students at home, as a useful reference and also to prepare for tests or progress checks.

The Workbook

The Workbook is a resource for both teachers and students, providing further practice in the language and skills covered in the Student's Book. It is organised unit by unit, following the Student's Book. Each Workbook unit has six pages, and the following contents:

Remember and check: this initial exercise encourages students to remember the content of the initial reading text in the Student's Book unit.

Exercises: an extensive range of supporting exercises in the grammatical, lexical and phonological areas of the Student's Book unit, following the progression of the unit, so that teachers can use the exercises either during or at the end of the Student's Book unit.

Everyday English and **Culture in mind**: extra exercises on these sections in the units corresponding to the Student's Book.

Skills in mind page: these pages contain a separate skills development syllabus, which normally focuses on two main skill areas in each unit. There is also a skill tip relating to the main skill area, which the students can immediately put into action when doing the skills task(s).

Unit check page: this is a one-page check of knowledge of the key language of the unit, integrating both grammar and vocabulary in the three exercise types. The exercise types are: a) a cloze text to be completed using items given in a box; b) a sentence-level multiple choice exercise; c) a guided error-correction exercise.

At the end of the Workbook, there is a **Grammar reference** section. Here, there are explanations of the main grammar topics of each unit, with examples. It can be used for reference by students at home, or the teacher might wish to refer to it in class if the students appreciate grammatical explanations.

The Workbook includes an **Audio CD / CD-ROM**, which contains both the listening material for the Workbook (listening texts and pronunciation exercises) and a CD-ROM element, containing definitions for the wordlist items with a spoken model for each one. A range of carefully graded grammar and vocabulary exercises provide further practice of language presented in each module.

The Teacher's Book

The Teacher's Book contains:

- clear, simple, practical **teaching notes** on each unit and how to implement the exercises as effectively as possible
- complete **tapescripts** for all listening and pronunciation activities
- complete **answers** to all exercises (grammar, vocabulary, comprehension questions, etc.)
- **optional activities** for stronger or weaker classes, to facilitate the use of the material in mixed-ability classes
- **background information** relating to the content (where appropriate) of reading texts and Culture in mind pages

- **language notes** relating to grammatical areas, to assist less-experienced teachers who might have concerns about the target language and how it operates (these can also be used to refer to the Workbook Grammar reference section)
- a complete **answer key** and **tapescripts** for the Workbook.

The Teacher's Resource Pack

This extra component, spiral bound for easy photocopying, contains the following photocopiable resources:

- an **entry test**, which can be used for diagnostic testing or also used for remedial work
- **module tests** containing separate sections for: Grammar, Vocabulary, Everyday English, Reading, Listening (the recordings for which are on the Class Audio Cassettes/CDs), Speaking and Writing. A key for the tests is also provided
- **photocopiable communicative activities**: one page for each unit, reflecting the core grammar and/or vocabulary of the unit
- **photocopiable extra grammar exercises**: one page of four exercises for each unit, reflecting the key grammar areas of the unit
- **teaching notes** for the above.

Web resources

In addition to information about the series, the *English in Mind* website contains downloadable pages of further activities and exercises for students, as well as other resources. It can be found at this part of the Cambridge University Press website:

www.cambridge.org/elt/englishinmind

Module 1
People and animals

YOU WILL LEARN ABOUT ...

Ask students to look at the pictures on the page. Ask students to read through the topics in the box and check that they understand each item. You can ask them the following questions, in L1 if appropriate:

1 *Who do you think the girls are?*
2 *Which city are the people in?*
3 *Do you have any pets?*
4 *What do you think is happening?*
5 *What do you do to show someone you are listening to them?*
6 *What is the girl on the left doing?*

In pairs or small groups students discuss which topic area they think each picture matches. Check answers.

Answers
1 Manufactured rock bands
2 Today's multicultural Britain
3 Animal friendship
4 Choosing a career
5 Sign language and body language
6 Teenage life in Britain

YOU WILL LEARN HOW TO ...

Use grammar

Students read through the grammar points and the examples. Go through the first item with students as an example. In pairs, students now match the grammar items in their book. Check answers.

Answers
Present simple vs. present continuous: People are using the Internet more and more but I prefer books.
Past simple vs. present perfect simple: My life has changed since I met him.
Present perfect simple vs. present perfect continuous: My friend has decided to study IT but I've been thinking about engineering.
Time expressions: I had dinner as soon as I got home.
Past simple vs. past perfect simple: When he turned round, the dog had disappeared.
Past simple vs. past continuous: It was raining when the train arrived.

Use vocabulary

Write the headings on the board. Go through the items in the Student's Book and check understanding. Now ask students if they can think of one more item for the *Phrasal verbs with up* heading. Elicit some responses and add them to the list on the board. Students now do the same for the other headings. Some possibilities are:

Phrasal verbs with *up*: *get up*; *look up*; *pick up*; *dress up* (SB2, Unit 6)

Expressions with *say* and *tell*: *say nothing*; *say 'hello'*; *tell a story*; *tell the time*

Jobs and work: *doctor, lawyer, salary, office*

Best of British

Unit overview

TOPIC: Aspects of British life

TEXTS

Reading and listening: a quiz about British teenagers
Reading: an interview with a foreign student living in Britain
Listening: statistics about teenagers in Britain
Listening: interviews with foreign visitors in Britain
Reading: an article about cultural influences in Britain
Writing: a report about the lifestyle of your family and friends

SPEAKING AND FUNCTIONS

Talking about how you spend your money
Presenting statistics
Describing recently completed or unfinished actions
Discussing influences from other cultures

LANGUAGE

Grammar: Present simple vs. present continuous review; Present perfect simple review; *for*, *since*, *just*, *already*, *yet* and *still*
Vocabulary: Giving statistics and making generalisations; Making new friends
Pronunciation: Schwa /ə/ in prepositions and articles

1 Read and listen

If you set the background information as a homework research task, ask students to tell the class what they found out.

BACKGROUND INFORMATION

Mobile phone cards: Many teenagers in Britain have their own mobile phone and buy mobile phone cards which allows them to pre-pay for calls. They are the size of a credit card and contain a code that you type into your phone. You can buy different value mobile phone cards of £5, £10, £20, etc. from many different shops.

Teenagers and part-time jobs: Between the ages of 13 and 16, children in the UK are allowed to do paid work for a maximum of 2 hours per school day. They are not allowed to start work before 7 am or finish after 7 pm. Paper rounds are a popular job with younger teenagers. They deliver newspapers to houses in the early morning or evening and are paid by a local newsagent. Working in a shop or café is popular with older teenagers and babysitting is also

popular, particularly with girls, who take care of someone's baby or child while the parents are out (usually in the evening).

Warm up

Ask students what adjectives they would associate with their country. Write each suggestion on the board. Choose some of the adjectives and ask students to give reasons for their answers.

(**a**) In the class, brainstorm some typical British images, e.g. *red telephone boxes, cricket, fish and chips.* Students write four adjectives they associate with Britain. Encourage them to think of reasons for their answers. Write all the adjectives on the board and check that all students understand their meaning. Then ask students to give brief reasons for their choices.

(**b**) Pre-teach vocabulary e.g. *paper round, part-time, run away (from home).* Students read the quiz and guess the answers. Ask students to compare their answers in pairs.

(**c**) 🔊 Briefly go through the questions with the class. Elicit answers but do not comment at this stage. Play the recording. Check answers and play the recording again as necessary.

Language note

You may want to point out the following phrases from the listening:

Most means the largest number or majority: *Most [teenagers] say 'going to the cinema'.*

Most is also used to form superlatives with adjectives: *The most common job is babysitting.*

TAPESCRIPT

Britain has 12 million people under the age of 16 – around 20% of the population.
If you ask teenagers what they do on a day they enjoy, most say 'going to the cinema', followed by 'seeing friends'. If you ask what they do on a day they don't enjoy, watching TV is the top answer – although on average, 11–16-year-olds actually watch 11 hours of TV a week!
Internet fans might think British teenagers spend all their time online, but surprisingly under 10% of 15–16-year-olds have the Internet at home (just 1 in 13). However, this number is increasing all the time.
11–16-year-olds spend about £12 a week. Girls tend to spend £2 a week more than boys. In the past, this was usually spent on sweets, but now

teens are spending most of their money on mobile phone cards.

If children are spending so much, that means some of them are working. It's illegal to work if you are under 13, but it is quite common for 10–16-year-olds to have some kind of job. 2 million schoolchildren with part-time jobs are earning an average of £14 a week. The most common job is babysitting, followed by newspaper rounds.

25% of under-19s are living with just one parent. About 100,000 young people run away from home every year, with up to 350 of them sleeping on the streets of London each night.

Answers
1 b   2 a   3 c   4 c   5 b   6 c   7 a   8 c   9 c

(d) 🔊 Students read the sentences. Encourage them to guess the answers before listening. Play the recording again and check answers.

Answers
1 T   2 T   3 F – girls spend £2 a week more than boys.   4 F – £14 a week.

Discussion box
Weaker classes: Students can choose one question to discuss.
Stronger classes: In pairs or small groups, students go through the questions in the box and discuss them.
Monitor and help as necessary, encouraging students to express themselves in English and to use any vocabulary they have learned from the text. Ask pairs or groups to feedback to the class and discuss any interesting points further.

2 Grammar

Present simple vs. present continuous review

Students covered these areas in SB2, Unit 1.

(a) **Weaker classes:** Books closed. Write on the board:
She plays the piano.
She's playing the piano.

Check students know the names of the tenses in each sentence and how they are constructed. Ask students to briefly explain the difference in meaning (*the sentence in the present simple talks about a regular habit and the sentence in the present continuous talks about an action happening at the moment of speaking*). Students open their books to page 7 and follow the procedure for stronger classes.
Stronger classes: Read through the examples. Ask students which sentence talks about a situation that is changing and which sentence talks about a permanent situation (*the first situation is about a changing situation, the second is permanent*). Check students understand trend (*a general direction in which a situation in changing*). Students complete the rules.

Answers
present simple; present simple; present continuous; present continuous

(b) Read some of the quiz together as a class and identify a few examples of the present simple and present continuous. Ask students to underline other examples of each these. Students then identify the reasons why each tense is used in their underlined examples, using the rule in Exercise 2a. Tell students that there may be more than one answer as there is often more than one reason of using a particular tense.

Answers
Present simple:
Question 1 fact   Question 2 regular habits/routines
Question 3 fact   Question 6 fact
Question 7 fact   Question 9 fact
Present continuous:
Question 4 changing situations / actions around now
Question 5 changing situations / actions around now
Question 8 changing situations / actions around now

Language notes
1   Students may still be making mistakes with these tenses because of the way their own language works. Students may produce statements like: *I am doing my homework every day. *My brother is work in a hospital at the moment.* If necessary, remind them of the main differences between the two tenses and emphasise that the present simple tense is generally used for permanent situations only.
2   The –*ing* form in question 2 in Exercise b may confuse students. Remind them that –*ing* forms also occur after some verbs such as *enjoy*, *like*, *hate*, and *go*. Point out that these are not connected with the present continuous tense.

— OPTIONAL ACTIVITIES —
Weaker classes
If your students need practice in the use of the present simple and present continuous, write these sentences on the board:
1   *Be quiet. The baby* .... *(sleep).*
2   *More and more people* .... *(use) the Internet every day.*
3   .... *Chris* .... *(go) jogging every day before school?*
4   *Dad's in the bathroom.* .... *he* .... *(have) a shower?*
5   *That new Ferrari* .... *(cost) £120,000.*

Go through the first sentence with students. Ask them why the verb is in the present continuous rather than the present simple (Be quiet *indicates that the speaker is talking about an action happening at the moment of speaking*). Students complete the sentences with the verbs in brackets in either the present simple or the present continuous. Check answers and encourage students to give reasons for their use of each tense.

Answers
1 is sleeping (use 3)
2 are using (use 4 from the rules)
3 Does, go (use 3)
4 Is, having (use 1)
5 costs (use 2)

c Remind students of the use of the present continuous for changing situations and trends. Ask students to think of any examples of trends in their country, e.g. *more people are giving up cigarettes*. Encourage students to phrase their examples in the present continuous. Write the topics on the board.
Elicit verbs that are commonly used with each topic and write them around each topic. For example, *music – listen, play, download*, etc.; *fashion – wear, buy*, etc. Go through the first example with students. Students complete the other sentences with their own ideas. If students finish early, encourage them to write more than one sentence for each sentence beginning. Check answers and make sure that students are not using verbs such as *be* in the present continuous tense.

Possible answers
1 More and more people my age are downloading music from the Internet.
2 Teenagers are buying more and more clothes.
3 People in my country are playing less sport.
4 My parents are watching more television.

Grammar notebook
Remind students to note down the rules for the present simple and present continuous and to write a few examples of their own.

3 Vocabulary
Giving statistics and making generalisations

a 🔊 Books closed. Ask students: *How many people in this class have a mobile phone / have the Internet at home / like 'The Simpsons' / cook for their family / like shopping?* Elicit key language from the table on page 7, e.g. *a lot, the majority, percent* /pə'sent/, *a quarter, a half, two thirds*. Students open their books and read the title and the table. Elicit some generalisations based on the questions you asked above, e.g. *The majority of students in this class have a mobile phone.*
Check students understand sentences 1 to 4 from the listening. Play the recording, pausing as necessary for students to write.

TAPESCRIPT/ANSWERS
1 Surprisingly, under 10% of 15–16-year-olds have the Internet at home.
2 Girls tend to spend £2 a week more than boys.
3 It is quite common for 10–16-year-olds to have some kind of job.

Language note
Make sure that students do not confuse the *prefer* + *–ing* structure with the present continuous tense. Remind students that this construction of verb + *–ing* is common in English. Other common examples include *enjoy, like* and *hate*. If necessary remind them of Unit 8 in Student's Book 2.

b Ask students to choose two of the categories and write three questions for each one using the structures given. Check students understand that the questions are about things which are always true or regular habits and therefore the structures given are in the present simple. Make sure that students are using the present simple tense appropriately.

Possible answers
Do you prefer fish to meat?
How often do you play football?
Do you ever play computer games?
What do you usually do in the evenings?

c This is a whole-class activity or you might find it more practical to do it in small groups of four to six students. Explain to students that they are going to do a class or group survey on the categories in Exercise 3b. Quickly ask each student to read out one of their questions and make sure that each student has a different question. Start with the weaker students so that they have the greatest choice of questions. When everyone has a different question, ask students to move around the classroom, asking their question and briefly recording the answers, e.g. *Do you prefer talking to friends to watching TV?*
friends – 22 students
watching TV – 8 students

When students have finished they should try and make a generalisation based on their results, e.g.
More than half of my classmates prefer talking to friends to watching TV.

⎡ OPTIONAL ACTIVITY
The results of 3b could be presented as a poster and put on the classroom wall. This is a good exercise for the group dynamic, especially in new classes at the beginning of a school year.

Vocabulary notebook
Encourage students to start a section called *Making generalisations* and to note down the words from this exercise. They may find it useful to note down translations of the words too.

4 Pronunciation

Schwa /ə/ in prepositions and articles

(a) 🔊 Students turn to page 120 and read the sentences. Tell students that schwa /ə/ is the most common vowel sound in English and is the sound in unstressed syllables with a vowel sound. Play the recording and ask students to listen to the pronunciation of the underlined words. Point out that prepositions and articles are rarely stressed and therefore they often have this sound.

TAPESCRIPT/ANSWERS

1 <u>The</u> majority <u>of</u> girls prefer music <u>to</u> sport.
2 Over half <u>of</u> us think shopping is better <u>than</u> school.
3 Less <u>than</u> <u>a</u> third <u>of</u> our class prefer books <u>to</u> films.
4 Girls tend <u>to</u> spend £2 <u>a</u> week more <u>than</u> boys.
5 It is quite common <u>for</u> 10–16-year-olds <u>to</u> have some kind <u>of</u> job.

(b) 🔊 Play the recording again, pausing after each sentence for students to repeat. Check students are pronouncing the vowel sound as /ə/.

OPTIONAL ACTIVITY

The *schwa* is the most common sound in English and therefore is found in many words. Open a page of the coursebook at random and give students a minute to find as many words as possible. Before feedback ask them to check with a partner. The winners are the pair with the most words with the schwa sound.

5 Read

If you set the background information as a homework research task, ask students to tell the class what they found out.

BACKGROUND INFORMATION

A-Levels: These British exams are usually taken in the final year of school at the age of 18. They are taken in a particular subject, such as History, English Literature, Chemistry, and are required for students to attend university.

IELTS: The International English Language Teaching System (IELTS) is a test required by many Australian, British, Canadian and New Zealand academic institutions before accepting a non-native English speaker on a course. It assesses the range of skills students need to study a subject such as Maths or Economics in English.

Ask students to read the questions and check potentially confusing vocabulary, e.g. *hard = difficult*, *cold = emotionally cold*. Ask students to read the interview and match the questions to each paragraph.

Encourage students to underline words in each paragraph that justify their answers.

Stronger classes: Before starting the activity, point out that there are two ways of doing this type of exercise. Students can read the question and then search for the matching paragraph. Or students can read a paragraph and search for the matching question. Divide the class into two halves and ask half the students to try the first method and the other half to try the second. During feedback briefly discuss with students which method they think was more successful.

Answers

2 E   3 A   4 C   5 B   6 H   7 G
Unused question: D

OPTIONAL ACTIVITY

If you would like your students to do more close comprehension work on the text, then use the following true / false / don't know exercise. The statements are in the order of the text so to make the exercise more challenging, write them on the board in a different order:

1 *Pietro is studying English to go to an English university.* (DK)
2 *Pietro likes salads.* (T)
3 *Pietro's mother is staying with Pietro and his English family.* (DK)
4 *Pietro was surprised by how much the English like football.* (T)
5 *He thinks that ice cream and coffee are always terrible in England.* (F)
6 *He has made some good English friends.* (T)

6 Listen

🔊 Ask students why Pietro, in Exercise 5, is visiting England (*he is studying English to prepare for A-Levels in Maths and Computing*). Elicit other reasons for visiting another country, e.g. holiday, visiting friends/relatives, work/business. Tell students they are going to listen to four other students talking about their visit to Britain. Briefly discuss what they might like or dislike about Britain. Play the recording. Students complete the table. Repeat the recording again, with pauses if necessary.

TAPESCRIPT/ANSWERS

Gözde My name is Gözde and I'm visiting my cousin and her English husband in Birmingham. I like the cafés and shops in the centre – it's very different from Izmir, where I'm from in Turkey. I don't like the rain, but it does make everything beautiful and green. I love England.

Marco I'm Marco, and I'm here for the game. I'm a big Bayern fan. I never miss a match in Munich. I think English football is much better than it was, but the German teams are still the best in Europe. I like the way some people dress here,

like me, a lot of black clothes, but the food is terrible –
I can't wait to get back to Germany.

Chris   I'm Chris, and I'm here on holiday with my wife
– we're from Little Rock, Arkansas – and we just love
this architecture, the castles, those pretty little houses,
Buckingham Palace. We sure don't have anything like
this back home. You guys sure have a lot of history. But
what we really don't like is the public transport. Your
buses and trains are just too crowded.

Rebecca   I'm Rebecca from Caracas in Venezuela. I'm
having English lessons at a school here in York. I'm
staying for six months and I think I made a very good
choice to come here because it's such a beautiful city. I
love English music and there are a lot of CDs I want to
buy, but the only problem is England is very expensive.

Answers

	Reason for being in UK	Likes	Doesn't like
Gözde	family	cafe's and shops	weather
Marco	football	fashion	food
Chris	holiday	architecture	public transport
Rebecca	learning English	music	expensive

7   Grammar

Present perfect simple with *for* and *since*

Students covered the present perfect simple in SB2, Unit 7.

a   **Weaker classes:** Write on the board:
We have been in this classroom since ....
(complete with correct time).
We have been in this classroom for ....
(complete with correct time).
Ask students if they are still in the classroom (*yes*). Explain
that when we are talking about a situation or action that
started in the past and leads to the present time, we use the
present perfect. Students open their books at page 9 and
follow the procedure for stronger classes.

Stronger classes: Students read the sentences and explain
why the present perfect simple is used. If necessary, ask
students:
1   When did Pietro arrive in Britain? **(at the beginning of summer)**
2   Is he still in Britain? **(yes)**
3   When did Pietro's mother arrive in Britain? **(two weeks ago)**
4   Is she still in Britain? **(yes)**

Explain the use of the present perfect simple to talk about
situations/actions that started in the past and continue to
the present. Briefly elicit the construction of the sentences
(*have/has* and the past participle). Point out that the past
participle of regular verbs is the same as the past tense form
(irregular verbs have irregular past participles) and point out
the table of irregular verbs on page 123.

b   Explain that in each sentence there is a
choice of three time periods. Ask students to
work in pairs and read the sentence stems,
e.g. *Life has changed since* ... . Go through the
example with students. Ask students which
word in the sentence stem will help them
decide (*for* or *since*).

Answers
2   a couple of weeks, such a long time
3   the last six weeks, most of my life
4   Frankie's party, last Friday

┌── **OPTIONAL ACTIVITY** ──────
│ Write the table on the board:

for		since
a day	→	*yesterday*
.... hours	←	8.00am
two days	→	....
.... months	←	Christmas
ten minutes	→	....
.... years	←	I was born
ten years	→	....

Tell students that each time period leading to
the present has an equivalent with *for* or *since*.
If necessary give them an example with the
sentence *We've been in this classroom for ...
minutes or since ... o'clock*. Tell students to
complete the table with equivalent time
phrases in each column.

Possible answers

for		since
three hours	←	8.00am
two days	→	*Monday*
10 months	←	Christmas
ten minutes	→	*11.30am*
15 years	←	I was born
ten years	→	*1995*

Present perfect with *just, already, yet* and *still*

c   Books closed. Ask students what Pietro said
about: fish and chips, new friends, football
matches, his English course. If students need
help, ask them:
Has he finished his English course? **(yes)**
Has he tried fish and chips? **(no)**
Has he seen a football match? **(no)**
Has he made any new friends? **(yes)**

Ask students to complete the sentences by looking back at the text in Exercise 5. Quickly check answers in open class.

Answers
1 just   2 still   3 yet   4 already

> **Language note**
>
> These four adverbs can be very confusing so students will inevitably make mistakes. For some students there will only be one word for *already* and *yet* in their language. Remind students that in English both words express the same idea. However, *already* is used in positive sentences and *yet* is used in negatives and questions.

(d) Explain that the words *just*, *already*, *yet* and *still* are commonly used with the present perfect tense. Their meaning and position in a sentence are different. Ask students to complete the rules using the sentences in Exercise c. Encourage students to use the text to help them where necessary.

Answers
yet; just; already; still

(e) Ask students to read the sentences and to complete them with *just*, *already*, *yet* or *still*. Check answers.

Answers
1 just   2 yet   3 still   4 already   5 yet

Grammar notebook
Remind students to note down the rules for the present perfect simple and to write a few examples of their own.

8 Speak

(a) Read the example with students. Remind students that if they are talking about general truths, e.g. what team you support, then use the present simple tense. If they are talking about specific times in the past, e.g. the last time you went to a match, then use the past simple tense. *How long* questions, if they refer up to the present, should be in the present perfect. Write the topics (*best friend, clothes*, etc.) on the board. Ask students for suitable verbs for each topic (best friend – *meet, know, be*; clothes – *buy, wear, have*; hobbies – *start, have*; possessions – *buy, have*). Encourage students to build short dialogues with their partners using the verbs. Check students are using the present perfect tense where relevant and that they are using an appropriate time phrase with *for* or *since*.

(b) In open class, read the list of 'Things to do by the age of 16'. Check potentially difficult vocabulary: *Shakespeare play, poem, continent*. Tell students to work in pairs and guess what their partner has or hasn't

done. Encourage students to use *already*, *just*, *still* or *yet*. Remind students that *already*/*just* are used in positive sentences and *still*/*yet* are used in negative sentences. Make sure students change roles after each sentence.

Culture in mind

9 Read

If you set the background information as a homework research task, ask students to tell the class what they found out.

BACKGROUND INFORMATION

Immigration: has always been an important issue in Britain. More recently the growth of asylum seeker applications has been a daily topic in the news and media. Asylum seekers are people who apply to live in a country for fear of religious or political persecution in their own country. In 2002, there were over 110,000 applications from asylum seekers in the UK – more than in any other country in the world.

Multiculturalism in London: There are probably few cities in the world more multicultural than London. Many groups of nationals that settle in London keep their own cultures and establish areas with specialist shops, restaurants and ways of life.

Emigration: According to a recent survey* of the British, the most popular destinations for emigration are the USA, followed by Australia. Destinations in Europe such as France and Spain are also popular.

*YouGov survey of 2,000 British adults for the *Daily Telegraph*, 2002

David Beckham: is a world-famous English football player who has played for Manchester United (1991–2003) and Real Madrid (2003–present). The film *Bend It Like Beckham* takes its title from the way Beckham is able to kick and dramatically 'bend' the path of the ball.

The Mercury Prize: is an annual prize celebrating the best in British music. Most types of music are entered for the prize, including pop, rock, dance, folk, jazz and contemporary classical music. Judges choose a selection of albums and meet in September each year to decide the winner. Past winners include Pulp, Badly Drawn Boy and Ms. Dynamite.

Warm up

Ask students to look at the photo and ask which city it is from (*London*). Can students give a reason for their answer? Check students understand the term *immigration* (*the process of coming to live in a country which is not your own*). Ask students which countries immigrants in their country come from.

(a) Students read the text quickly and find the countries (not nationalities or continents) mentioned. It is a good idea to give a time limit of just two minutes to encourage the students to skim the text. Tell them not to worry about words they do not understand.

Answers
12: Britain, Iraq, Afghanistan, Bosnia, Germany, Italy, France, Spain, Bangladesh, Pakistan, England, Jamaica

(b) Check students understand difficult vocabulary in 1 to 6: *apart from, percentage, reggae (music)*. Students read the text to find out the information. Point out that the information for 1 to 6 is not in order in the text so they will probably need to read the text more than once or scan the text to find the relevant paragraphs. Encourage students to work without a dictionary, or your help, at this stage. Instead, ask students to write down specific words and phrases they don't understand. Students check answers in pairs before open class.

Answers
1 The Romans   2 Iraq, Afghanistan and Bosnia
3 Over 300   4 *Bend It Like Beckham* and *East Is East*
5 Turkeys / animal rights   6 UB40

Discussion box
Weaker classes: Check difficult vocabulary in the questions: *influence, emigrate* (to leave your country to live in another). Students choose one question to discuss.
Stronger classes: In pairs or small groups, students go through the questions in the box and discuss them.
Monitor and help as necessary, encouraging students to express themselves in English and to give details in their answers. Ask pairs or groups to feedback to the class and discuss any interesting points further.

---

10 Vocabulary
Making new friends

(a) Tell students that sentences 1 to 5 are all from the text. Students match the underlined phrase with the definitions. Encourage students to reread relevant sections of the text to guess the meaning of difficult phrases. This is also a good opportunity for students to write the phrases in their vocabulary notebook with example sentences of their own. Students compare answers in pairs before checking.

Answers
1 a   2 e   3 d   4 c   5 b

(b) Students put the letters in order to complete the sentences. (Depending on the sensitivity of your class, you may want to leave out the discussion.) Students check in pairs before discussing each question. Ask some pairs to report back to the class on their discussion.

Answers
2 fit in   3 feel left out   4 join in   5 bond with

Vocabulary notebook
Encourage students to start a section called *Friends* and to note down the words from this exercise. They may find it useful to note down translations of the words too.

11 Write

(a) The planning for this exercise can be done in class and the interviews and writing can be set as homework. Elicit the meaning of the headings from students. If the structure of this report is different from students' normal report-writing style, explain that this is the common structure for reports in Britain (and many other countries).

Answers
First paragraph – Introduction
Second paragraph – Findings
Third paragraph – Conclusion

Ask students to read the model report and point out the useful language, e.g. generalisations with *(Well) over three quarters, About two thirds, the majority of* ... etc. Finally, in the conclusion point out that Ayşe has said what surprised her about her results.

(b) Students interview their family or friends using the questions they wrote in Exercise 3b on page 7. In a subsequent lesson, encourage students to read each other's reports and vote on the most interesting.

② Ways of talking

Unit overview

TOPIC: Communication

TEXTS

Reading and listening: an article about two deaf teenage friends
Listening: information about communicating with deaf people
Listening: a radio interview about body language
Reading and listening: Story: *Meeting up again*
Writing: a description of a friendship

SPEAKING AND FUNCTIONS

Discussing problems of being deaf
Talking about recently completed actions
Discussing how body language helps communication
Exchanging information

LANGUAGE

Grammar: Past simple vs. present perfect simple
Vocabulary: Body language; *say* and *tell*; Phrasal verbs with *up*
Pronunciation: Sentence stress: rhythm in questions
Everyday English: *How's life/things?*; *Talking of …*; *All right, mate?*; *Anyway*; *Got to be going*; *Nice seeing you*; *Long time, no see*; *Take care*

1 Read and listen

If you set the background information as a homework research task, ask students to tell the class what they found out.

BACKGROUND INFORMATION

California: This state is on the West coast of the USA. The largest cities are Los Angeles, San Diego, San José and San Francisco. Major tourist attractions in the state include Disneyland and the Golden Gate Bridge.

Mexico: This country has borders with the USA in the north and Guatemala and Belize in the south. The capital is Mexico City and its official language is Spanish. The population is about 105 million (July 2004).

The US school system: Each state is different but many children go to pre-school kindergarten at the age of 5. Compulsory education generally starts at elementary school, which children attend between the ages of 6 and 11. Between 12 and 14 students attend junior high school and then senior high school between the ages of 14 and 17. Students can skip grades or be held back for poor performance.

Drive-thru (restaurant): This is a restaurant, often fast-food, which you can visit without getting out of your car by ordering at one window and picking up your food at the next.

Sign language: This is a method of communication, especially used by people who are deaf or hard of hearing. It uses a system of facial, hand and other body movements to express meaning. Each sign has three distinct parts: the hand shape, the position of the hands, and the movement of the hands. Sign language is not universal – British Sign Language is different from American Sign Language and neither is based on English or any other spoken language.

Warm up

Ask students, in pairs, to think of as many methods of communication as possible. Give them one minute and then elicit all their answers. Do not write them on the board.

(a) Check the meaning of the words in the box. Students write down how they communicate. Help students with vocabulary as necessary (see possible answers).

Possible answers

whales: make noises (e.g. clicks, whistles), sing, body language (e.g. moving their tail)
people and their animals: speaking, gestures, touching (patting, stroking), whistle
deaf people: sign language (making symbols with their hands), lip-reading, body language, writing

(b) Read through the questions with students and encourage them to read the text quickly to find the answers. Remind them they do not need to understand every word in the text to answer the questions.

Answers

1 Since the first day of kindergarten school (About 11 or 12 years)
2 They put food in bags at a local supermarket

(c) ◀ᴗ)) Ask students to read through questions 1 to 6. Check any problems. You may want to pre-teach the following vocabulary: *majority*, *regular* (American English for *normal*), *sign* (the deaf equivalent of *say*), *drive-thru*. Play the recording, pausing it at the end of the second paragraph as ask students to give you the answer to question 1. Play the recording while students read and listen to answer the questions. Check answers. Play the recording again, pausing as necessary to clarify any problems.

TAPESCRIPT

See the reading text on page 12 of the Student's Book.

Answers

1 F – Para 2: Orlando lost his hearing at the age of one.   2 T   3 F – Para 5: ... can't talk on the phone ... call an emergency service ... or order food in a drive-thru   4 T   5 F – Para 8: They [the other employees] even sign sometimes.   6 F – Para 9: After high school, they hope to attend the National Technical Institute for the Deaf in New York.

Discussion box

Weaker classes: Students can choose one question to discuss.

Stronger classes: In pairs or small groups, students go through the questions in the box and discuss them.

Monitor and help as necessary, encouraging students to express themselves in English and to use any vocabulary they have learned from the text. Ask pairs or groups to feedback to the class and discuss any interesting points further.

---

2 Listen

🔊 Remind students about a common way for deaf people to communicate (*signing*). Tell students they are going to hear about ways to communicate with deaf people if you don't know how to sign. Ask students to predict some answers. Play the recording. Students make notes of four things to do. Play the recording again, with pauses if necessary.

TAPESCRIPT

When two deaf people meet, they communicate with sign language – they 'sign'. But what can you do if you meet someone who is deaf and you don't know how to sign? Well, remember that most deaf people can also lip-read – they watch your mouth and see the sounds that you're making. So, when you meet a deaf person and you want to communicate, here are some things to remember:

First, make sure that the person is looking at you, and you are looking at them.

Secondly, don't cover your mouth with your hand. Let the deaf person see your lips move!

Thirdly, use your hands – point with your fingers, point to yourself and the other person, make shapes and so on.

And lastly, speak a little more slowly and a lot more clearly than you normally speak. Remember that deaf people can lip-read, but it helps them if you move your mouth more slowly and clearly.

Answers

1 Look at the person
2 Don't cover your mouth with your hand
3 Use your hands
4 Speak more slowly and more clearly than normal

---

3 Grammar

Past simple vs. present perfect simple

(a) Weaker classes: Books closed. Write on the board:
Paul lived in Paris for three months.
Sally has lived in Paris for three months.

Ask students who lives in Paris now (*Sally*). Ask students to identify the tenses in each sentence. Elicit or explain the use of the present perfect simple to indicate unfinished time and elicit the construction of each tense. Point out that regular verbs have the same past form and past participle. Students now open their books at page 13 and follow the procedure for stronger classes.

Stronger classes: Students decide which sentences are in the past simple and the present perfect simple. Remind students of the construction of the present perfect simple (*have/has* + past participle).

Answers

present perfect simple, past simple, past simple, present perfect simple

(b) Students underline sentences in the past simple from the text in Exercise 1b and circle sentences in the present perfect simple. Go through a few examples if necessary.

Answers

Past simple:
Para 2: Orlando lost; German was born; his parents moved; where he could learn; He met
Para 3: We were; I didn't know; I was deaf; I was different
Para 4: was very hard; kids didn't understand; we didn't understand them
Para 6: They got their jobs
Para 7: Orland started
Para 8: we were nervous

Present perfect simple:
Para 1: (Orlando and German) have been friends; (They) have had
Para 4 we've all grown up
Para 6: the two boys have found
Para 7: German has worked
Para 8: the other employees have been; we've learned a lot
Para 9: has been exciting

(c) Write on the board:
Orlando and German have been friends since kindergarten.
They were in a special class with 25 other deaf children.
Ask students if they are friends now (*yes*). Ask students if they are still in a special class with deaf children (*no*). Students complete the rules with the name of the tense.

Answers

past simple; present perfect simple

Students look at the timeline. Elicit the time that they met (*on their first day of kindergarten*). Elicit the time they have been friends (*from the day they met until today*).

Time expressions

(d) Explain that there are often time expressions which determine which tense you should use. Ask students to find examples of some phrases from the first two paragraphs of the text (*present perfect simple – since kindergarten; past simple – at the age of one, on their first day of kindergarten*). Then students read the rules and complete with the correct tense name. If necessary, remind students of the work they did in Unit 1, Exercise 7.

Answers
past simple; present perfect simple; present perfect simple; present perfect simple

> **Language note**
> Students may produce statements like **I am working here since two years ago*. Remind them that in English we use *ago* only with the past simple.

(e) Students complete the paragraph with verbs in the present perfect simple or the past simple. Encourage students to decide using time expressions to help them.

Answers
1 left   2 got   3 Did, learn   4 didn't learn
5 has worked   6 has written   7 Has, visited
8 spent   9 haven't been   10 have saved

OPTIONAL ACTIVITY

Weaker classes
Write these questions on the board:
1 When _____ Sally _____ (leave) university?
2 Where _____ she _____ (get) a job?
3 _____ she _____ (learn) English in Sweden?
4 How many countries _____ she _____ (work) in since Sweden?
5 How many books _____ she _____ (write)?
6 How long _____ she _____ (spend) in Rio de Janeiro?
Students complete the questions in the past simple or present perfect simple using the text in Exercise 3e as a reference. Then students take it in turns to ask and answer with a partner based on the information in the text.

Answers
1 did, leave   2 did, get   3 Did, learn
4 has, worked   5 has, written   6 did, spend

Stronger classes
Ask students to write questions about the text in Exercise 3e using the past simple or present perfect simple tense, e.g.
When did Sally leave university?
Where did she get a job?
Did she learn any Swedish while she was there?
Students take it in turns to ask and answer the questions with a partner.

Grammar notebook
Remind students to note down the rules for this and to write a few examples of their own.

4 Speak

Warm up

Tell students something *you've just done*, e.g. *bought a new car, had lunch with someone important at the school*. Elicit the communicative meaning of the sentence. Ask students to imagine that they also want to impress you. Elicit what they could say about a situation. For example,
You: *I've just had lunch with the headmaster.*
Student: *Oh, really? I have lunch with him most days.* or *I'm having lunch with him tomorrow.*

> **Language note**
> Students have seen that *just* is used with the present perfect simple to describe recently completed actions. One communicative function of this structure is when you want to impress people, e.g. *I've just bought a new car!*

(a) Students work in pairs and invent five things they *have just done* that are impressive. If they need ideas, write these verbs on the board: *meet, buy, see, had lunch/dinner with, read (a book), write*. Remind students to use the present perfect simple with *just*.

(b) When students have written five sentences, ask them to find a different partner. Read the example with students and check they understand the function behind the short dialogues (two people trying to impress each other). Students take turns at being A and B.

Weaker classes: If students work with the same partner as they did in Exercise 4a, they will find the task easier. They could also prepare B's replies together before acting out the dialogue.

5 Listening and vocabulary

If you set the background information as a homework research task, ask students to tell the class what they found out.

BACKGROUND INFORMATION

Body language: An important part of our communication is *non-verbal*. That is, it does not involve words. Instead, it consists of gestures, body movements and facial expressions. However, these gestures and expressions are not always universal. For example,

Nodding the head means 'yes' in most countries. However, it also means 'no' in some parts of Greece, Yugoslavia, Bulgaria and Turkey.

Eye contact is important in America and Europe, but it can be rude in most Asian countries and in Africa. Closing your eyes in Western cultures often means 'I'm bored or sleepy'. However, in Japan, Thailand and China it can mean 'I'm listening and concentrating'.

Warm up

Ask students what the body language in the background information means in their country. Do they know any examples of body language which mean different things in different countries? Discuss the general importance of body language in the students' country and compare it with their experience in other countries.

a 🔊 Students read through items 1 to 10 and look at the pictures. Go through the first item as an example and see if they can match any more items. Students complete the exercise. Play the recording for students to check answers. Play the recording again, pausing after each item for students to repeat.

TAPESCRIPT/ANSWERS

a 8   look nervous
b 9   give someone a warm smile
c 1   make eye contact
d 2   cross your arms
e 7   raise your eyebrows
f 4   sit back
g 3   lean forward
h 5   avoid eye contact
i 6   gesture
j 10   nod your head

b Explain that some kinds of body language 'help' communication, that is, they encourage communication, and some kinds are more negative. Students decide which of the examples of body language (1–10) help and do not help communication. If necessary, discuss a few examples with students. Ask students to decide which types of body language they use.

Possible answers

Body language that helps communication: 1, 3, 6, 7, 9, 10

Body language that does not help communication: 2, 4, 5, 8

c 🔊 Explain that students are going to listen to a psychologist talking about body language. Ask the students to read through questions 1 to 6 and explain any difficult vocabulary: *mirroring* – displaying the same body language as the person you are talking to, *flash* – a short and quick expression. Encourage students to predict the answers first and then play the recording. Students choose the correct answers, a, b or c. Ask students to check their answers with a partner. Then play the recording again, with pauses if necessary.

TAPESCRIPT

Interviewer   ... and now it's my pleasure to welcome Dr Anna Forbes, a specialist in body language.

Dr Forbes   Thank you.

Interviewer   Dr Forbes, is it easy to know what is going on in someone's mind by reading their body language?

Dr Forbes   No, quite the opposite. Let me give you an example. If someone crosses their arms when they're talking to you, it could be a sign that they're feeling insecure and protecting themselves. But it might also mean the person's just very cold. So, it's just not that easy, really.

Interviewer   I see.

Dr Forbes   90 percent of what we say isn't verbal. It's your body language – your gestures, expressions, eye contact and touch – that does most of the talking.

Interviewer   So how can I communicate better by using my body language?

Dr Forbes   Well, for example, through mirroring. Just watch two friends sitting in a café – whatever one person does, the other one does too. If one person leans forward to say something, the other one leans forward too. If one sits back and takes a sip of their drink, so does the other.

Interviewer   Right. But isn't it a bit annoying?

Dr Forbes   Well, maybe, but the theory behind mirroring is that we like people who are similar to us. If someone is doing what we're doing, we feel they're in harmony with us. We like being with them.

Interviewer   That's interesting. Can you tell us another secret?

Dr Forbes   Well, try the eyebrow flash.

Interviewer   The eyebrow flash? What on earth is that?

Dr Forbes   Well, scientists have found out that when we first see someone we're attracted to, our eyebrows go up, then down. If they're attracted to us, too, they raise their eyebrows in return. Never noticed? It's not surprising, since the whole thing lasts about one fifth of a second! Some experts say it's the most instantly recognised non-verbal sign of friendly greeting in the world.

Interviewer   So how can I use it?

Dr Forbes   Well, when you meet someone you like, raise your eyebrows for up to one second – in this way your body is 'telling' the other person that you like them.

Interviewer   Hmm. Before we say 'goodbye' – any other tricks you can tell our listeners about?

Dr Forbes   Well, they're not tricks really. The most 'attractive' people in the room make others feel attractive and interesting. Their bodies say 'I hear you, I like you.' Lots of nods, gestures, eye contact and most important of all: a nice, warm smile.

Answers

1 c   2 b   3 a   4 a   5 b   6 a

6 Speak

a Tell students they are going to practise being a good listener using positive examples of body language. Student A talks about one of the subjects in the box for one minute. Student B should listen and give positive examples of body language. Then, students change roles and repeat the exercise. Ask students to decide who they thought was the better listener.

b Ask students to choose another topic and repeat the exercise with Student B as a bad listener.

c Ask students to think about the differences between the conversations. With the class, discuss the differences the role of B made to the conversations.

OPTIONAL ACTIVITY

If your students enjoy this exercise, repeat it in groups of three. This time, Student C is an observer. They watch the speaker and the listener and record the number of times B shows positive kinds of body language. When they have finished, they should change roles until they have all had the opportunity to play each role. Ask groups to decide who the best listener was.

7 Pronunciation

Sentence stress: rhythm in questions

a Tell students that sentence stress is stress on certain words within a sentence and it gives English its rhythm. Students turn to page 120 and read through sentences 1 to 5.

Weaker classes: Play the recording, pausing after each sentence for students to mark the stress. Play each sentence twice. Students compare answers with a partner before class feedback.

Stronger classes: Students can mark where they think the sentence stresses fall before they listen and then listen to check.

TAPESCRIPT/ANSWERS
1 Can you <u>tell</u> us another <u>secret</u>?
2 Was it <u>really</u> that <u>easy</u>?
3 So <u>how</u> can I <u>use</u> it?
4 What on <u>earth</u> is <u>that</u>?
5 <u>What</u> can I <u>do</u> to <u>communicate</u> better?

b Play the recording again, pausing after each sentence for students to repeat. Check students are stressing the correct words.

8 Vocabulary

say and tell

a Ask students to complete the sentences from the interview in Exercise 5c using the correct form of *say* or *tell*.

b Check that students understand the difference between *say* and *tell* (see Language note). Play the recording from Exercise 5 again for students to check their answers.

Answers
1 say   2 tell   3 telling   4 say, tell   5 say

c Students complete the sentences using the correct form of *say* and the phrases in the box. Remind students that they will need to work out the necessary tense for each sentence. Students check their answers in pairs before feedback.

Answers
1 said goodbye   2 say a prayer   3 say thank you
4 saying sorry   5 say it out loud   6 say it again

> **Language note**
> The difference between *say* and *tell* is simple.
> Both have the same meaning but:
> We use *say* with some particular nouns,
> e.g. *say a prayer/goodbye/sorry.*
> We use *tell* with other particular nouns,
> e.g. *tell a joke/lie/story.*
> You *say* something, e.g. *Alex said he was tired.*
> You *tell* someone something, e.g. *Alex told me he was tired.*

d Students complete the sentences with the correct form of *tell* and the phrases in the box. Point out the illustrations that help students with some sentences.

Answers
2 tell me the time   3 told my parents a lie
4 tell the difference   5 told me off
6 telling the truth   7 tell you a secret
8 tell me a story

Vocabulary notebook
Encourage students to start a section called *say* and *tell* and to note down the words from this exercise. They may find it useful to note down translations.

9 Speak

Student A completes the questions with the correct form of *say* or *tell*. Student B turns to page 122 and does a similar exercise. Check that students are using the correct forms.

Answers (Student A)
1 say   2 said   3 tell   4 say   5 told

Answers (Student B)
1 say   2 said   3 tell   4 telling   5 told

Then students take turns in asking and answering their partner's questions.

Meeting up again

10 Read and listen

Warm up

Write these questions on the board:

When was the last time you met an 'old friend'?
What did you say?
Did they tell you anything interesting?

Ask students to ask and answer the questions in pairs. Elicit feedback from one or two pairs of students. If students have used levels 1 or 2 of *English in Mind*, ask if they can remember the characters from the Photostory (*Dave, Amy, Joanne and Matt*).

a ◁)) Read through the questions as a class and ask students to predict the answers but do not comment at this stage. Play the recording while students read and listen to check their predictions. Check answers in open class. If students ask questions about vocabulary, write the words on the board but do not explain the meaning at this stage.

TAPESCRIPT
See the story on page 16 of the Student's Book.

Answers
Ben's just got back from Hong Kong. His parents have probably separated (*Things didn't work out between Mum and Dad*). Ben's unemployed at the moment. Joanne's at college.

b **Weaker classes:** Students read through the questions. Play the recording, pausing after the first question and go through it as an example. Play the recording again for students to listen and complete the exercise. Check answers, playing and pausing the recording as necessary to clarify any vocabulary problems.

Stronger classes: Students read through the questions and answer them without playing the recording again.

Answers
1 The last time they met was on their last day at school
2 He's been in Hong Kong
3 She's hoping to find a job in music
4 He's not sure whether to go back to college or get a job
5 met (unexpectedly or by chance)

11 Everyday English

a Ask students to locate the expressions 1 to 8 in the story on page 16 and decide who says them.

Weaker classes: Check answers at this stage.

Answers
1 Ben   2 Ben and Matt   3 Joanne
4 Ben and Matt   5 Joanne   6 Joanne   7 Matt

Students then match the expressions with the situations. Go through the first item with them as an example if necessary. Check answers.

Answers
a 1, 2, 3
b 5, 6, 7
c 4

b Ask students to read through the sentences and complete the answers. Go through the first sentence with them as an example if necessary.

Answers
1 Anyway   2 All right mate?, how's things
3 got to be going, nice seeing you

> **Language note**
> There are some interesting phrases in the dialogue that are commonly used in informal conversation.
>
> | Phrase | An informal way of saying: |
> |---|---|
> | All right, mate? | Hello |
> | How's life? | How are you? |
> | How's things (with you)? | How are you? |
> | Long time, no see. | It's been a long time since I last saw you. |
> | What are you doing with yourselves? | What are you doing? |
> | Nice seeing you again. | It was good to see you again. |
> | Take care. | Goodbye (literally Take care of yourself) |

┌─ OPTIONAL ACTIVITIES ─────
These optional activities can be used after every Everyday English exercise in the Student's Book.

Weaker classes
Students can act out the dialogues. Make sure they are saying them with the correct intonation and expression and in the right context.

Stronger classes
Students can write their own short dialogues using the expressions. They can then act them out in front of the class. Make sure they are saying them with the correct intonation and expression and in the right context.

Vocabulary notebook
Encourage students to start a section called *Everyday English* and to note down the expressions from Exercise 11. They may find it useful to note down a translation for each expression too.

12 Vocabulary

Phrasal verbs with *up*

a Explain that phrasal verbs are very common in English, especially in informal conversation. (See Language notes.) Ask students if they know any phrasal verbs with *up*, e.g. *get up*, *look up*, *grow up*. Ask students to match the underlined verbs in sentences 1 to 4 with the definitions a to d. Encourage students to use the text on page 16 to help them and to record the verbs in their vocabulary notebooks.

Answers
1 c   2 a   3 d   4 b

> ### Language notes
> 1 Phrasal verbs are verbs with more than one word. They consist of a verb, e.g. *get*, and a particle (preposition), e.g. *up*. There are two types of phrasal verbs: separable and non-separable. This will be focused on in detail in Unit 16.
> 2 Separable phrasal verbs can have an object between the verb and the particle. For example, *take off* (something) = to remove clothing
> *She took her jacket off.* ✓ or
> *She took off her jacket.* ✓
> but <u>not</u> **She took off it.* ✗
> 3 Non-separable phrasal verbs must stay together. For example,
> *take off* = depart
> *The plane took off at ten.* ✓
> but <u>not</u> * *The plane took at ten off.* ✗

b Students complete the sentences with one of the phrasal verbs in Exercise 12a. Remind students to think about the form of the verb.

Answers
1 broken up   2 look me up   3 turned up
4 meet up

┌ OPTIONAL ACTIVITY ═══════════════════

This activity works as a review of any new vocabulary. Students work with a partner. Ask one student in each pair to turn their back to the board. Write three items of vocabulary that students have recently studied on the board: *look up*, *tell* and *meet up*. Give students a time limit of a minute. Students must try and describe the word or phrase without using any of the words, e.g. for *look up* students might say 'a phrasal verb that means to get in touch'. The student who can't see the board must try and guess the word. When students have finished, ask them to change positions, and write three new words or phrases on the board.

Vocabulary notebook
Encourage students to start a section called *Phrasal verbs* and to note down the words from this exercise under the heading *up*. They may find it useful to note down translations of the words too.

13 Write

a The planning for this exercise can be done in class and the writing can be set as homework. Ask students to read the composition quickly and answer the question (*No – Rebecca moved last year*).

> ## BACKGROUND INFORMATION
> **Techno:** This is a type of fast, electronic dance music with a regular beat.
> **Green Day:** This band, from California, USA, are a pop/punk band and have released albums called *Dookie* (1994), *Warning* (2000) and *Shenanigans* (2002).

b Ask students to read the composition again and find the two tenses she uses (*present perfect simple* and *past simple*). Point out the structure of the text – the first paragraph is about how they met, the second and third paragraphs are about things that happened a few years ago and also about the situation now.

c Students think of one of their good friends and write a similar text. Remind them about the tenses they should use. In a subsequent lesson, encourage students to read each other's descriptions and vote on the most interesting or use them for a peer-correction exercise.

3 A true friend

Unit overview

TOPIC: Friendship and loyalty

TEXTS
Reading and listening: a ghost story
Reading: a questionnaire about friendship
Reading: an extract from a story about friendship
Writing: rewriting a short story about a relationship

SPEAKING AND FUNCTIONS
Predicting what happens next in a story
Telling a story
Discussing the events in a story

LANGUAGE
Grammar: Past simple vs. past continuous review;
Time conjunctions; Past simple vs. past perfect simple
Vocabulary: Friends and enemies
Pronunciation: Linking sounds

1 Speak and read

If you set the background information as a homework research task, ask students to tell the class what they found out.

BACKGROUND INFORMATION

2nd World War: This war lasted from 1939 to 1945. The war was initially between Germany and Britain. However, other countries became involved during the war and in 1941 Japan attacked the US Navy at Pearl Harbor. The USA then entered the war on the side of Britain.

Kentucky: A state in south-eastern USA. It has borders with the states of Indiana, Ohio, West Virginia, Virginia, Tennessee, Missouri and Illinois. Coal-mining and agriculture are important industries in the state.

Apple pie: Apples are considered one of America's symbols because they have often been used in recipes throughout the country's history. Apple dishes of some kind were very common during Colonial times in America, especially in New England. If something is said to be as 'American as apple pie', it means it is truly American.

Warm up

Ask if any students have a pet. Elicit the kind of pet and its name. Then write three types of pets on the board: *dogs, cats, fish.* Ask students to decide which is the best and the worst pet and why. Discuss the answers with the class and elicit common qualities of a dog (*faithful/loyal, friendly, enthusiastic, full of energy*, etc.).

(a) Ask students to make a list of stories and films that involve dogs or other animals. Point out the characteristics of a dog, e.g. *faithful* (*loyal*), and encourage them to give characteristics of other animals.

Possible answers
Films: *Free Willy* (whale), *Antz* (ants), *The Lion King* (lions)
Books: *Aesop's Fables*, *The Jungle Book* (bear, wolf, tiger)

(b) Ask students to match phrases 1 to 5 with pictures a to e. Check answers and point out difficult vocabulary using the pictures: *pat, bark.*

Answers
a 5   b 3   c 4   d 1   e 2

(c) Tell the students that the pictures illustrate the first part of the story. Ask students to work with a partner and put them in order to tell the first part of the story. Ask a few pairs to tell their version of the start of the story.

(d) (◀)) Play the recording. Students check their stories with the first part of the story.

TAPESCRIPT
See the reading text on page 18 of the Student's Book.

(e) Ask students to predict what happens next in the story. Point out that *Hugh* is pronounced /hjuː/. Ask students questions if they need help, e.g. *Why is the dog barking? What will happen if Hugh walks across the bridge?*

2 Grammar
Past simple vs. past continuous review

Students covered these areas in SB2, Unit 2.

(a) Students read the sentences and identify the verb tense. Point out the similarity in construction between the past continuous and the present continuous. Ask students what the difference is (*the past continuous uses the verb* be *in the past*).

Answers
past simple: came, got
past continuous: was waiting, were walking

(b) Students underline other examples of both tenses from the text. Then students complete the rules.

Answers
past simple:
thought, arrived, came out, were, patted, started, got, decided, started, started, stopped, looked around, kept, looked down
past continuous:
was finally going, was travelling, It was raining, Shep was there waiting, were walking
Rule: past simple, when; past continuous, while

(c) Students complete the sentences using the correct form of the verbs in brackets. Encourage students to think about the actions happening at one point in the past and actions happening in the background.

Answers
2 came, were watching
3 phoned, was doing
4 was playing, hit
5 was surfing, found
6 were walking, started

Time conjunctions: *as / then / as soon as*

(d) Read through the explanation about the other time conjunctions. Check students understand that *as* is very similar in meaning to *while*, and *as soon as* is very similar to *when*. Point out that *as soon as* emphasises the fact that something happened immediately after something else happened.

> **Language notes**
> If students are getting confused with the use of these time conjunctions, you may want to point out the following.
> 1 *As* and *as soon as* are two time conjunctions used in complex sentences. This means that there are at least two parts to the sentence. With *when, while, as* and *as soon as*, there is no change in meaning if the order of the clauses in these sentences is changed. For example, *As soon as I got home, the phone rang.* This means the same as *The phone rang as soon as I got home.*
> 2 If the time conjunction is used at the start of the sentence, we commonly put a comma (,) between the two clauses.

(e) Read through the sentences with students. Check that they understand the time conjunction can be used at the beginning or in the middle of the two sentences and that the order of the sentences can be changed if necessary.

Answers
2 While I was walking, I heard a strange noise.
3 As I looked up, something hit me on the head.
4 As soon as the thing hit me, everything went black.
5 When I woke up, I was lying in a hospital bed.
6 As soon as I rang the bell, a nurse came to talk to me.
7 While the nurse was talking to me, I fell in love with her.

─── OPTIONAL ACTIVITY ───

Stronger classes
Students can write a few more sentences to finish the story. Give them the start to help.
As soon as I was better, …
Ask pairs to read out their sentences and vote on the best ending.

(f) Students complete the dialogue by putting the verbs in either the past simple or the past continuous tense. In feedback ask a few pairs of students to read the different parts. Encourage students to act out the dialogue rather than simply read it.

Answers
2 had   3 happened   4 was singing   5 went
6 did you do   7 came   8 wasn't working
9 were fixing   10 started

─── OPTIONAL ACTIVITY ───
Write on the board:
When Mum arrived home, I …
While she was taking off her coat, I …
When she came into the living room, I …
As soon as she saw me, she …
Students complete the sentences in pairs to make a short story. Ask pairs to read out their stories and check they are using the correct tenses. Students vote on the funniest / most original story.

Grammar notebook
Remind students to note down the rules for the past simple and the past continuous and to write a few examples of their own.

3 Speak and read

(a) **Weaker classes:** Write these words and phrases on the board: *soldier, war, travelling home, apple pie, station, Shep, walk home, storm, bridge, barking* and ask students to use them to retell the story of Old Shep with their partner. Encourage them to use time conjunctions as appropriate.

Stronger classes: Ask students to retell the story of Old Shep without putting any prompts on the board.

(b) Students read the second part of the story and find out what happened in the end (*the dog died two years before*). Ask students if they enjoyed the story and if the ending of the story surprised them.

4 Listen

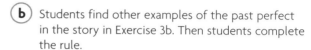 Tell students they are going to listen to a girl telling a similar story. Students note five differences from the story they read. Play the recording and repeat if necessary.

Weaker classes: Write these sentences on the board before the listening:
He was thinking about his mother's apple pie.
The soldier was coming home on the train.
The bridge was over a river.
When he got home, he met his mother.
The soldier's dog died two years ago.

Tell students to read the sentences and listen for five differences in the girl's story. Elicit some possible answers before playing the recording.

TAPESCRIPT

I heard this really, really old story the other day – from the 1940s, I think. It was about this soldier, he'd been in the war somewhere for a long time, and he was coming home and he was thinking about his old dog and his mother's home-made ice cream. Anyway, when he got home it was dark and rainy, and when he got off the bus his dog was there waiting. They started walking home and they got to a bridge over a road, and the dog started barking to stop the man going onto the bridge – because the bridge was broken. So the dog saved the man's life. When the man got home, he met his mother and father, they hugged, you know, and then the soldier told them about the bridge and the dog. 'Oh, no,' his mum said. 'That's impossible. Your dog died five years ago.' Sad story, huh?

Answers
1   He was thinking about his mother's home-made ice cream, not apple pie.
2   The soldier was coming home on the bus, not the train.
3   The bridge was over a road, not a river.
4   When he got home, he met his mother and father, not just his mother.
5   The soldier's dog died five years ago, not two years ago.

5 Grammar

Past simple vs. past perfect simple

Students covered the past perfect simple in SB2, Unit 15.

(a) Read the sentences with the class. Elicit the construction of the past perfect simple tense (*had + past participle*). Read the questions with the class and elicit answers (*before* for both questions). Point out that when we talk about an event in the past we use the past simple. Then if we talk about something that happened *before* this event we use the past perfect.

Weaker classes: Books closed. Present a situation of a famous person coming to a student's house for lunch. Ask students what they would need to do before they

arrived, e.g. *go shopping, cook lunch, clean the house,* etc. Now write on the board:
When Eminem (or other famous person) *arrived, I …*
Present and elicit possible endings to the sentence:
I had cooked lunch; I had cleaned the house.
Point out the structure of the past perfect (*had + past participle*) and its use. Give students other situations, e.g. other people coming to their house, and help them to construct similar examples. Students now open their books at page 20 and answer the questions.

Answers
1 before   2 before

(b) Students find other examples of the past perfect in the story in Exercise 3b. Then students complete the rule.

Answers
had cooked, had made, had saved, had gone
Rule: past simple; past perfect

OPTIONAL ACTIVITY

The following might help students if they are having difficulties with the past perfect. Write on the board:
Hugh turned round.
Ask students to look at the text and identify which event happened before it (*dog disappeared*). Get students to write the two events in the correct order on a timeline.

Write the full sentence underneath, using the past perfect: *When Hugh turned round, the dog had disappeared.* Do the same with the examples below, sometimes choosing the first action and sometimes the second.
- *bridge fell – Hugh looked down*
- *mother cooked dinner – they sat down for supper*
- *Shep saved Hugh's life – Hugh told his mother a story*
- *mother's face went white – Hugh looked up at his mother*

Point out that when we use the past perfect there is always another past event in the past simple.

Language notes
1   Students may confuse the past perfect with the present perfect and produce statements like:
    *I have finished my homework when the phone rang. Remind them of the use of the past perfect in English.
2   Remind students that we don't repeat the main verb in short answers. We don't say: **Yes, I had played.*

(c) Students complete the sentences with the correct form of the verbs in brackets. If students find this difficult, encourage them to think about which event happened first. This is the event that is in the past perfect.

Answers
1 arrived, had left   2 had finished, turned
3 got, had eaten   4 had gone, got

(d) If you set the background information as a homework research task, ask students to tell the class what they found out.

BACKGROUND INFORMATION

Ronaldo: Born in Rio de Janeiro, Brazil on 22 September, 1976, Ronaldo has become one of history's greatest strikers in football. He signed for his first club at 12 and has been awarded FIFA World Footballer of the year three times and was top scorer in the 2002 World Cup.

Real Madrid: Formed on 6 March, 1902, Real Madrid Football Club plays in the Spanish first division. The team play in all-white and their home stadium is the Santiago Bernabéu. Real Madrid has consistently been ranked as one of the top football clubs in Europe and they have won the Champions League eight times, more than any other team.

Inter Milan: This team is generally known in Italy as *Inter*. They play in black and blue stripes and their stadium is the San Siro, which they share with their great rivals, A.C. Milan.

Lecce: play in the first division in Italy. They play in red and yellow and their stadium is the Via del Mare.

Students complete the text with verbs in the correct tense. Ask students to check their answers with a partner before checking in open class.

Answers
1 ended   2 ran   3 cheered   4 hadn't played
5 had damaged   6 fell down   7 didn't get up
8 had injured   9 were   10 left

Grammar notebook
Remind students to note down the rules for the past simple and past perfect simple and to write a few examples of their own.

6 Read

Warm up

Write on the board:
My best friend is ...
a
b
c, etc. (list the alphabet until *z*)

Ask students to work with a partner and write an adjective for as many letters as possible of the alphabet. For example, *amazing*, *brave*, *clever*, etc. Give students a time limit, say 2 minutes. Check answers and see which pair has completed adjectives for the most letters.

(a) Ask students which adjectives from the warm up are real characteristics of a good friend. Elicit *loyal* and check students understand the meaning. Students read and complete the questionnaire. Help students with difficult vocabulary as necessary but leave detailed explanation until Exercise 7.

(b) Students check their answers with the key. Do they agree with it? Ask students who is the most loyal in the class.

7 Vocabulary
Friends and enemies

Remind students of the importance of phrasal verbs in English. Students choose the best meaning for the phrasal verbs from the questionnaire.

Answers
1 b   2 b   3 a   4 b   5 b   6 a

Vocabulary notebook
Encourage students to add this to the *Friends* section that they made in Unit 1 and to note down the words from this exercise. They may find it useful to note down translations of the words too.

8 Pronunciation
Linking sounds

Students covered this area in SB2, Unit 1.

(a) Students turn to page 120 and read through the sentences. Ask students what they notice about the underlined parts (*consonants at the end of words are immediately followed by a vowel*). Write the first sentence on the board and ask students how the underlined part is pronounced. Then play the rest of the recording.

TAPESCRIPT/ANSWERS
1   I always stick up for my friends.
2   I can't lie, but I don't want to tell on a friend.
3   Why should I get into trouble for something I haven't done?
4   That's a good reason to fall out.
5   I'm surprised anyone gets on with you.

(b) Play the recording again, pausing for students to repeat each sentence. Encourage students to link the consonant at the end of words with the vowel sound that begins the next work.

9 Speak

Students write another question for the quiz. Encourage students to use the phrasal verbs they studied in Exercise 7. Ask students to compare their answers to the questionnaire with a partner. Encourage them to give reasons for their answers. Students also ask the question they wrote. Tell students to decide which of them is more loyal.

Weaker classes: Give students situations and ask them to choose one and write possible answers, for example:

You are invited to a party but your friend isn't. Do you ...?
Your friend gets a higher mark for a piece of homework but it's a mistake. Do you ...?

> **Language note**
> You may want to help students with appropriate language for the comparison of their answers. For example:
> *I answered ... for question ... because ...*
> *Marco said ... for question ... while I said ...*
> *I chose ... for question ... but Ana chose ...*

┌ OPTIONAL ACTIVITY ═══════════════════
In pairs, students decide if they have ever been in any of the situations. They describe the situation they have been in and what they did.

Fiction in mind

10 Read

If you set the background information as a homework research task, ask students to tell the class what they found out.

BACKGROUND INFORMATION

Japan: is an island chain between the North Pacific Ocean and the Sea of Japan. There are four main islands: Hokkaido, Honshu, Shikoku, and Kyushu. The population is about 127 million (July 2003). Compulsory education begins at six in Japan with six years in elementary school. Then students spend three years in either junior high or lower secondary school. After this, students can optionally choose to spend three years in high school.

Staying Together: is a book published as part of the Cambridge English Readers series.

(**a**) Students read the question and look at the title and the cover of the book. Elicit *romance* and *love story*. Read the *blurb* (short description of the story) and check that students understand that Ikuko is female and Hiroshi is male.

(**b**) Ask students to read through the extract. Tell them not to worry about difficult vocabulary. You may like to read it aloud with them or alternatively the extract is recorded on track 32 of the Workbook CD/CD ROM.

Students read through the questions. Check difficult vocabulary: *fix, considerate.* Ask students to read the extract again and choose the best answers. They can

compare with a partner before feedback. Tell students to underline the reasons for their answers in the text.

Answers
1 c lines 2, 3
2 a lines 11–36
3 b lines 41, 42
4 a lines 49, 50
5 c lines 70, 71

> **Discussion box**
> **Weaker classes:** Students can choose one question to discuss.
> **Stronger classes:** In pairs or small groups, students go through the questions in the box and discuss them.
> Monitor and help as necessary, encouraging students to express themselves in English and to use any vocabulary they have learned from the text. Ask pairs or groups to feedback to the class and discuss any interesting points further.

11 Write

Warm up

Students look at the picture. Ask students what they think the note says. How does the woman feel?

(**a**) Students read the story quickly and answer the questions.

Answers
They met in London.
She had an accident

(**b**) This exercise can be set as homework. Ask students what they think of the story. Elicit the fact that the story doesn't have enough detail so it's not very interesting. Tell students that they are going to make the story more interesting by adding more details. Students answer the questions, adding as much detail as possible. Ask students for possible answers to the first few questions as an example.
Students re-write the story in 120–150 words.
Encourage students to use:
- relevant vocabulary from the unit
- linking words like *when, while, as soon as, then*
- appropriate tenses – past continuous, past simple, past perfect.

4 A working life

Unit overview

TOPIC: Jobs and work

TEXTS
Reading and listening: short texts about teenagers' career plans
Listening: a conversation about a dream job
Listening: a job interview
Reading and listening: Song: *So You Want to Be a Rock 'n' Roll Star*
Writing: a job application letter

SPEAKING AND FUNCTIONS
Discussing your future job
Discussing someone's ambitions
Role-playing a job interview
Discussing the events in a story
Discussing manufactured pop bands

LANGUAGE
Grammar: Present perfect simple and continuous review; *had better / should / ought to*
Vocabulary: Jobs and work
Pronunciation: /ɔː/ sh*or*t

1 Read and listen

If you set the background information as a homework research task, ask students to tell the class what they found out.

BACKGROUND INFORMATION

Work experience: Some school-age teenagers in Britain go on *work experience* programmes. This involves students spending some days or weeks at a company, school, hospital, etc. experiencing the environment and the kind of skills needed for work. Many companies organise work experience programmes in cooperation with local schools and colleges.

Warm up

Write these jobs on the board and check their meaning: *doctor, teacher, football player.* Ask students to put the jobs in order according to the: *salary, stress, number of hours.* Ask a few pairs to explain their answers. Elicit useful work-related vocabulary such as *earn (a salary), well/badly paid, stressful job, work long hours.* Finally, ask students which job they would most like to do of the three.

a Ask students to look at the photos and answer the questions. Check answers and ask students to give reasons. Make sure they understand the different jobs and industries.

Answers
1 engineer, (primary) school teacher
2 banking, computing or IT (information technology)

b Quickly ask the students if they have thought about their future jobs. Ask a few students what they hope to do. Give students a minute to read the article quickly and match each teenager with jobs and industries a to d.

Answers
a Lauren   b Gemma   c Mark   d Rob

c 🔊 Ask students to read the questions. Play the recording. Students answer the questions, checking their answers in pairs before feedback.

TAPESCRIPT
See the reading text on page 24 of the Student's Book.

Answers
1 Lauren   2 Gemma   3 Rob, Gemma   4 Mark
5 Rob
6 Rob: programming course at home.
   Lauren: watching what her father does.
   Mark: letters to banks.
   Gemma: visit to a primary school on work experience.

Vocabulary notebook
Encourage students to start a word map called *Work* and to note down the words from this exercise. They may find it useful to note down translations of the words too.

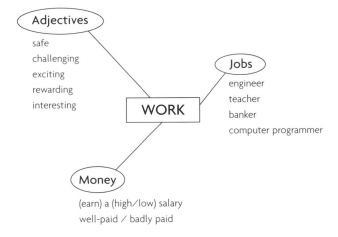

OPTIONAL ACTIVITY

Point out that Gemma talks about *work experience* (see background notes). Does the same system exist in the students' countries? Do students think this is a good idea?

Discussion box

Weaker classes: Students can choose one question to discuss.

Stronger classes: In pairs or small groups, students go through the questions in the box and discuss them.

Monitor and help as necessary, encouraging students to express themselves in English and to use any vocabulary they have learned from the text. Ask pairs or groups to feedback to the class and discuss any interesting points further.

2 Grammar

Present perfect simple vs. continuous review

Students covered these areas in SB2, Unit 12.

(a) **Weaker classes:** Books closed. Write on the board:
Tom has read the Harry Potter books.
Mark has been reading the Harry Potter books.

You can replace *Harry Potter* with more suitable books if necessary. Ask students which person has definitely finished reading the books (*Tom*) and which person has not necessarily finished reading them (*Mark*). Elicit how to form each tense (present perfect simple: *have/has* + past participle, present perfect continuous: *have/has + been + –ing* form of verb). Students now open their books at page 25 and follow the procedure for stronger classes.

Stronger classes: Ask students to read the examples in the book. Ask students which sentence talks about a completed action (*have decided*) and which action is probably incomplete (*have been thinking*). Elicit the construction of each tense and ask students to complete the rule.

Answers
simple; continuous

(b) Students underline other examples of present perfect simple and present perfect continuous in the text.

Answers
present perfect:
I've always wanted to be, I've already started, I've written, It's been

present perfect continuous:
I've been doing, I've been spending, I've been visiting

(c) Students complete the sentences with the verbs in the box. Check answers, encouraging students to decide if the action is finished or unfinished.

Answers
2 written   3 been writing   4 read
5 been playing   6 been reading

(d) Ask students to read through questions 1 to 7 and match them with answers a to g. Then students complete the answers using the present perfect simple or continuous. Encourage students to think about whether the action has finished or is continuing into the present.

Answers
1 b – 've eaten
2 e – 's been arguing
3 g – haven't seen
4 f – Has he been working
5 c – Have you cleaned
6 d – hasn't been learning
7 a – haven't finished

Grammar notebook

Remind students to note down the rules for the present perfect simple and present perfect continuous and to write a few examples of their own.

3 Speak

Explain that students should take turns to tell their partner about the different subjects on the page. Their partner should ask questions using the prompts and the present perfect simple or continuous.

Look

Students read the Look box. Elicit other verbs that are not normally used in the continuous form, e.g. *see, hear, want, prefer, like, love, hate, think, feel, forget, remember.*

Language note

Students may make pronunciation errors with the present perfect continuous tense. If they don't hear the contracted auxiliary, students may produce sentences like: **I been reading.*
Students may think that the contracted *s* is *is* and produce sentences like: **He is been writing a letter.* *Been* sounds like *being* so students may say: **He's being writing a letter.*

OPTIONAL ACTIVITY

Ask each student to write four true facts about themselves in the present simple or continuous tense. For example,
I live in Bologna.
I want to be a doctor.
I am studying English.
Write a few sentences about yourself on the board and then add a sentence in the present perfect to explain how long these facts have been true. For example:
I have lived in Bologna since 1995.
I have been teaching English for ten years.

Ask students to write a sentence about their facts in the present perfect simple or continuous.

If students write each sentence on a different slip of paper, you can play a guessing game where students try to guess who wrote each sentence.

4 Listen

If you set the background information as a homework research task, ask students to tell the class what they found out.

BACKGROUND INFORMATION

Muse: This UK rock band is from Devon in south-west England. School friends Matthew Bellamy (guitar/vocals), Chris Wolstenhome (bass) and Dominic Howard (drums) first formed the band as teenagers. Their first record deal was with Madonna's Maverick Records. Their albums include *Showbiz* (1999), *Origin Of Symmetry* (2001) and *Absolution* (2003).

a Ask students to look at the picture and decide what they can say about Claire's interests.

Possible answers
She's interested in music
She plays the electric guitar

b Students read the conversation. Check answers.

Answers
She has a gig, supporting another band called Muse. She should think about her future and talk to her mum and dad.

c Ask students to read through the words in the box (it is not necessary for them to understand what they mean at this stage). Students then try to complete the dialogue. Play the recording while students read and check their answers. Play the recording again, pausing where necessary to clarify any problems. Encourage students to guess the meaning of the words in the box from the context and to add new words to their vocabulary notebooks.

TAPESCRIPT
See the dialogue on page 26 of the Student's Book.

Answers
1 advertisement   2 application form   3 fill it in
4 CV   5 interview   6 job   7 career

d Students work with a partner and discuss the questions. Monitor students and encourage them to use *should* when they are giving advice. Ask a few pairs for their advice for Claire and what they think her parents will say.

e Students listen and check their answers to the second question. Ask students what their parents might say in this situation.

TAPESCRIPT

Claire   Err, Dad – can I speak to you for a minute?

Dad   Sure, what is it, sweetheart?

Claire   Well, I've got a gig with the band. We're going to play at The Ballroom.

Dad   Oh, that's fantastic! When?

Claire   In a couple of weeks. We're going to open for Muse. They're really famous, you know.

Dad   Wonderful! I know Muse, they're great. I hope there's free tickets for us! Jeanie! That's great news, Claire. You must be really excited.

Claire   Well, there is one more thing.

Dad   Yes?

Claire   Hi, Mum. Well, I've been thinking. Now that the band's getting some success I'm not sure I really want to apply for a job.

Mum   So you mean you want a career as a singer?

Claire   Well, I mean, I know that this is difficult to understand, but, erm, yes.

Mum   You're right it's difficult to understand. It's one thing to have a hobby – singing's not a bad hobby – but if you seriously think you can—

Dad   Now, hold on, Jeanie, you should be pleased for Claire. Muse are a great band—

Claire   Thanks a lot, Mum, it's really nice to have your support. I'm going out.

Dad   Now look what you've done!

Mum   You're a great help, aren't you! You just want to be a pop-star-dad ...

Answer
Claire's dad thinks it's great news but her mum thinks music is a hobby.

5 Grammar
had better / should / ought to

Students covered this area in SB1, Unit 14.

a Students try and complete the advice from memory. Encourage students to guess even if they don't remember the exact words. Students check answers in the dialogue.

Answers
1 ought to
2 should
3 'd better

Look

Read through the rule and the *Look* box with students. Point out that with *you had better* is used for giving strong advice or indicating that something is the right thing to do, e.g. *You'd better see a doctor about that.*

Language notes

1 *Should* and *ought to* are modal verbs. You may want to remind students about some common features of modal verbs:
There is no infinitive, e.g. **to should*
There is no third person, e.g. **shoulds, oughts to*
Question forms are constructed by inversion, e.g. *Should I ...? Ought I to ...? not *Do I should ...?*
The negative form of *ought to* is *ought not to* (or *oughtn't to*).
2 Make sure students are not saying **should to go*
3 *Had better* is used with *you* to give strong advice. When we use *had better* with *I* or *we*, we commonly indicate an intention, e.g. *I'd better go to bed* implies that I am going to bed. *Had better* can imply a threat and therefore is not appropriate for giving polite advice.

OPTIONAL ACTIVITY

Write these sentences on the board:
1 *I'd never been to England before last year.*
2 *He's thinking about the question.*
3 *I think we'd better go home now.*
4 *It's been raining all day.*
5 *I'd like a drink.*
6 *She's not here – she's gone shopping.*

Ask students to identify the contractions in each sentence. Check answers and that students understand which construction(s) are being used in each sentence.

Answers

1	had	–	past perfect
2	is	–	present continuous
3	had	–	had better
4	has	–	present perfect continuous
5	would	–	would like
6	is, has	–	present simple, present perfect

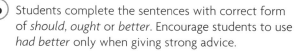 Students complete the sentences with correct form of *should, ought* or *better*. Encourage students to use *had better* only when giving strong advice.

Answers

2 ought   3 should   4 shouldn't   5 better not (see Language note about *had better*)   6 ought

Grammar notebook

Remind students to note down the rules for this structure and to write a few examples of their own.

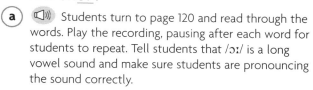

6 Pronunciation

/ɔː/ *short*

a Students turn to page 120 and read through the words. Play the recording, pausing after each word for students to repeat. Tell students that /ɔː/ is a long vowel sound and make sure students are pronouncing the sound correctly.

TAPESCRIPT

1 more   2 four   3 before   4 saw   5 short
6 bought   7 caught   8 court   9 ought   10 forty

b Students read through the sentences and underline the /ɔː/ sounds. Go through the first one with them as an example, if necessary. Play the recording, pausing after each sentence for students to check and repeat.

TAPESCRIPT/ANSWERS

1 I s<u>aw</u> the b<u>all</u>, and I c<u>augh</u>t it.
2 We can't play tennis here – the c<u>our</u>t's too sh<u>or</u>t!
3 We <u>ough</u>t to buy f<u>our</u> m<u>ore</u>.
4 But we b<u>ough</u>t f<u>or</u>ty bef<u>ore</u>!

7 Vocabulary

Jobs and work

a Students match the expressions with the definitions. Encourage students to match as many as possible and check answers in pairs. Play the recording, pausing as necessary for students to check their answers and repeat the phrases.

TAPESCRIPT/ANSWERS

1	h	apply for a job
2	g	employee
3	j	employer
4	a	full-time
5	c	part-time
6	i	qualifications
7	e	resign
8	f	salary
9	d	trainee
10	b	unemployed

Vocabulary notebook

Students can add these words to their word map on *work*.

OPTIONAL ACTIVITY

Stronger classes

Point out the suffixes *–er* and *–ee* in *employer* and *employee*. Ask students to write words and their meanings using the suffixes and the words *train* and *interview*.

Answers

trainee	–	someone being trained
trainer	–	someone training
interviewee	–	someone being interviewed
interviewer	–	someone interviewing

(b) Students complete the questions using the expressions. Check students use the correct form of the words as necessary, e.g. verbs without *to*, plural forms of nouns.

Answers
2 unemployed 3 salary 4 apply for 5 resign
6 part-time 7 employees 8 qualifications
9 employer 10 trainee

8 Listen

Tell students they are going to listen to a job interview. Ask them to look at the picture and decide who is the interviewer and who is the applicant. Play the recording while students take notes under the headings. Point out that students do not need to write full sentences. Ask students to check answers with a partner. Play the recording again, pausing as necessary to check answers.

TAPESCRIPT

Interviewer Ms Hill, come in and sit down. So, tell me – why have you applied for the job of sales assistant at PC Paradise?

Ms Hill Well, I've always been interested in computers. My parents bought me one when I was seven, and I spend hours on it. Also, I think I have the right qualifications. I like working in teams, and, I'd love to work for your company.

Interviewer I see from your CV that you have experience as a sales assistant.

Ms Hill Yes. I had a Saturday job at TechWorld while I was at school. Then when I finished college I got this job at Computer City in town. I've been working there as a sales assistant for more than two years. It's been great. The problem is, there doesn't seem to be any chance of getting a better position there. You know, maybe assistant manager …

Interviewer Would you be interested in training to be a manager?

Ms Hill Well, yes, definitely.

Interviewer OK. Tell me a bit about your qualifications.

Ms Hill I've taken various courses in computing. I did IT at school, of course, and then I did programming at college. I'm also doing a part-time web page design course two evenings a week. I thought about doing IT at university, but I wanted to start work.

Interviewer Right. Are you still at your present job?

Ms Hill Yes. I've been thinking about resigning, but people say it's much better to find another job while you're actually working.

Interviewer That's true, and it's not much fun being unemployed. How much …

Answers

Job wanted	–	sales assistant
Experience	–	Saturday job at TechWorld (a computer shop), while at school
Current job	–	Sales assistant at Computer City (a computer shop)
Qualifications	–	did IT at school, did programming at college, is now doing a part-time web page design course

9 Speak

Tell students they are going to roleplay a job interview. In pairs they should decide who is the interviewer and who is the applicant. The interviewer should prepare the questions and the applicant should prepare the answers. Remind students to use appropriate tenses to talk about their experience (past simple for past experience and present perfect for their present job).

Weaker classes: Put the students in small groups of interviewers and applicants. Students prepare the role with their group before roleplaying with a partner from a different group. Students could also write the dialogue of their interview before speaking. Encourage them to use their written work as little as possible.

Students roleplay the interview and then change roles. Ask a few pairs to act out their interviews for the class. Ask the class to decide if the applicant should get the job.

┌─ **OPTIONAL ACTIVITY** ─────────────

Stronger classes
If your students enjoy this kind of activity, you can use the following ideas for different interviews. Tell the applicants that they:
i) should exaggerate their experience as much as possible, or
ii) are feeling really nervous about the interview.
Tell the interviewers that:
i) the applicant arrived really late, or
ii) this is their fifth interview today and they are really bored.

10 Speak and listen

If you set the background information as a homework research task, ask students to tell the class what they found out.

BACKGROUND INFORMATION

The Byrds: Formed in California, USA, in 1964, The Byrds were a folk music group. They were heavily influenced by the folk singer Bob Dylan and their first major hit was a cover of his song *Mr Tambourine Man*. In 1966, they released the album *Younger Than Yesterday*, which included the song *So You Want to Be a Rock 'n' Roll Star*, which reached number 29 in the US charts in 1967.

The Monkees: Mickey Dolenz, Davy Jones, Peter Tork and Mike Nesmith were chosen from 437 applicants for an American television series. TV executives wanted an American band that might be as successful as The Beatles. On 12 September 1966, the first episode of The Monkees was broadcast and the show quickly became very popular. The songs *Last Train to Clarksville* and *I'm a Believer* reached number one in the US charts. However, the public were shocked when they found out that the band didn't actually play any instruments or do much singing on their songs. The band split up in 1968

Manufactured bands: The Spice Girls is a good example of this: in 1993 five girls were selected, from 400 applicants, for an all girl pop band. However, the idea of record companies creating bands to appeal to as many people as possible is not new. In the 1980s New Kids on the Block sold millions of records. In fact, the idea started in the 1960s with the hugely popular band The Monkees.

Warm up

Books closed. Ask students to tell their partner about their dream job and why they would like to do it. Ask a few students to tell the class about their choice. Discuss briefly the advantages and disadvantages of jobs that make you famous.

(a) Students now open their books at page 28 and read the things rocks stars do. Check difficult vocabulary: *autograph*, *agent*, *contract*. Ask students to think of other things rocks stars do.

Possible answers
rehearse for concerts, practise singing, play musical instruments, go on tour, give a concert, make a CD, give interviews, go on television

(b) 🔊 Tell students that the song is about advice. Read the title and ask students who they think the advice is for (*someone who wants to be a rock and roll star*). Students listen and complete each space with a word. Play the recording and give students time to check their answers. Remind students that some of the words will rhyme. Play the recording again if necessary.

TAPESCRIPT
See the song on page 28 of the Student's Book.

Answers
1 say   2 guitar   3 play   4 all right   5 company
6 week   7 game   8 money

(c) Students match expressions 1 to 6 from the song with definitions a to f. Encourage students to use the lyrics of the song to help them decide.

Answers
2 a   3 c   4 b   5 f   6 d

Did you know ...?

Read the information in the box with students and ask for some differences between the bands (The Monkees are a lot smarter in appearance than The Byrds because their image had to appeal to the majority of the public). Check students understand the meaning of a 'manufactured band' (*a band specially put together by music companies*).

Discussion box
Weaker classes: Students can choose one question to discuss.

Stronger classes: In pairs or small groups, students go through the questions in the box and discuss them.
Monitor and help as necessary, encouraging students to express themselves in English. Ask pairs or groups to feedback to the class and discuss any interesting points further.

11 Write

(a) The planning for this exercise can be done in class and the writing can be set as homework. Tell students that the letter is a formal letter of application and it displays formal letter-writing conventions in English. Point out that these are very important when writing a letter in English. Students read the letter quickly and find the job Sophie is applying for (*website designer*).

(b) Read the questions together and explain any difficult vocabulary: *enclose, requested*. Students read the letter again and answer the questions. Check answers and elicit differences between English conventions and those in students' L1.

Answers
1 She puts her name at the bottom, under her signature. She puts her address in top right-hand corner.
2 She puts the date under her address, telephone number and email.
3 She starts the letter with *Dear Sir or Madam*. If you know the name of the person you are writing to you write *Dear Richard Clark* or *Dear Deborah Jenkins*.
4 The first paragraph talks about her reasons for writing.
5 She uses phrases such as *First of all, Secondly, Lastly* and starts each main reasons with a new paragraph.
6 She ends the letter with how she can be contacted and the formal phrase *I look forward to hearing from you*. If you know the name of the person you are writing to, you begin with their name and end *Yours sincerely*.

(c) Students choose an advertisement from page 27 and write a letter of application using formal letter-writing conventions. Encourage students to use appropriate vocabulary and organisation in describing their relevant experience. In a subsequent lesson, encourage students to read each other's letters and decide if they are good enough to get an interview.

┌─ OPTIONAL ACTIVITY ─────────────────
│ Students can make up their own advertisements
│ and write an appropriate letter of application.

Vocabulary notebook
Encourage students to note down the expressions from Exercise 11 and to use them whenever appropriate in their writing.

Module 1 Check your progress

1 Grammar

(a) 2 'm working   3 prefer   4 Does, go   5 don't like

(b) 2 've just painted   3 hasn't been, for   4 haven't finished, yet   5 've already seen   6 still haven't cleaned

(c) 2 left   3 didn't, tell   4 haven't sent   5 has, had   6 Did, go

(d) 2 were building, found   3 wrote, was waiting   4 was, talking, got   5 was climbing, arrived   6 didn't find, was cleaning

(e) 2 weren't, had eaten   3 had gone, got   4 arrived, hadn't started   5 took, hadn't finished   6 Had, seen, saw

(f) 2 've written   3 have, seen   4 haven't been learning   5 haven't finished   6 's been snowing

(g) 2 You ought to tell the truth   3 You shouldn't sit there   4 Hadn't you better stop now   5 She should apologise

2 Vocabulary

(a) 2 About   3 with   4 for   5 in   6 up   7 of

(b) 1 part-time   2 salary   3 qualification   4 resign   5 unemployed   6 employee   7 employer
mystery word: trainee

(c) 2 says   3 tell   4 told   5 saying   6 say

How did you do?
Student's work out their scores. Check how they have done and follow up any problem areas with revision work for students.

Module 2
Survival

YOU WILL LEARN ABOUT ...

Ask students to look at the pictures on the page. Ask students to read through the topics in the box and check that they understand each item. You can ask them the following questions, in L1 if appropriate:

1 *Where do you think you might see this face?*
2 *Where do you think she lives?*
3 *Why do you think she is famous?*
4 *Where is the man?*
5 *What did the man do?*
6 *What do you think she is eating?*

In pairs or small groups students discuss which topic area they think each picture matches. Check answers.

Answers
1 Intelligent computers
2 Tribes in danger
3 A famous sailor
4 Reality TV
5 A space tourist
6 The secrets of long life

YOU WILL LEARN HOW TO ...

Use grammar

Students read through the grammar points and the examples. Go through the first item with students as an example. In pairs, students match the grammar items in their book. Check answers.

Answers
Future plans and arrangements: I'm going to see the match tomorrow.
Future predictions: Steve might be there, but Sally probably won't be.
First conditional with *if* and *unless*: We won't win unless Andy plays.
Present perfect passive: Oh no! My bike's been stolen.
Future passive: The exam results will be announced next week.
Causative *have* (*have something done*): Alison's had her hair cut.
make / let / be allowed to: My parents let me drive their car.
Modal verbs for obligation, prohibition and permission: You mustn't talk in here.

Use vocabulary

Write the headings on the board. Go through the items in the Student's Book and check understanding. Ask students if they can think of one more item for the *Travel* heading. Elicit some responses and add them to the list on the board. Students now do the same for the other headings. Some possibilities are:

Travel: *tram, underground* (all SB2, Unit 5), *journey, emigrate* (SB2, Unit 1), *airport*

Television: *the News, quiz show, programme*

make and *do*: *make fun of someone,* make *someone laugh, make a funny face* (all SB2, Unit 7), *do your homework, do the shopping*

Extreme adjectives: *hot – boiling, frightening – terrifying* (SB2, Unit 8)

5 Travel

Unit overview

TOPIC: Unusual and interesting journeys

TEXTS
Reading and listening: an article about a solo woman sailor
Listening: an interview about a sailing project
Reading: an article about a man who paid to travel into space
Reading: texts about travellers who completed significant journeys alone
Writing: an email about a trip

SPEAKING AND FUNCTIONS
Discussing a modern female heroine – Ellen MacArthur
Discussing space tourism
Predicting future events in a story
Talking about crime stories

LANGUAGE
Grammar: Future review
Vocabulary: Travel; Movement
Pronunciation: /ɡənə/ *going to*

1 Read and listen

If you set the background information as a homework research task, ask students to tell the class what they found out.

BACKGROUND INFORMATION

Ellen MacArthur: was born in 1976 in Derbyshire, a county in England that has no borders with the sea. Although she has been well known in France since racing there in 1997, the British public only discovered her in 2001 during the 100-day Vendée Globe Round-the-World solo race. This was partly due to the modern technology which meant that the race could be reported in 'real time'. For example, her daily diary was published in a Sunday newspaper in England. Also, during the race she answered questions live on the Internet. Everything she wrote and said revealed Ellen MacArthur as an incredibly brave and determined woman.

Vendée Globe Round-the-World solo race: This race has been held five times between 1989 and 2004. In the 2001 race, 15 out of 24 competitors finished, and the winner, Michel Desjoyeaux of France, set a new record for the race of just over 93 days. Ellen MacArthur was the youngest ever competitor to finish, the fastest woman around the planet and only the second solo sailor to get around the world in less than 100 days.

Warm up

Ask if students know the names of any famous sailors, past or present. Discuss briefly what students know about the people they suggest. If necessary, prompt students with names such as Cabot (Giovanni Caboto), Columbus (Cristóbal Colón), Cook, Drake, Magellan and Vasco de Gama.

a Ask students to look at the pictures and elicit anything they know or think about the woman in the photo. Point out the map and encourage them to guess what she has done but do not comment at this stage. Use the photo to pre-teach *sails* (the material that catches the wind), *mast* (the central pole that holds the sail) and *hull* (the main part of the boat that is normally underwater).

b Students read the questions and the text quickly to find the answers. Encourage students to look for the answers to their questions and not to spend time on new words.

Answers
1 In 2001 because she came second in a round-the-world solo race.
2 She only sleeps for 20 minutes at any one time.

c ◁)) Read the questions with the students and pre-teach difficult vocabulary: *fix/repair, single-handed, exhausted, worthwhile*. Play the recording. Students read and listen to the text and then answer the questions. Students check their answers with a partner before feedback.

TAPESCRIPT
See the reading text on page 34 of the Student's Book.

Answers
1 When she was 18. (para 1)
2 100 days. (para 2)
3 She lived in a hut. (para 2)
4 She slept under the boat. (para 3)
5 Because she is sailing on her own. (para 4)
6 Because it's dangerous to sleep for a long time while at sea. (para 4)

Write these sentences on the board. Ask students to read the last two paragraphs again and decide if the sentences are true or false. Students correct false sentences:

1 *Ellen climbed the mast of the boat during the night.* (F – She climbed the mast very early in the morning)
2 *The sea was quite calm.* (F – The winds were blowing at 100 kph)
3 *She repaired the sails very quickly.* (F – It took her many hours to make the repairs)
4 *She was very tired when she had finished.* (T)
5 *Someone was kicking her while she was up the mast.* (F – The wind feels like someone kicking you)
6 *Ellen thinks she is lucky to have a diary.* (F – She thinks she is lucky to be at sea)

Discussion box

Weaker classes: Students can choose one question to discuss.

Stronger classes: In pairs or small groups, students go through the questions in the box and discuss them.
Monitor and help as necessary, encouraging students to express themselves in English and to use any vocabulary they have learned from the text. Ask pairs or groups to feedback to the class and discuss any interesting points further.

2 Listen

If you set the background information as a homework research task, ask students to tell the class what they found out.

BACKGROUND INFORMATION

Trimaran: This is a fast sailing boat with three hulls (the body of a boat or ship, most of which goes under the water). There is a large centre hull and two smaller outer hulls. The first trimarans were built by the Polynesians almost 4,000 years ago.

a 🔊 Point out the photo of the trimaran. Ask students if they know how many hulls the boat has (*three*). Explain that Ellen is preparing for a series of new challenges by building a special boat. Students listen to the recording to find the three pieces of information about the boat. Play the recording and check answers.

TAPESCRIPT

Interviewer Ellen, perhaps you could tell us about your latest project.

Ellen Well, at the moment we're working on a project to build a new boat, a trimaran ...

Interviewer A trimaran – that's a boat with three hulls, yes?

Ellen That's right. And this one's going to be a bit different, because usually, trimarans are about 20 metres long, erm, that's because there are lots of sailing races where the rules say that you can only have a 20 metre boat, but this one's going to be 25 metres long.

Interviewer Won't that be a problem?

Ellen No, no, it won't be a problem, because we aren't going to use the new boat for races, we're going to use it for solo round-the-world records umm, records like the 24 hour record, the transatlantic record, and perhaps the round-the-world record.

Interviewer I see. So do you have any limits on how you design and build this new trimaran?

Ellen Sort of. We can use any technology we want, but it's important to think about safety too. I mean, it has to be a boat that I can sail alone. It's the most important part of the design process, to make it bigger but still manageable for one person.

Interviewer When will it be finished?

Ellen Well, they're starting in four weeks' time and it's going to take about seven months to build. Hopefully, umm, it will be finished in December.

Interviewer So why are you building the boat in Australia?

Ellen Because it'll be summer there in December. It means that when the boat's launched we'll be able to train and sail it every day if we want to. The weather is much better there at that time of year than in Europe.

Interviewer Yes, I can imagine.

Ellen Anyway, then we'll bring the boat back to Britain, by sea, you know, and then I can learn about the boat by sailing her.

Interviewer Well, Ellen, we wish you the very best of luck.

Ellen Thank you.

Answers
size – 25 metres long
when it will be finished – December
where they are building it – Australia

b 🔊 Students read the questions. Elicit possible answers to the questions from the students. Then play the recording again. Students check answers with a partner before repeating the recording, pausing if necessary.

Answers
1 Because the rules of lots of races say the maximum length of the boat is 20 metres.
2 She wants to beat records like the 24-hour record and the transatlantic record.

3 To make a big boat that can be controlled by only one person.
4 About seven months.
5 Because it will be summer in Australia when they launch it.
6 They will sail it back.

3 Grammar
Future review

Students covered some of this area in SB2, Unit 4.

(a) Books closed. Ask students which ways they can talk about the future in English. Elicit *(be) going to*, present continuous and *will*. Write these sentences on the board:
I can't see you tomorrow night. I .... football.
Wait a few minutes. He .... home soon.
You need some help. I .... your bags for you.
I've decided. I .... be a doctor.

Elicit the future forms that complete the sentences (*'m playing, 'll be, 'll carry, 'm going to be*) and the difference in their meaning (*present continuous* for arrangements, *will* for predictions, promises and offers, *(be) going to* for intentions made before the time of speaking).
Students now open their books at page 35 and read through the example sentences from the listening and the different forms of future reference. Point out that the present continuous for arrangements is often used with a time reference to indicate that we are talking about a future, rather than present, event.

(b) Students look at the pictures and the sentences and circle the correct future form. Check answers and encourage students to give reasons for their choice.

Answers
1 We're going to have (intention)
2 it's going to rain (present evidence)
3 won't be (prediction)
4 I'm not going to study (intention)
5 I'm seeing (arrangement)
6 will be (prediction)

(c) Students complete the sentences with the verb in the correct future form. Point out that the word at the end of the sentence gives them a clue for the appropriate future form. Ask students to read their sentences aloud. Check pronunciation of the contracted *will* /əl/.

Answers
1 'm meeting   2 'm going to walk   3 'll be
4 'll break   5 are visiting   6 's going to study

Language notes
1 Deciding between different future forms in English can be difficult. Students sometimes do not distinguish between the present continuous for arrangements and *going to*. Sometimes this is acceptable, e.g. *I'm going to play tennis tomorrow* instead of *I'm playing tennis tomorrow*.
2 Many students prefer *will* as a future form because it is closer to their L1, e.g. *What are you doing in the holidays? *I will go to Spain* instead of *I'm going to Spain*.
3 Remind students that the negative form of *will* is *won't*.

Grammar notebook
Remind students to note down the rules for the future and to write a few examples of their own.

4 Pronunciation
/gənə/ *going to*

(a) 🔊 Students turn to page 120 and read the sentences. Ask students how they think *going to* is pronounced. Play the recording.

TAPESCRIPT
1 Hurry up – we're <u>going to</u> be late!
2 She's <u>going to</u> sail round the world.
3 I think I'm <u>going to</u> sneeze.
4 He isn't <u>going to</u> come.
5 Do you think it's <u>going to</u> rain?

(b) 🔊 Point out that in informal speech *going to* is often pronounced /gənə/. Play the recording again, pausing after each sentence for students to repeat. Point out that /gənə/ replaces *going to* and check students are saying /gənə/ not /gənə tuː/.

5 Read

If you set the background information as a homework research task, ask students to tell the class what they found out.

BACKGROUND INFORMATION

Dennis Tito: was born on 8 August, 1940 in New York, USA. He is a multimillionaire and has university degrees in Astronautics and Aeronautics, and Engineering. He was a scientist at NASA and in 1972 he started an investment company.

The International Space Station (ISS): This is a permanent space station built with the cooperation of the USA, Russia, Canada, Japan and Europe. It was built for scientific research and observation in space. At least two people have been on the ISS since November 2000. The space station orbits the earth at a height of approximately 386 km. It takes about 92 minutes for the ISS to orbit the earth.

ProSpace: is a non-profit group based in the USA that wants to make space travel available to the public as soon as possible. It asks the government to invest in space programmes and tries to ensure that space remains the property of everyone in the world, not just government organisations. Charles Miller is the founder of ProSpace.

Warm up

Books closed. Write on the board:
The place I would most like to visit is ...
Ask students to complete the sentence for themselves and discuss their answer with a partner. Ask some students for their answers and reasons. Students can vote on the most unusual or interesting place.

(a) Students now open their books at page 36 and look at the photo of Dennis Tito. Ask students if they know anything about the story. Elicit answers but do not comment at this stage.

(b) Make sure students understand that the main subject is the most important message in the text. Give students a time limit of one minute to read the text and decide on an answer.

Answer 2

(c) Students read the text again and underline words in each paragraph that mean the same as phrases 1 to 7. Encourage students to add the words to their vocabulary notebook and write example sentences.

Answers
1 setting off   2 routine   3 cosmonauts   4 the sum (of)   5 recovered   6 commented   7 depart

┌─ OPTIONAL ACTIVITY ─────────────
Write these sentences on the board. Students decide if they are true or false and correct the false sentences:
1 *Dennis Tito is very wealthy.* (T)
2 *There were four people on the spacecraft.*
   (F – There were three people – Dennis and two cosmonauts)
3 *Dennis was sick when he arrived at the space station.* (F – Dennis was sick as the spacecraft left the earth's atmosphere)
4 *ProSpace is the name of Dennis's company.* (F – ProSpace is the name of Charles Miller's company)
5 *Charles Miller thinks that space tourism will increase in the future.* (T)

Discussion box
Weaker classes: They can choose one question only to discuss.

Stronger classes: In pairs or small groups, students go through the questions in the box and discuss them.

Monitor and help as necessary, encouraging students to express themselves in English and use *will* and *going to* appropriately. Ask pairs or groups to feedback to the class and discuss any interesting points further.

6 Vocabulary
Travel

(a) Students work with a partner and discuss where they would find the things in the box.

Possible answers
terminal – airport
customs – airport, border between countries, ferry port
check-in desk – airport
boarding card – airport, ship/ferry
platform – train station, underground station, sometimes in a bus station
departure lounge – airport, large bus stations, ferry port
timetable – train station, underground station, bus stop, bus station

(b) Students choose the correct words. Encourage them to guess before checking their answers in a dictionary.

Answers
1 cruise   2 flight   3 journey   4 trip (cruise and tour refer to holidays)   5 tour

Look
Read through the Look box with students. Point out that we use *on* with *plane/train/bus/bike* and *in* for *car/taxi*.

(c) Students complete the text with the correct form of the verbs in the box. Check answers.

Answers
1 get in   2 arrived at   3 checked in   4 get on
5 had taken off   6 missed   7 arrived in

┌─ OPTIONAL ACTIVITY ─────────────
For further practice of the travel vocabulary, write the following halves of sentences on separate slips of paper:
1 *I couldn't find my boarding card because I ...*
2 *The bag was so heavy that he couldn't ...*
3 *We arrived at ...*
4 *His plane is going to arrive in ...*
5 *I couldn't find my train ticket because I ...*

a *the airport very early.*
b *had left it in the departure lounge.*
c *had left it on the platform.*
d *check it in.*
e *Madrid at 12.30.*

You can duplicate the halves of sentences according to the number of students in your class but make sure every half sentence has a match. Ask students to memorise the half of their sentence. Then students walk round the class trying to find someone with the other half. Ask each pair to read their sentence to check answers.

Answers
1 b 2 d 3 a 4 e 5 c

Vocabulary notebook
Encourage students to start a word map called *Travel* with the categories *places*, *verbs*, *at the station*, *at the airport*, *confusing words*, etc. and to note down the words from this exercise. They may find it useful to note down translations of the words too.

7 Speak

Read the situations with students. Give students a few minutes to think of ideas by themselves before making predictions with their partner. Make sure students are using *will* and encourage them to use the travel words they learned in Exercise 7. Ask each pair for some of their answers.

Possible answers
He'll discover his problem at the check-in desk.
He won't be able to get into the departure lounge.
He'll miss his flight and arrive in New York late.

OPTIONAL ACTIVITY
Ask students to make notes on their next holiday or their ideal holiday. Tell students to use the questions below. Check that students understand that an ideal holiday can be anywhere.

1 *Where are you going?*
2 *How are you going to travel?*
3 *How long are you going to stay?*

Students work with a partner and compare their answers. Make sure that students are expressing their plans using *going to* and not *will*. In feedback, ask students to tell the class about their partner's plans. Students should use *going to* to express these opinions.

Culture in mind

8 Read

If you set the background information as a homework research task, ask students to tell the class what they found out.

BACKGROUND INFORMATION

Harriet Quimby: was born in 1875, in Michigan, USA and was a journalist and theatre critic. In 1910 she learned to fly and qualified in 1911 – the first woman in the USA to get a pilot's licence. Her achievement of being the first woman to fly across the English Channel

did not receive as much attention as it should have – the *Titanic* had sunk just a few days earlier.

Francis Chichester: was born in 1901, in Devon, England and moved to New Zealand at the age of 18. He set up an airline and between 1927 and 1930 it carried 9,000 passengers without one serious accident. In 1929 he returned to England and learned to fly. His first solo flight was from New Zealand to Australia. Over the next 30 years he made several important solo flights and in addition to his achievements in the text, in 1967 he sailed from England to Australia in 107 days. In 1971, at 70 years old, he sailed from England to West Africa, then on to the Caribbean and then back to England. He died in 1972. In Westminster Abbey in London, there is a plaque dedicated to him, Sir Francis Drake and Captain James Cook.

Libby Riddles: was born in 1956 in Wisconsin, USA and moved to Alaska when she was 17 years old. She became interested in sled dogs and two years later entered her first race, where she came first. She entered the Iditarod for the first time in 1980, when she finished in 18th place. She is still raising sled dogs and competing in dog races. She is also a public speaker and an author.

David Hempleman-Adams: was born in 1956 near Swindon, England, and became an enthusiastic climber while at university. In 1983 he attempted to walk to the geographic North Pole but a bad fall stopped him from getting there. A year later an attack by a polar bear stopped him from reaching the magnetic North Pole. In 1993 he eventually climbed Mount Everest and by 1995 David had become the third Briton to climb the highest mountains in each of the seven continents: Africa (Kilimanjaro), Antarctica (Vinson Massif), Asia (Everest), Australia (Kosciusko), Europe (Elbrus), North America (McKinley) and South America (Aconcagua).

The geomagnetic North Pole: This is just one of the earth's four north poles – the others are the geographic North Pole, the magnetic North Pole and the northern pole of inaccessibility.

(a) Tell students that each of the people in the photos has made an important journey alone. Elicit answers, encouraging students to use appropriate vocabulary, but do not comment at this stage.

(b) Students read the headings in the text and check their ideas, matching the names to the photographs. Encourage students not to worry about unknown words and just confirm their predictions from 8a.

Answers
1 David Hempleman-Adams 2 Libby Riddles
3 Francis Chichester 4 Harriet Quimby

c) Read the questions and check students understand difficult vocabulary: *awards*, *apart from*. Students read the texts and answer the questions. Set a time limit, of 4 minutes if appropriate. Ask students to check their answers in pairs before feedback.

Answers
1 He stopped in Sydney 2 11 months 3 He told her he was going on a skiing holiday 4 Her dogs, Duhan and Sister 5 Francis Chichester's journey around the world was the longest in time and distance: 47,000 kilometres and 225 days

Discussion box
Weaker classes: Students can choose one question to discuss.

Stronger classes: In pairs or small groups, students go through the questions in the box and discuss them. Monitor and help as necessary, encouraging students to express themselves in English and to use any vocabulary they have learned from the text. Ask pairs or groups to feedback to the class and discuss any interesting points further.

9 Phrasal verbs
Movement

a) Ask students to find the phrasal verbs in the text about Harriet Quimby with the same meaning as the underlined phrase in sentences 1 to 4. Encourage students to write the infinitive of the verbs, their definition and an example sentence in their vocabulary notebooks.

Answers
1 took off 2 head towards 3 touched down
4 went back

b) Students complete the sentences with the correct phrasal verb. Remind students to think about the form of the verb.

Answers
1 headed towards 2 took off 3 went back
4 touched down

10 Write
Students covered email-writing in SB2, Units 5, 7 and 10.

BACKGROUND INFORMATION

Barcelona: is the second-largest city in Spain and the chief city of the region of Catalonia. It is situated on the Mediterranean coast of north-east Spain and its population is approximately 1.5 million (2003).

Emoticons: Also sometimes called *smileys,* emoticons are characters used to represent an emotion. Emoticons are meant to be viewed by tilting your head left so the right side of the emoticon is at the bottom of the 'picture'. They are used in email messages or in chat on the Internet. The creator of the original emoticons :-) and :-(was Scott Fahlman.

a) The planning for this exercise can be done in class and the writing can be set as homework. Students read the text quickly and find how long Hannah is staying in Barcelona.

Answer
three or four days

b) Read the questions with students. Check that students understand this is an informal email and so questions 1 to 3 are about informal conventions in emails. Students answer the questions and check their answers in pairs, before feedback.

Answers
1 Arrived here …; Have had great fun …; Left my bag …; Have to finish …
2 :-) means that the writer is being humorous and also a little sarcastic as it is unlikely the weather is good at home.
3 She starts with *Hi!* and ends with *Love.*

c) Tell students they are going to write an email to a friend from Ellen MacArthur or Dennis Tito. Encourage students to use the plan and the email conventions in Hannah's email.
In a subsequent lesson, encourage students to read each other's emails and choose one they would most like to answer.

┌─ **OPTIONAL ACTIVITY** ─────────────
If your students enjoy the idea of emoticons, ask them to match the following signs with their meaning.
1 |-O   a I'm crying
2 :'-(b I'm laughing
3 :-s   c I'm sending you a kiss
4):[d I'm tired
5 :-x   e I'm confused
6 :-D   f I'm angry or frustrated

Answers
1 d   2 a   3 e   4 f   5 c   6 b

6 Live forever!

Unit overview

TOPIC: Future and cutting-edge technology

TEXTS
Reading and listening: an article about amazing technology in medicine
Listening: a programme about the secrets of long life
Reading and listening: Story: *Ben calls Caroline*
Writing: a composition about life in the future.

SPEAKING AND FUNCTIONS
Discussing computer chips in your brain
Talking about the causes of stress

LANGUAGE
Grammar: Future predictions; First conditional review, *if* and *unless*
Vocabulary: Verbs with prepositions; Phrasal verbs with *into*
Pronunciation: Weak and strong forms of prepositions
Everyday English: *believe it or not*; *between you and me*; *the fact is*; *I know what you mean*

1 Read and listen

If you set the background information as a homework research task, ask students to tell the class what they found out.

BACKGROUND INFORMATION

Ray Kurzweil: was born in 1948 in New York, USA, and is widely regarded as one of the leading inventors of our time. His range of work is huge and has included the first machine to turn print to speech, the first music synthesizer, and the first commercially successful speech recognition technology. Kurzweil's website, www.KurzweilAI.net, is a leading resource on artificial intelligence with over 100,000 readers. He is author of *The Age of Intelligent Machines* (1990), a best-selling book which made many accurate predictions about the development of technology over the next few decades including the importance of the Internet. Overall, Kurzweil's inventions have involved combining major advances in computer science while also producing practical products that meet important needs. He has also started several very successful businesses to bring these inventions to the public. His inventions have helped disabled people, enriched the world of music, and increased the usefulness of computers for everyone.

Warm up

Ask students how many of them have Internet access and/or mobile phones. Point out that before 1996 few people had access to the Internet and before 1998 mobile phones were only used by businessmen or the very wealthy. Ask students what kind of technology they expect to see over the next ten years. Discuss students' ideas in L1 if necessary.

a Students look at the picture and predict which of the things Ray Kurzweil does. Check students understand *compose music, people with disabilities* and *research*. Encourage students to give reasons for their answers but do not comment at this stage.

b 🔊 Students read and listen to the text and check their ideas. Play the recording. Check answers and ask students to give reasons for their answers.

TAPESCRIPT
See the reading text on page 40 of the Student's Book.

Answers
1 Ray Kurzweil, author of ... (Para 1)
5 ... interested in using this technology to help people with physical disabilities (Para 3)
6 ... is one of the world's leading computer research scientists ... (Para 1)

c Pre-teach difficult words in the text: *computer chip, Parkinson's disease, virtual hostess, disability*. Students match titles A to F to paragraphs 1 to 6. Check students understand *immortality*. Ask students if they would like to be immortal. Check answers and encourage students to give reasons.

Answers
1 B   2 D   3 E   4 A   5 C

┌─ OPTIONAL ACTIVITY ─────────
If students find matching exercises difficult, encourage them to use the following techniques:
- If they don't know the answer to one question, do the easier questions in the matching exercise. This will give them fewer choices with the harder items.
- Try and discount the obviously wrong answers and then choose the best of the remaining answers.

Discussion box
Weaker classes: Students can choose one question to discuss.

Stronger classes: In pairs or small groups, students go through the questions in the box and discuss them.
Monitor and help as necessary, encouraging students to express themselves in English. Ask pairs

or groups to feedback to the class and discuss any interesting points further.

2 Grammar
Future predictions
Students covered some of this area in SB2, Unit 4.

a Books closed. Students think back to some of their predictions from the warm up exercise. Ask students which verb they used to make predictions about the future (*will*). Now students open their books at page 41 and complete the sentences using the text in Exercise 1.

Answers
1 might   2 will, will probably   3 are likely to
4 probably won't

b **Weaker classes:** Write on the board:
In ten year's time ...
everyone has a computer
people live for an average of 90 years
you speak excellent English
you are married
Ask students to decide in pairs which of the events are certain (*will happen*), likely (*are likely to happen*), possible (*might happen*) or impossible (*won't happen*). Students now follow the procedure for stronger classes.

Stronger classes: Students complete the chart. Point out that both 2 and 3, and 6 and 7, give the same idea of the chance of something happening. Check answers and summarise the main points about the scale: *will* and *won't* are at opposite ends of the scale (100% and 0%), *might* and *might not* are in the middle, and *is (not) likely to* and *will probably / probably won't* have similar meanings.

Answers
1 will
2 will probably   3 is likely to
4 might   5 might not
6 probably won't   7 isn't likely to
8 won't

> **Language note**
> Remind students of the difference in word order between the positive and negative of *will*:
> *I will probably go* but in the negative *I probably won't go.*

c Students read the sentences and decide if the speaker in these situations is sure or not sure about something happening. Check answers.

Answers
1 'll   2 might not   3 might   4 won't

d Read through the example with students. Students rewrite the second part of the sentences using the word in brackets. Check answers and that students are using *be* appropriately with *likely to*.

Answers
2 He isn't likely to win   3 The traffic will probably be bad   4 He's likely to fail   5 It probably won't rain tomorrow

e Ask students to look at the pictures. Elicit *pregnant*, *dinosaur*, *life on other planets*. Read the first statement and ask students if they think this will happen in the future. Ask a few students for their opinion and check that students understand the strength of the sentence that each student makes. Refer students to the language in Exercise 2b for making predictions. If students are having difficulties, do a second example together. Then students make predictions for the rest of the statements. Ask a few pairs to tell you their answers to different statements.
Weaker classes: Students can write sentences about their predictions first.

Grammar notebook
Remind students to note down the rules for future predictions and to write a few examples of their own.

3 Listen
If you set the background information as a homework research task, ask students to tell the class what they found out.

BACKGROUND INFORMATION
The Bible: is the sacred book of Christianity. There are two sections of the Bible: the Old and the New Testament. Each section consists of a number of separate books, written at different times by different authors.

Methuselah: was the oldest man in the Bible. He died at the age of 969 years.

Iceland: This country is an island in northern Europe between the Greenland Sea and the North Atlantic Ocean, north-west of the UK. Its population is about 280,000 (July 2003) and the capital is Reykjavik.

The Vikings: Scandinavian traders and pirates who aggressively raided much of northern Europe between the 8th and 11th centuries.

a Students answer the question. Encourage students to say who the person is, e.g. a relative or a friend, and see who knows the oldest person.

b Check students understand the activities in the box. You may want to pre-teach some difficult vocabulary: *lettuce, taking vitamins, doing crosswords*. Ask students to decide which activities they think help people to live longer and which do not. Encourage students to discuss the activities with their partner and give reasons. Check students' ideas and discuss the most interesting activities but do not give the answers at this stage.

c ◁))) Play the recording while students listen and tick the activities mentioned. Play the recording again if necessary, pausing after each speaker. Check answers.

TAPESCRIPT

Presenter Some people can live to be nearly 130 years old. But what are the secrets of old age? What can we do to help us to live longer? We interviewed people in Cambridge to see what they thought.

Girl Someone told me it's good if you sing a lot. A lot of people have breathing problems when they get old, and singing is a good way to help.

Man It doesn't make any difference what I eat, I think that unless I do some exercise I won't live very long. I can't even run for the bus without getting tired.

Boy Have a laugh, have a bit of fun. I think until people realise life's not so serious, they can look older than they really are.

Man Well, I think keeping your emotions inside can make you ill. So when you're angry about something, you should tell someone, err, shout maybe. I don't mean hit someone or anything ...

Woman OK, now listen. Sit in the sun for twenty minutes a day, do a crossword to keep your mind busy, eat lettuce at night to help you sleep, go to bed at 10.00, and don't worry about anything! If you do all those things, you'll live as long as me.

Presenter There are, however, those who believe that it doesn't really matter what ...

Answers
singing; doing exercise; having fun; getting angry; sitting in the sun; doing crosswords; eating; lettuce at night; going to bed early

d ◁))) Students read the questions. Pre-teach difficult vocabulary: *genetics*, *genes*, *ancestors*, *Viking times* (between 8th and 11th centuries), *family tree* and *related to*. Then play the recording. Students check answers with a partner before repeating the recording, pausing if necessary.

TAPESCRIPT

Presenter There are, however, those who believe that it doesn't really matter what we do to our bodies, because, they say, the secret to living a long life is in our genes. Kari Steffanson, a genetics researcher from Iceland, explains.

Kari Here in Iceland we are very, very interested in our family trees – we have records that go back over a thousand years to the Vikings. So we looked at records for people who died at 70 years old, and compared them to people who lived to be more than 90. And we found that the people

who lived longer were much more likely to be closely related to each other – first cousins, uncles and so on.

Now, of course, you could say that maybe these people just lived a healthier life, but, you know, Iceland is a very small country, so people here have a very similar lifestyle. So we analysed their blood, and found that there was one gene that was different, and it seems to help us to live longer. We call it the Methuselah gene, and if we can find out exactly how it works, then we will be able to make drugs that could help us to live a lot longer.

Answers
1 b   2 b   3 a   4 c   5 b   6 c

4 Grammar

First conditional review, *if* and *unless*

Students covered the first conditional in SB2, Unit 4.

a **Weaker classes:** Read through the sentences with students. Check that students understand *unless* means *if ... not*. Ask students to choose the correct form of the verb in each clause of the sentence.

Stronger classes: Books closed. Write on the board:
Unless I _____ do some exercise, I _____ live very long.
If you _____ all those things, you _____ as long as me.

Ask students to complete the sentences from the listening. Play the first part of the programme for students to check. Then follow the procedure for weaker classes. Check the answers.

Answers
1 I do, won't live
2 you do, you'll live

Ask students whether the speaker in sentence 1 has stopped doing exercise (*no*). Then elicit whether the verb refers to the present or the future (*the future*). Point out that a present tense is used in the first conditional to refer to the future.

b Students choose the correct words in the rules.

Answers
future; present simple; will or won't

Language notes
1 Students often try to use *will* in both parts of the first conditional, e.g. **If it will rain tomorrow, I will stay at home.* Point out that the present simple is used after *if* or *unless* in the first conditional.
2 Remind students that the *If* phrase can come first or second in the sentence but the present simple tense always goes with the *If* phrase.

3 Remind students to use the contracted form in conditional sentences as it is more natural.

c **Weaker classes:** Students complete the sentences with the verbs in the box. Go through the first example with students and point out one verb in each sentence must be in the present simple and the other is formed with *will*.

Stronger classes: Books closed. Write these sentences on the board and ask students to complete them with the correct form of the verb:
1 *You'll fall if you .... (not be) careful.*
2 *If you .... (come) shopping with me now, I .... (help) you with your homework later.*
3 *Unless we .... (leave) the house right now, we .... (not get) there for the start of the film.*
4 *I .... (copy) this CD for you if you .... (want).*
5 *I .... (not call) you at the weekend unless you .... (want) me to.*

Answers
1 aren't   2 come, 'll help   3 leave, won't get
4 'll copy, want   5 won't call, want

d Students construct first conditional sentences. Do the first sentence as an example with students. Point out that students should use *unless* instead of *if ... not*. Check answers and make sure students are using the correct tenses. Tell students there maybe more than one possibility.

Answers
1 If you play with matches, you'll burn your fingers.
2 If you go near that dog, it'll bite you.
3 If you don't come and eat your pizza now, there won't be any left. or Unless you come and eat your pizza now, there won't be any left.
4 If you're tired, I'll do the washing up.
5 If you don't slow down, you'll crash the car. or Unless you slow down, you'll crash the car.
6 I'll buy you a new bike if you pass all your exams.

Time conjunctions: *if / unless / when / until / as soon as*

Students covered some of this area in SB2, Unit 4.

e Ask students to match the two parts of the sentences. Check answers and elicit the meaning of the conjunctions *when*, *until* and *as soon as*. Point out that sentence 1 refers to a general truth and therefore uses the present simple in both parts of the sentence.

Answers
1 e   2 d   3 a   4 c   5 b

Language notes
1 Remind students that *unless* means *if ... not*.
2 Students may produce statements like **Unless I don't work, I will ...* Remind them that *unless* is always followed by a positive verb.
3 *As soon as* is similar to *when* except that it means at the exact moment/time something happens or will happen, e.g. *As soon as I get home, I'll tell my brother.*
4 *Till* is another word for *until* and is more common in conversation, e.g. *I'll work till 4.*

f Students look at the illustrations and choose the correct time conjunction in the conversations. Students check answers in pairs before feedback.

Answers
1 unless, until   2 if, as soon as   3 If, unless
4 as soon as, when

OPTIONAL ACTIVITY ════════════
Write on the board:
1 *You'll get married ...*
2 *As soon as you get home today ...*
3 *When you pass your exams ...*

Students complete the sentences about their partner. Ask students to read their sentences to their partner. Check students are using an appropriate conjunction. Ask a few pairs to read out their sentences and find out whether their partner agrees with their predictions.

Grammar notebook
Remind students to note down the rules for the first conditional and to write a few examples of their own.

5 # Vocabulary and speaking
Verbs with prepositions

a Explain that many verbs in English often have a preposition after them, e.g. *listen to*. Point out that these verbs are not phrasal verbs – their meaning is more obvious than with phrasal verbs. Elicit examples of verbs like this that students know already, e.g. *listen to*, *depend on*, etc. Students complete the verbs with the correct preposition. Check answers and that students understand the meaning of the verbs.

Answers
1 with   2 for   3 for   4 about   5 about

b Students complete the sentences with the verbs from Exercise 5a and the correct preposition. Check answers. Encourage students to write down the relevant preposition when they record verbs in their vocabulary notebooks.

Answers
1 get ready for   2 argue with   3 worry about
4 revise for   5 think about

(c) Ask students to decide how stressful the events are in Exercise 5a. Students give each verb a mark from 0 to 5. Students compare answers with a partner before feedback. Ask a few pairs for their scores and discuss interesting comments with students. Encourage students to use appropriate language, e.g. *I think revising for exams is (much) more stressful than arguing with your parents.*

(d) Students work in groups to discuss other stressful things in life. If necessary, give students some ideas to start the discussion, e.g. *doing exams, changing schools, family problems, arguing with friends*, etc. Encourage students to give ideas on how to make things less stressful and to use relevant verbs.

Vocabulary notebook
Encourage students to start a section called *Verbs with prepositions* and to note down the words from this exercise. They may find it useful to note down translations of the words too.

6 Pronunciation
Weak and strong forms of prepositions

(a) 🔊 Students turn to page 120 and read the sentences. Tell students that prepositions have a weak and a strong form. We pronounce the vowel sounds in prepositions in their weak form as schwa /ə/, for example *for* is pronounced /fə/. Play the recording and ask students to circle the prepositions that are pronounced in their weak form and underline those that are stressed.

TAPESCRIPT/ANSWERS
1 I'm revising (for) my exams.
2 What are you looking <u>for</u>?
3 I can't stand talking (to) him.
4 Who's John talking <u>to</u>?
5 Who are you looking <u>at</u>?
6 I think he's (at) work.
7 You can leave if you want <u>to</u>.
8 We're going (to) London for the weekend.

(b) 🔊 Ask students to identify the sentences where the preposition is pronounced in its strong form. Ask students why they are pronounced in their strong form (*they are the last word of the sentence and all prepositions in the final position are pronounced in their strong form*). Play the recording again, pausing after each sentence for students to check and repeat.

Ben calls Caroline
7 Read and listen

BACKGROUND INFORMATION
Indie music: The term indie music is short for independent music. This originally meant that the music was produced independently of major record labels. However, in Britain is has become a description of a type of music that is broadly guitar-based. Examples of indie bands include *Radiohead* and *Muse*.

Hong Kong: See background information in Unit 2.

Warm up

Ask students what they can remember about the last episode of the story. (*Ben has been living in Hong Kong but is now back in England. Ben's parents are probably separated. Ben hasn't got a job, yet. Joanne is at college.*)

(a) 🔊 Ask students to read the questions and predict the answers but do not comment at this stage. Play the recording while students read and check their predictions. Tell students to underline the answers in the dialogue. Check answers in open class. If students ask questions about vocabulary, write the words on the board but do not comment at this stage.

TAPESCRIPT
See the story on page 44 of the Student's Book.

Answers
Ben thinks Joanne is a bit full of herself (she thinks she is very important) but Caroline thinks she has changed and she's a nice person now. Matt's in trouble. She thinks he has a money problem.

(b) Ask students to read through sentences 1 to 5. You may want to pre-teach difficult vocabulary: *break up, indie music, go into* (talk about). Ask students to read the text again and decide if the statements are true or false. Students correct the false statements.

Answers
1 T   2 F – He doesn't want to talk about his parents.   3 F – He thinks Matt is crazy.   4 T   5 F – Caroline doesn't think it's strange as Matt hasn't seen Ben for a year.

8 Everyday English

(a) Ask students to find expressions 1 to 4 in the story on page 44 and decide who says them.

Weaker classes: Check answers at this stage.

Answers

1 Ben   2 Ben   3 Ben   4 Caroline

Students then match the expressions with the situations. Go through the first item with them as an example if necessary. Check answers.

Answers

a 4   b 1   c 2   d 3

(b) Ask students to read through the sentences and complete the answers. Go through the first sentence with them as an example if necessary.

Answers

1 believe it or not   2 The fact is   3 between you and me   4 I know what you mean

┌─ OPTIONAL ACTIVITIES ─────────
See Unit 2, Exercise 11: Everyday English, Optional Activities.

9 Vocabulary

Phrasal verbs with *into*

(a) Ask students to read through the phrasal verbs and encourage them to use the context to help them decide. Point out that all the phrasal verbs in this exercise are inseparable. Students check answers with a partner.

Answers

1 c   2 a   3 b   4 d

(b) Ask students to complete the sentences with the appropriate phrasal verbs. Go through the first item with them as an example if necessary. Remind students to use the correct form.

Answers

1 turned into   2 look into   3 bump into   4 go into

Vocabulary notebook

Encourage students to add these to the section *Phrasal verbs* from Unit 2 and to note down the words from this exercise under the heading *into*. They may find it useful to note down translations of the words too.

10 Write

> ### BACKGROUND INFORMATION
>
> **Chip:** Also known as a microchip, this is a very small piece of electronic equipment, especially in a computer, that contains extremely small electronic circuits, and can perform particular operations.
>
> **Parkinson's disease:** First described in 1817 by James Parkinson, a British surgeon, this disease affects communication between neurons in the brain and the muscles and therefore causes problems with coordination.

Students can do the preparation in class and the writing for homework.

(a) Read the title of the composition with students. Ask students to read the text quickly and see if the writer agrees or disagrees (*disagrees*).

(b) Elicit the basic organisation of a composition, e.g. introduction, argument/discussion and conclusion. Students read the composition again and find which paragraph matches each function. Point out that each paragraph has a topic sentence, where the main idea is given. (These have been underlined in the composition). Check answers.

Answers

1   second and third paragraphs
2   fourth paragraph
3   first paragraph

(c) Read the sentences with students and make sure they understand the idea of topic sentences. Tell students they are going to write a composition about one of the questions. Encourage them to plan their composition and to use the structure shown in the example text. In a subsequent lesson, encourage students to read each other's compositions and vote on the most convincing.

7 Campaigning for survival

Unit overview

TOPIC: Tribes in danger, environmental planning

TEXTS
Reading and listening: an article about a threatened tribe
Listening: speeches about town development
Reading: an extract from a thriller
Writing: a letter to a newspaper about plans to build a new hotel

SPEAKING AND FUNCTIONS
Discussing organisations which help tribal people
Talking about life in the future
Discussing a thriller

LANGUAGE
Grammar: Present passive and past passive review; Present perfect passive; Future passive; Causative *have*
Vocabulary: *make* and *do*
Pronunciation: Stress pattern in *have something done*

1 Read and listen

If you set the background information as a homework research task, ask students to tell the class what they found out.

BACKGROUND INFORMATION

Jarawa: The Jarawa are a largely un-contacted people, living on the Andaman Islands in the Indian Ocean. Both British and Indian settlers have moved onto their islands over the last 150 years, but the Jarawa have chosen to maintain an almost complete isolation. They are very different in appearance from their Indian neighbours, and DNA tests suggest that their closest relatives are African. Because of the Jarawa's voluntary isolation, and the fact that no one outside the tribe really speaks their language, very little is known about them. We do know that they live a hunter–gatherer lifestyle, hunting pig and monitor lizard, fishing with bows and arrows, and gathering seeds, berries and honey. They are nomadic, living in bands of 40 to 50 people.

Andaman Islands: Belonging to the Andaman and Nicobar Islands Union Territory of India, this is a group of approximately 200 islands situated midway between India and Burma. The islands are hilly, covered in forest and mostly uninhabited. Port Blair is the major community on the islands.

Warm up

Ask students to imagine a life without school, work, television, supermarkets, etc. Discuss the following questions with students, in L1 if necessary:
Would you like this kind of life?
What would you do in your spare time?
Would school be important in this kind of life?
What about work?
What do you think would happen if you were suddenly given all the things you have today?

a Students read the questions. Encourage students to use the information in the pictures to answer the questions. Elicit/pre-teach: *tribe, organisation, nomadic, hunt, self-sufficient*. Elicit answers but do not comment at this stage.

b Students read the first two paragraphs quickly to check their ideas. Encourage students not to look up every new word but just note down any new words they feel important. Check answers.

Answers
1 The person is from the Andaman Islands.
2 A simple life without work or money. They eat small animals, fish, berries and honey.

c Ask students to read through the questions. Point out that *settlement* comes from *settlers*, which was covered in Unit 1 of Student's Book 2. Check the meaning of *forced settlement*.

Ask students to match topics A to D with paragraphs 1 to 4. Again, encourage students not to look up every new word but just find the general theme of each paragraph. Check answers and encourage students to give brief reasons for their choices.

Answers
1 D   2 B   3 A   4 C

d ◁)) Ask students to read through the questions. Check students understand the questions and explain difficult vocabulary: *give up, sense of identity, campaigns, respect, rights, court case*. Play the recording and encourage students to take brief notes about the questions during the listening. Then give students time to read the text closely again and to check their answers with a partner.

TAPESCRIPT
See the reading text on page 46 of the Student's Book.

Answers

1 No one outside the tribe speaks their language.
2 Tribes are no longer self-sufficient; they become more likely to catch new diseases and they are exposed to alcohol; the culture of the tribe and their sense of identity is easily destroyed.
3 Survival carried out a number of campaigns and asked the Indian government to respect the rights of the tribe.
4 The road is now closed and the settlers have gone.

OPTIONAL ACTIVITY

Write these definitions on the board. Ask students to find words in the text that match the definitions:

1 *People from the same family.* (para 1) **(relatives)**
2 *A word to describe a group of people that does not live in any one place for a long time.* (para 2) **(nomadic)**
3 *Able to provide everything you need, especially food, for yourself without the help of other people.* (para 2) **(self-sufficient)**
4 *A set of ideas or a plan of what to do in particular situations.* (para 3) **(policy)**
5 *Actions taken to achieve a political aim.* (para 4) **(campaign)**

Discussion box
Weaker classes: Students can choose one question to discuss.

Stronger classes: In pairs or small groups, students go through the questions in the box and discuss them.
Monitor and help as necessary, encouraging students to express themselves in English. Ask pairs or groups to feedback to the class and discuss any interesting points further.

2 Grammar

Present passive and past passive review

Students covered these areas in SB2, Units 6 and 9.

Warm up

Books closed. Write these sentences on the board:
1 *We don't know much about the Jarawa.*
  Not much ...
2 *The government built a road through the forest.*
  A road ...

Ask if students can complete the phrases to mean the same as the sentence above. Give students a minute to decide their answers in pairs and then elicit their answers. Ask students if they remember the name of this construction (*the passive*). Ask if students notice any differences between the two sentences. Elicit that the first sentence is in the present and the second is in the past.

(a) Students open their books at page 47 and quickly label each sentence. Remind students that the construction is usually used when we are more interested in the person/thing the action was done to and that we only include the person/thing that did the action if it is important.

Answers
present simple passive
past simple passive

(b) Students find further examples of the passive in the text. Ask students to decide whether each example is present or past passive. Then students complete the rules.

Answers
Survival was founded ... (past)
A road was built ... (past)
A tribe's sense of identity can easily be destroyed. (present)
Rule: be, past participle; by

(c) Students complete the sentences using the verb in brackets in the present or past passive form. Do the first question as an example if necessary and point out that time phrases often help them decide if the sentence is present or past. Ask students to check answers with a partner.

Answers
1 is supported   2 was given   3 was interviewed
4 is (not) funded   5 were discovered
6 are treated   7 was made   8 is known, are brought

Grammar notebook
Remind students to note down the rules for present passive and past passive and to write a few examples of their own.

3 Grammar

Causative *have* (*have something done*)

(a) Books closed. Choose one of these examples and ask students what they would do in the following situations: *their hair is too long; their bike is broken; they want to know the value of a piece of jewellery*

Use more relevant examples for your group if necessary. Elicit the idea that we don't usually do anything in these situations ourselves. Point out that we normally go to someone else for the service. Ask students who would provide the service in each case (*a hairdresser, a bike shop, a jeweller*). Ask students what the person would do (*cut their hair; repair their bike; value their jewellery*).

Write these sentences on the board:
The hairdresser cut my hair.
The bike shop repaired my bike.
The jeweller valued my jewellery.

Now ask students to think about how they can rewrite the sentences beginning I ... Students can try and complete the sentences themselves. Give them an example of *I had my hair cut* and try and get them to rewrite the other two sentences (*I had my bike repaired*; *I had my jewellery valued*). Tell students that this construction is called the *causative* and is used to talk about situations where someone provides a service for us. Ask students to think of other examples.

Students open their books at page 47 and read the examples.

(b) Ask students what the subject is in each sentence (*They*, *I*, *My mum*). Ask them who might provide the service in each sentence (*probably the authorities*, *a hairdresser*, *a telephone engineer*).

(c) Students complete the rule.

Answers
someone, us

(d) Read the situation and ask students to look at the cartoon. Point out the construction of 'He always has his hair cut.' You may want to do this exercise in open class as examples of the causative. Otherwise, students complete the sentences. Check answers.

Answers
1 He always has it washed.   2 He always has it cut.
3 He always has it made.

─── OPTIONAL ACTIVITY ──────────
Students work with a partner and write down other things that Mr Hill never does himself, e.g. *He never feeds his dog*, *He never irons his shirts*, etc. Give pairs a time limit of 3 minutes. The students swap their sentences with another pair and each pair rewrites the sentence using causative *have*, e.g. *He always has it fed*, *He always has them ironed*.

(e) Students make sentences using the prompts, causative *have*, and the words from the box. Check students understand the regular verbs *pierce*, *dye*, *shave*, and *tattoo*. Point out that students need to think about the appropriate tense, e.g. the present perfect for things your friends *have had done*. Complete a few examples with students.

Possible answers
Many of my friends have had their ears pierced.
None of my friends have had their body tattooed.
My parents wouldn't allow me to have my hair dyed.
I would love to have my ears pierced.
I would hate to have my body tattooed.
My parents don't want me to have my head shaved.

Grammar notebook
Remind students to note down the rules for causative *have* and to write a few examples of their own.

4 Pronunciation
Stress pattern in *have something done*

(a) 🔊 Students turn to page 120 and read the sentences. Ask students which words they think are stressed. Play the recording and ask students to mark the stressed words.

TAPESCRIPT/ANSWERS
1 Have you had your <u>hair</u> <u>cut</u>?
2 Dad's going to have a <u>phone</u> <u>installed</u>.
3 They had the <u>road</u> <u>closed</u>.
4 They had the <u>people</u> <u>removed</u>.
5 Have you had your <u>camera</u> <u>fixed</u>?
6 He's having a <u>garage</u> <u>built</u>.

(b) 🔊 Play the recording again, pausing after each sentence for students to check and repeat. Make sure they are stressing the correct words.

5 Listen

(a) Ask students to look at the pictures and decide who is supporting the plan (*Phil*) and who is against it (*Samantha*).

(b) 🔊 Tell students they are going to listen to Samantha talking about the plans. Ask them to read through the sentences. Check difficult vocabulary and pre-teach: *cut down*, *developer*, *(make) a mess*, *factory*. Then play the recording. Students check answers with a partner before repeating the recording, pausing if necessary.

TAPESCRIPT
Samantha   Hello everybody – thanks for coming. I'm Samantha – Samantha Bailey – and I'm part of the campaign to stop the new hotel in the park.

I think you all know what the plans are – they want to use part of the parkland to build a new hotel so that more tourists will come to the town. We've got too many tourists already, haven't we? You all know that two hotels have been built here in the last five years – when's it going to stop?

If they build this hotel, a lot of really nice trees in the park will be cut down to make room for the hotel, and some of the places where children go to play, well, they'll be lost. These developers are going to make a mess of the town. They're only interested in making money.

I know what we've been told: 'Build a new hotel and more jobs will be created'. Well, maybe. But why not build the new hotel outside the town? There's a lot of land out there that could be used – out where the old factory was. It doesn't make sense to build another hotel in the town. We need to do something – now! Let's all do our best to keep this town a really nice place! Let's all make a big effort to stop them destroying the town that we want to live in!

Answers

1 F (Two hotels have been built in the last five years.)
2 T   3 F   4 T

c 🔊 Tell students they are now going to listen to Phil. Ask students to read the paragraph and encourage them to predict possible answers. Then play the recording. Students check answers with a partner before repeating the recording, pausing if necessary.

TAPESCRIPT

Phil   Well, hello everyone, I'm Phil. I don't want to make fun of Samantha but I have to say that I disagree with a lot of what she says. First of all, she talks about 'destroying the town' – well, this new hotel has got nothing to do with 'destroying' the town. It's to do with bringing the town into the twenty-first century. We need to make progress here! I'm sorry, Samantha, but the old factory site has been bought by other developers, and a new sports centre will be built on that land. Now isn't that a great idea? Isn't that better than having a piece of park for children to play in? I think it is – and I think that a new hotel will make a big difference to the town. More tourists will mean more jobs and a better life for everyone here. This plan will do the town a lot of good – we should be supporting the idea, not fighting against it. Let's have the new hotel!

Answers

1   destroyed
2   into the twenty-first century
3   other developers
4   a sports centre
5   more jobs (and a better life)

d Students decide who they agree with. Encourage students to give reasons for their opinion.

6 Vocabulary
make and do

a 🔊 Tell students that *make* and *do* are common verbs in English. Tell students that *make* is used to talk about constructing something. There are also several phrases that use either *make* or *do*, e.g. *make money* or *do your best*. Students read the sentences and complete them with the correct form of *make* or *do*. Ask students to compare their answers with a partner. Then play the recording from Exercise 5 for students to check their answers.

Answers

1 make   2 make   3 making   4 make   5 do
6 make   7 make   8 make   9 make   10 do

b Students decide if the phrases go with *make* or *do*. Encourage students to say the phrases aloud and think whether they sound right or wrong. Check answers.

Answers

make – money, fun of (someone), a difference, sense, an effort, a mess, room
do – your best, a lot of good

Language note

Students often confuse *make* and *do*, especially when their L1 has only one verb as an equivalent. Make is used to talk about building, constructing, producing, creating:
We make yoghurt at home.
I've made you a drink.
Do is used to describe an action without saying exactly what the action is:
We did some things around the house at the weekend.
Do is used to talk about work and jobs:
I didn't do any work today.
Have you done your homework?

OPTIONAL ACTIVITY

For further revision of phrases with *make* or *do*, students can play a game in pairs. Tell them to write each phrase in the table in Exercise 6b, e.g. *progress*, *your best*, etc., on a separate slip of paper. Students put the slips of paper in a bag and take it in turns to choose a phrase and read it to their partner. Their partner must simply say *make* or *do* according to which verb is used with the phrase. If students get it right, they get a point. If students get it wrong, they should put the phrase back into the bag. Students continue until the bag is empty.

Vocabulary notebook

Encourage students to start a section called *make* and *do* and to note down the words from this exercise. They may find it useful to note down translations of the words too.

7 Grammar
Present perfect passive

a Remind students of the passive tenses they studied earlier in the unit.

Weaker classes: Books closed. Write on the board: *Developers have built two hotels in the last five years.* Ask students to identify what is doing the action (*the subject – developers*), and what is being done by the verb (*the object – two hotels*). Ask students to identify the tense (*present perfect simple*). Point out that we are more interested in the two hotels and elicit how a passive construction would begin (*Two hotels ...*). Ask students to complete the sentence and write the passive construction on the board (*Two hotels have been built by the developers in the last five years*).

Ask students which part of the sentence can be omitted (*by the developers*). Students turn to page 49 and complete sentences 1 to 3 with the verbs given. Check answers. Then students complete the rule.

Stronger classes: Ask students to complete the sentences with the verbs given. Check answers and elicit the tense of the passive construction (*present perfect*). Then students complete the rule.

Answers
1 have been built   2 have been told
3 has been bought
Rule: be, past participle

b Elicit the difference between the past simple passive and the present perfect passive with the following sentences:
A hotel was built last year.
Two hotels have been built in the last five years.

Point out that we form the past simple passive with the past simple form of *be* (*was/were*) + past participle. The present perfect passive is formed according to the rule in 7a.

Ask students to read the sentence and decide if the sentence is past simple or present perfect. Students complete the sentences with the present perfect simple passive or past simple passive using the verb in brackets.

Answers
2 were sent   3 have been sold   4 were given
5 have not developed   6 have been criticised

Grammar notebook
Remind students to note down the rules for the present perfect passive and to write a few examples of their own.

8 Grammar
Future passive

a Students should now be familiar with passive constructions. Ask students to complete the sentences with the passive forms. Check answers and elicit the construction of the future passive (*will + (not) + be* + past participle).

Answers
1 will be cut   2 won't be destroyed   3 will be built

b Students complete the rule about the future passive.

Answer
will or won't, past participle

c If you set the background information as a homework research task, ask students to tell the class what they found out.

BACKGROUND INFORMATION

Bobby Moore: This English footballer, who played in defence, was the captain of West Ham United (a London football club). He also captained England in 1966 when they won the World Cup. He died in 1993.

Elicit/pre-teach the background information on Bobby Moore. Students read the text about the sports centre and complete the text with the correct passive form of the verb in brackets. Students check answers in pairs before feedback.

Stronger classes: you could set this exercise as homework.

Answers
1 will be built   2 will be named   3 will be held
4 won't be announced   5 will be chosen
6 will be made

─ OPTIONAL ACTIVITY ─────────────
Write these sentences on the board:
1 *I think the sports centre .... (build) in the High Street.*
2 *I'm sure it .... (not build) outside the town.*
3 *They say a lot of money .... (give) to the winning architect.*
4 *A lot of new equipment .... (buy) for the sports centre.*
5 *But the new equipment .... (not put) into the sports centre until later.*
6 *Perhaps the new building .... (open) by Prince William.*

Read the sentences with students and check difficult vocabulary. Students complete the sentences with the future passive form of the verbs in brackets. Check answers.

Answers
1 will be built   2 won't be built   3 will be given
4 will be bought   5 won't be put   6 will be opened

Grammar notebook
Remind students to note down the rules for the future passive and to write a few examples of their own.

9 Speak

Read the topics with students and elicit some ideas about what will be done in the future. Encourage students to use future passive forms in their answers. Ask two students to read the example dialogue below the box. Students work in pairs to make predictions using the future passive form. In feedback discuss interesting ideas further.

Weaker classes: Students can write their ideas before speaking. Encourage them to look at their notes as little as possible.

Fiction in mind

10 Read

BACKGROUND INFORMATION

But Was it Murder?: is a book published as part of the Cambridge English Readers series.

(a) Write *Thriller* on the board and ask students what they understand by the word. Elicit types of *thrillers*, e.g. books, television programmes and films. Ask students for examples of thrillers they have read or seen. Do they know any titles in English? Ask students to read the blurb for *But Was it Murder?* Ask students if they think Alex was murdered and, if so, who killed him. If it wasn't murder, what could explain his death?

(b) Ask students to read through the extract. Tell them not to worry about difficult vocabulary. You may like to read it aloud with them or alternatively, the extract is recorded track 33 of on the Workbook CD/CD ROM.

Students read through the questions. Check students understand *unwilling*. Ask students to read the extract again and answer the questions. They can compare with a partner before feedback.

Answers
1 It might be suicide or murder.
2 He hasn't met her before. We know because Detective Inspector Rod Eliot doesn't recognise Amanda when she answers the door.
3 Because Amanda Grant's room was so peaceful.
4 He wonders whether she was really as cool as she seemed.

--- OPTIONAL ACTIVITY ---
Write these definitions on the board. Ask students to find words and expressions in the text that match the definitions:
1 *in the middle of* (line 12) **(halfway)**
2 *stay away from* (line 13) **(avoid)**
3 *living room* (line 23) **(sitting room)**
4 *without much colour* (line 44) **(pale)**
5 *not worried or unhappy* (line 45) **(calm)**
6 *gave a signal with his head meaning yes* (line 56) **(nodded)**

Discussion box
Weaker classes: Students can choose one question to discuss.

Stronger classes: In pairs or small groups, students go through the questions in the box and discuss them.
Monitor and help as necessary, encouraging students to express themselves in English. Ask pairs or groups to feedback to the class and discuss any interesting points further.

11 Write

The planning for this exercise can be done in class and the letter can be set as homework.

Warm up

Ask students if they have ever read the letters page of a newspaper. Ask if any students have ever written to a newspaper.

(a) Students read the letter quickly and find Hilary's reasons for writing (*she is concerned about plans to build a motorway through her village and she is worried about the motorway reducing house prices*).

(b) Students read the questions and then read the letter. Remind students about topic sentences they studied in Unit 6.

Answers
1 (I am writing) to express my concern about ...
2 The first sentence in each paragraph is the topic sentence. The writer supports the ideas by explaining the topic sentence in more detail and giving examples of the consequences of the plans to build a motorway.
3 She wants to tell the politicians who support the plan what the villagers think of the plan.

(c) Tell students they are going to write a letter from either Samantha or Phil to the editor of a newspaper about the hotel plan. Encourage students to use suitable expressions from the model letter and to use topic sentences. Remind students that the relevant information is in Exercises 5 and 6 on page 48. You may also want to give your students the tapescript of the meeting to help them.

In a subsequent lesson, encourage students to read each other's letters and decide on the best letters from Samantha and Phil that they would publish in the newspaper.

8 Reality TV

1 Read and listen

If you set the background information as a homework research task, ask students to tell the class what they found out.

BACKGROUND INFORMATION

Endurance: This very popular Japanese television show introduced Britain to the idea of putting contestants in difficult situations. Over 1,000 contestants started the programme, each competing for an unknown prize. Examples of the challenges included holding people underwater while hungry fish bit their faces.

Survivor: This show was initially shown in Sweden and called *Expedition Robinson*. The programme has been produced and broadcast in over 25 countries.

That'll Teach 'em: Every year, there is a heated debate about falling education standards in Britain. The first series attempted to look at this by putting 30 16-year-olds, who had just taken their national GCSEs, through the tough regime of a 1950s state grammar boarding school. At the end of the month, they took O-levels (the exams their parents took) in English, Maths and History. Although all the students passed all their GCSEs with exceptionally good grades, most failed the O-level examination in the same subjects.

Shattered: In January 2002, 12 contestants competed for £100,000 by staying awake for as long as possible. Every day for a week, they had special tests to find out just how well they were coping without sleep. Each day, the contestant who got the lowest score in the tests was eliminated from the competition. The winner was 19-year-old Clare Southern, a trainee policewoman, who stayed awake for a total of 178 hours. There were many complaints from viewers and the show was investigated by an independent body who concluded that the show had not broken any codes of conduct.

Warm up

Ask students to discuss the following questions in small groups:
How much television do you watch a week? Be honest! Which are your favourite / least favourite types of programmes?
Ask students to feedback on their answers. Write some examples of students' favourite and least favourite shows on the board and use them to pre-teach the type of TV programme: *sitcom, soap opera*, etc. Finally, make a total for the amount of TV watched by the class a week: *Our class watches .... hours of TV a week.*

a Students look at the pictures. Ask students if they recognise any of the TV shows in the photos. Encourage students to talk about the reality TV shows that they have seen. Students read the text quickly to check how they compare. Encourage students not to look up every new word but just to read and get the general idea of the text.

b 🔊 Use the pictures to pre-teach *contestants, island, school uniforms*. Students read the questions. Play the recording while students read the text again. Students decide if the sentences are true or false and correct the false sentences. Students check answers in pairs before feedback.

TAPESCRIPT
See the reading text on page 52 of the Student's Book.

Answers
1 T   2 F – Contestants stay on an island for more than a month   3 F – Students weren't allowed to take anything from their modern lives into the school   4 F – There was no prize money in this programme   5 T   6 F – *Shattered* had many complaints from viewers

Discussion box
Weaker classes: Students can choose one question to discuss.

Stronger classes: In pairs or small groups, students go through the questions in the box and discuss them.

Monitor and help as necessary, encouraging students to express themselves in English and to use any vocabulary they have learned from the text. Ask pairs or groups to feedback to the class and discuss any interesting points further.

┌─ OPTIONAL ACTIVITY ─────────────────
Write these definitions on the board. Ask students to find the words in the text which mean the same as the definitions:
1 *a group of TV programmes* **(series)**
2 *a person who leads a TV programme* **(presenter)**
3 *a person who takes part in a TV competition show* **(contestant)**
4 *the number of people who watch a TV programme* **(viewing figures)**
5 *the people who watch a TV programme* **(viewers)**
6 *to show / send out a television programme* **(broadcast)**

2 Grammar
make / let / be allowed to
Students covered some of this area in SB2, Unit 6.

(a) Books closed. Write on the board:
My parents let me ...
I am not allowed to ...

Ask students to complete the sentences with their own ideas. Give students three minutes to write examples and then ask them to compare their sentences with their partner's. Encourage them to check their partner's sentences for grammatical accuracy. Elicit some examples and explain that we use *let* to talk about permission and *not allow* to talk about prohibition.

Students open their books at page 53 and read the sentences from the text. Point out the new structure of *make someone do something*. Ask if the students had to have cold showers (*yes*) and if they had to wear 1950s school uniforms (*yes*).

(b) Students find other examples of the structures in the text. Point out the structure of *be allowed to* + verb, *let* + object + verb, *make* + object + verb. Remind students that *let* is the same in its infinitive, past and past participle forms.

Answers
Presenters made them do ...
... are made to stay there
The producers let the contestants take ...
We weren't allowed to take anything ...

(c) Ask students to read the rules and choose the correct option. Point out that *be allowed to* and *let* talk about similar ideas of permission.

Answers
permission; prohibition; permission; obligation

(d) Students look at the two examples with *make* and answer the questions. Remind students that passive constructions are always made with *be*.

Answers
1 The first sentence is passive, the second is active.
2 In the active construction there is an object (*me, us, etc.*) followed by the verb without *to*. In the passive construction the verb is followed by an infinitive with *to*.

Language notes
1 Students may produce statements like **My dad let me to stay out late*. Remind them that in English we don't use *to* after the expression *let someone do something*.
2 Students may produce statements like **I'm allowed stay out late*. The expression *allow someone to do something* is always followed by the infinitive with *to*.

(e) Read the sentences with students and check difficult vocabulary: *lend*. Do the first sentence as an example with students. Students complete the sentences with the correct form of *make, let* or *be allowed to*. Encourage students to think about whether it is a case of permission, prohibition or obligation to help them choose the correct verb. Students check answers in pairs before feedback.

Answers
1 are not allowed to   2 Do, make   3 let
4 make   5 Are, allowed to   6 am, allowed to
7 let   8 made

(f) Read the items in the box and ask students to think about rules at home. Elicit the question forms relating to each verb (*Are you allowed to ...? Do your parents let you ...? Do your parents make you ...?*). Read through the example conversation with students and elicit answers to the same question about music. Ask students how to make the same question with *let* (*Do your parents let you listen ...?*). Students talk about the ideas in the box in pairs. In feedback ask a few students to tell you about their partner's answers.

Weaker classes: Students can write their answers as preparation.

Grammar notebook

Remind students to note down the rules for this and to write a few examples of their own.

3 Vocabulary

Television

BACKGROUND INFORMATION

Who Wants to Be a Millionaire?: This show is now made and broadcast in over 60 countries around the world. It is a simple quiz show where contestants answer multiple-choice questions in order to win money. The top prize in Britain is £1,000,000.

Soaps: In Britain soaps run for many years. The two most popular soaps are *Coronation Street,* which started in 1960, and *Eastenders,* which started in 1985. Both soaps have been broadcast every week since that time.

Friends: This sitcom started in 1994 and lasted for 10 years. It was about a group of friends living in New York. The programme was very successful and the actors who appeared in the programme have also become famous film stars.

Ask students to read the text through once before they complete it with the words in the box. If necessary, students check the meanings of words in a dictionary. Students check answers in pairs before feedback.

Answers

1 presenter   2 contestant   3 audience
4 viewers   5 series   6 episode   7 Sitcoms
8 viewing figures   9 celebrities

Look

Read the definitions of the words in the Look box. Check students understand the use of each word is specific to the kind of event that people are watching.

Vocabulary notebook

Encourage students to start a section called *Television* and to note down the words from this exercise. They may find it useful to note down translations of the words too.

4 Pronunciation

/aʊ/ *allowed*

(a) ◁)) Students turn to page 120 and read through the words. Play the recording, pausing after each word for students to repeat. Tell students that /aʊ/ is a long vowel sound, and make sure students are pronouncing the sound correctly.

TAPESCRIPT

1 cow   2 house   3 round   4 town   5 shower
6 allowed

(b) ◁)) Students read through the sentences and underline the /aʊ/ sound. Go through the first one with them as an example, if necessary. Play the recording again, pausing after each sentence for students to check and repeat.

TAPESCRIPT/ANSWERS

1   H<u>ow</u> are you n<u>ow</u>?
2   I'm all<u>ow</u>ed to have a m<u>ou</u>se in the h<u>ou</u>se.
3   You aren't all<u>ow</u>ed to sing l<u>ou</u>dly in the sh<u>ow</u>er.
4   We're all<u>ow</u>ed to walk the c<u>ow</u> ar<u>ou</u>nd the t<u>ow</u>n.

5 Listen

(a) Ask students to read through the questions about the television programme. Check difficult vocabulary: *put people under pressure, limit, bad effects, humiliate.* Check students' understanding by eliciting a few of their own answers to the questions.

(b) Students predict the order in which the questions are asked.

(c) Explain that students will hear an interview with a psychologist about reality TV. Ask students to predict the answers the psychologist will give. Tell students to take brief notes.

(d) ◁)) Play the recording while students listen and check their answers to Exercise 5b. Check answers.

TAPESCRIPT

Interviewer   There has been some controversy recently concerning reality TV programmes. *Shattered* was the programme in which people had to stay awake as long as possible. The question is: is this reality TV or humiliation TV? Does it put people's health at risk, or risk psychological damage? To talk about these questions, we've invited Dr Martha Wright into the studio. Dr Wright is a social psychologist. Dr Wright – do you think that programmes like this humiliate the contestants?

Dr Wright   Well, I think there's a risk of that – but in this particular case, no, I don't think so, I don't think there was any humiliation at all.

Interviewer   So, do you think reality TV shows like this one are OK?

Dr Wright   Well, I certainly don't enjoy them – I only watch them with professional interest. I think it's a shame that people enjoy being on these shows. People don't have to become contestants on these programmes, they aren't made to do it – they choose to. And, if they want to, they can leave.

Interviewer   But don't these programmes put people under enormous pressure?

Dr Wright Yes, that's the whole point, of course. That's what viewers want to see. But in this case, the contestants weren't doing anything very extreme. I mean, there are lots of people in various situations who don't sleep very much. They survive very well.

Interviewer Do you think the contestants in this programme will suffer bad effects?

Dr Wright Not really – well, perhaps for a few days, but they'll be absolutely fine. And I must say, I think the contestants were fantastic. If there is a risk at all, I think it's more to do with the way the winner handles the momentary fame of being the winner. Going without sleep might have a short-term physical effect – but that's not very difficult to deal with for young people like these. But fame – that's another thing altogether. There are lots of people, in sports, in cinema, on TV, who find it very, very hard to deal with fame and money.

Interviewer Is there any limit to what the programme-makers will think of? What can we expect next? A hunger programme where people mustn't eat for a week, until they're starving?

Dr Wright Well, I hope never to see that one – and actually people have complained, the producers know this. I think they'll be a little more careful in the future. It's really important not to upset viewers too much, otherwise they won't watch any more.

Interviewer Well, let's see. Dr Wright, thank you very much.

Dr Wright Thank you.

Answers

5   3   1   4   2

e 🔊 Play the recording again while students listen and make notes about the psychologist's answers. Quickly check answers before starting the next stage of the exercise.

Answers

1 The psychologist doesn't think *Shattered* humiliates anyone.
2 The psychologist doesn't enjoy them but watches them for professional interest.
3 She thinks that the pressure is part of the programme.
4 She thinks they might suffer for a few days but in the long term they probably won't suffer.
5 The psychologist doesn't think there will be a hunger programme and thinks that *Shattered* was useful because people complained. **This will mean that the producers will be more careful in the future.**

f Explain that all the statements are false. Students use their notes to correct the statements. Check answers. You may want to play the recording again, pausing as necessary.

Answers

1 Dr Wright watches the programmes for professional interest.
2 She thinks the contestants were fantastic.
3 She thinks that might have a short-term physical effect.
4 Lots of people find it hard to deal with fame and money.
5 Dr Wright hopes that there won't be a reality TV show about hunger.

6 Grammar

Modal verbs of obligation, prohibition and permission

a 🔊 **Stronger classes:** Write these sentences on the board:

1 *Shattered was the programme in which people .... stay awake as long as possible.*
2 *People .... become contestants on these programmes.*
3 *If they want to, they .... leave.*
4 *What .... we expect next?*
5 *A hunger programme where people .... eat for a week.*

Play the recording from Exercise 5 again and ask students to complete the sentences with the correct verb. Check answers and then follow the procedure for weaker classes.

Answers

1 had to   2 don't have to   3 can   4 can
5 mustn't

Weaker classes: Students read the examples from the interview and answer the questions. Check answers. Remind students that the negative form of *have to* (*don't have to*) indicates a choice not prohibition.

Answers

a 3   b 4   c 2   d 1

b Read through sentences 1 to 6 with students. Students match the pictures and sentences. Check answers and whether each sentence indicates obligation, prohibition or permission.

Answers

a 5 – prohibition
b 1 – permission
c 4 – obligation
d 6 – permission
e 2 – prohibition
f 3 – obligation

c Ask students to read through the sentences before they complete them with the appropriate modal verbs in the correct positive or negative form. Remind students that there may be more than one possibility. Go through the first sentence as an example.

Answers
2 have to / must
3 can
4 must
5 don't have to
6 mustn't / can't

OPTIONAL ACTIVITY
Ask students if they can remember some of the rules for the reality TV programmes in the text, e.g. *Survivor*: *you can't leave the island*. Ask students to write some more of the rules for reality TV programmes in the text, or those they have seen in their own country. Encourage students to use the modals of obligation, prohibition and permission. In feedback, ask students not to read the name of the show. Encourage other students to guess which show's rules are being described.

Language notes
1 Remind students of the correct use of *to* with these modal verbs:
I have to go now and not **I have go now.*
I must go now and not **I must to go now.*
2 Students might want to use **haven't to* as the negative for *have to*. Remind them that the correct negative form is *mustn't*, e.g. *You mustn't eat that!* and not **You haven't to eat that!*

Grammar notebook
Remind students to note down the rules for these modal verbs and to write a few examples of their own.

7 Vocabulary
Extreme adjectives and modifiers

a Students read the sentences from the interview. Check students understand the meaning of *enormous* (very, very big), *fantastic* (very, very good) and *starving* (very, very hungry). Tell students that these are example of extreme adjectives.

b Students match the adjectives to their extreme form. If necessary, do the first few as examples. Check answers.

Answers
1 b   2 e   3 d   4 c   5 g   6 a   7 f

Language note
Words like *enormous*, *fantastic* and *starving* are sometimes called limit or extreme adjectives. Normally, extreme adjectives are not used with *very*. Instead we use adverbs such as *really* or *absolutely*, e.g. *I'm absolutely starving* not **I'm very starving*. Most extreme adjectives have an equivalent adjective, a scale adjective, which can be modified with *very*. For example, *very, very big = enormous*. Scale adjectives, e.g. *big*, *hungry*, can be modified with *very* and *really*.

OPTIONAL ACTIVITY
Write adjectives 1 to 7 from Exercise 7b on the board. But do not write the extreme adjectives. Students work in pairs and take it in turns to form the exchange:
A: *I'm really, really hot!* (*I'm really, really* + adjective)
B: *I'm boiling!* (*I'm* + extreme adjective)

c Read the example sentences. Point out that adjectives that can have more or less of a quality can be modified with *very* or *really* but extreme adjectives are modified with *really* or *absolutely*. Students tick or cross the correct and incorrect combinations in the box.

Answers

really tiny	✓	very tiny	✗	absolutely tiny	✓
really hot	✓	very hot	✓	absolutely hot	✗
really boiling	✓	very boiling	✗	absolutely boiling	✓

d Students complete the sentences with the correct adjectives from Exercise 7b. Point out that more than one adjective may be possible when the modifier is *really*.

Answers
1 boiling   2 hungry   3 exhausted   4 small
5 cold/freezing   6 fantastic

e Tell students that extreme adjectives can make language more dramatic and more interesting. Students read the topics in the box and talk about their opinions using extreme adjectives and modifiers *really* or *absolutely*. Do an example with a student and, in feedback, ask a few students to tell you about their partner's answers.

Vocabulary notebook
Encourage students to start a section called *Extreme adjectives* and to note down the words from this exercise with their scale adjective equivalents. They may find it useful to note down translations of the words too.

8 Listen and speak

If you set the background information as a homework research task, ask students to tell the class what they found out.

BACKGROUND INFORMATION
Rockwell: Kennedy Gordy was born on 15 March, 1964 and changed his name to avoid favouritism from his father, who was Motown Records founder Berry Gordy. The single *Somebody's Watching Me* reached number 2 in the US charts in 1984.

***Twilight Zone*:** This TV series was a collection of strange stories all with an unexpected ending. The name is taken from the period just before it becomes completely dark in the evening, where it is thought that two different states of existence meet.

***Psycho*:** This film was originally made by Alfred Hitchcock in 1960. In the film there is a famous scene where someone is murdered while they are having a shower and, even though you don't actually see the murder, in 2004 the film received an award for the best death scene in a film.

The IRS: Internal Revenue Service (IRS) is the USA government department that collects taxes. It mainly collects business and personal income tax.

a 🔊 Ask students to look at the picture and the title of the song. Ask students what they think the song is about and how the man feels (he feels like he is being watched all the time). Tell students to close their books and play the recording. Students check their answers.

b 🔊 Students read the lyrics of the song. Check difficult words, e.g. *privacy, real tight* (= *very tight*), *paranoid, play tricks, mailman* (US English for *postman*). Tell students there are nine incorrect words and phrases in the song. Then play the recording again. Students check answers with a partner before repeating the recording, pausing if necessary.

TAPESCRIPT
See the song on page 56 of the Student's Book.

Answers
Line 2:   price not *money
Line 3:   home not *school
Line 9:   come home not *go out
Line 11:   avoid not *invite
Line 12:   TV not *the radio
Line 13:   in the shower not *on the street
Line 15:   crazy not *healthy
Line 23:   neighbours not *teachers

c Ask students why the singer feels so paranoid. In pairs students try and invent an interesting reason. In feedback ask pairs to tell the class their reasons and vote on the most interesting.

Did you know ...?

Before you read the box, ask students if they know any other recording artists who use just one name (*Madonna, Eminem, Beyoncé, Shakira, Dido*). Read the information in the box with students.

9 Vocabulary

Collocations with *on*

Point out the line from the song *Who's playing tricks on me*? Tell students that *on* is part of a phrase: *to play a trick on someone*. Ask students if they know any other phrases with *on*, e.g. *on time*. Ask students what it means if you arrive *on time* for an appointment (*you arrive at the right time, not late*). Students complete the sentences with the correct word from the box. In feedback, check students understand the meaning of each phrase.

Answers
1 TV   2 strike   3 time   4 the phone
5 offer   6 holiday

Vocabulary notebook
Encourage students to start a section called *Collocations with on* and to note down the words from this exercise. They may find it useful to note down translations of the words too.

10 Write

The planning for this exercise can be done in class and the letter can be set as homework.

BACKGROUND INFORMATION

Wales: Part of the United Kingdom, Wales is a small country with a population of about 3.5 million. It is bordered by the Irish Sea and in the east by England. Much of Wales is mountainous.

Warm up

Look at the picture. Tell students the article is about a new reality TV show. Ask students to predict what the programme is about (*a reality TV programme about celebrities living the life of cave people*). Students read the text quickly to check their ideas.

a Ask students to read through questions 1 to 6. Check difficult vocabulary: *scene, prize*. Students read the article and answer the questions. Check answers.

Answers
1 Celebrities   2 In a cave in the mountains of Wales
3 One personal item   4 Six times a day
5 Viewers will vote each week   6 £1,000,000 for charity and a recording contract for a CD

b Tell students they are going to write an article about a reality TV show they have invented. Students should use the questions in Exercise 10a to plan their writing. Remind students to use extreme adjectives to make the article sound more exciting. In a subsequent lesson, encourage students to read each other's articles and decide on the most interesting reality TV programme.

Module 2 **Check your progress**

1 **Grammar**

a 2 are, going to wear 3 'm not doing
4 'll know 5 is taking

b 2 'll call, get 3 don't come, 'll miss
4 won't let, aren't 5 'll see, asks

c 2 Mr Hart has his hair cut every month.
3 Our teacher has had her car repaired.
4 Sally is having a cake made for her birthday.
5 We're going to have a new phone installed tomorrow.

d 2 were used 3 have been sent 4 have been received 5 weren't understood

e 2 will be sent 3 will be found 4 will be brought
5 will be examined 6 won't be answered

f 1 lets 2 makes 3 Does, let 4 aren't allowed to
5 Do, make

g 2 mustn't 3 can't 4 Do, have to
5 don't have to

2 **Vocabulary**

a 2 boarding card 3 flight 4 timetable
5 arrive at 6 tour 7 arrive in 8 platform

b 2 did 3 made 4 did 5 making 6 makes
7 making

c *Across*
3 audience 4 celebrities 5 contestant
6 viewing figures

Down
1 presenter 2 series 6 viewers 7 episode
8 sitcom

Module 3
Right and wrong

YOU WILL LEARN ABOUT ...

Ask students to look at the pictures on the page. Ask students to read through the topics in the box and check that they understand each item. You can ask them the following questions, in L1 if appropriate:

1 *Who is the man?*
2 *Where is the person?*
3 *Who is the woman?*
4 *Where can you see these statues?*
5 *What is the girl doing?*
6 *Do you have this in your town?*
7 *What do you think he is doing?*

In pairs or small groups students discuss which topic area they think each picture matches. Check answers.

Answers
1 The filming of *The Beach*
2 The 1969 moon landing
3 A computer game
4 Mysterious places
5 Teenage crime
6 Graffiti
7 Some classic 'monsters' from fiction

YOU WILL LEARN HOW TO ...

Use grammar

Students read through the grammar points and the examples. Go through the first item with students as an example. In pairs, students now match the grammar items in their book. Check answers.

Answers
Verbs + gerunds and infinitives: I remembered to post the letter.
Second conditional: If I knew where she lived, I would tell you.
I wish / if only + past simple: I wish I had a car.
Linkers of contrast: Although it was difficult, we all passed the test.
Modals of deduction in the present: They might be Spanish.
Indirect questions: Do you know where she lives?
Modals of deduction in the past: The murderer must have been a man.

Use vocabulary

Write the headings on the board. Go through the items in the Student's Book and check understanding. Now ask students if they can think of one more item for the *Crime* heading. Elicit some responses and add them to the list on the board. Students now do the same for the other headings. Some possibilities are:

Noun suffixes: *discussion, spelling, happiness, dancer*

Phrasal verbs with *down*: *sit down, lie down, turn down*

Crime: *steal, murder, prison, thief*

Problems: *think about, solve, help someone*

Good and evil

Unit overview

TOPIC: Fictional characters that fight the forces of evil.

TEXTS

Reading and listening: short introductions to classic novels

Listening and speaking: a conversation about a video game

Reading: an article about graffiti

Writing: a discursive competition giving advantages and disadvantages

SPEAKING AND FUNCTIONS

Talking about video games

Guessing about your partner's habits

Discussing graffiti and hip-hop culture

LANGUAGE

Grammar: Verbs with gerunds or infinitives

Vocabulary: Noun suffixes; Belonging to a group

Pronunciation: Stress in nouns, adjectives and verbs

1 Read and listen

If you set the background information as a homework research task, ask students to tell the class what they found out.

BACKGROUND INFORMATION

Oscar Wilde (1854–1900): was an Irish writer. He was famous for his wit and his flamboyant sense of dress and when touring America he told a customs officer that he had 'nothing to declare but my genius'. *The Picture of Dorian Gray* (1891) was his only novel but he wrote several successful plays including *The Importance of Being Earnest* (1895).

Robert Louis Stevenson (1850–1894): was a Scottish writer. *The Strange Case of Dr Jekyll and Mr Hyde* was published in 1886 and was based partly on the true story of Deacon Brodie, a local government worker in Scotland who had a double life. The book became an immediate best-seller in England and America. However, Stevenson's most famous book is probably *Treasure Island* (1883).

Johann Wolfgang von Goethe (1749–1832): was a German writer and university teacher. *Faust* is a poetical drama that was written in two parts. The second part was published just after Goethe's death.

Mary Shelley (1797–1851): was a British writer. Her most famous novel was *Frankenstein*, started when she was 18. When *Frankenstein* was published in 1818, it became a huge success. Many people believed it was written by Mary's husband, the famous English poet Percy Shelley.

Warm up

Books closed. Write the title of the unit (*Good and evil*) on the board. Ask students to think of examples of books, films, TV programmes which have that theme. In feedback, concentrate on any books that students mention.

a Ask students to look at the pictures and match them to the texts. Encourage them to ignore unknown words at this time. Check answers and ask students to give reasons. Ask students if they have read any of the books and allow students to give their opinion of the book(s) in L1 if necessary.

Answers

a 3   b 4   c 1   d 2

b 🔊 Use the pictures to pre-teach *portrait*, *detest*, *invent*, *scientist*, *bolt of lightening* and *monster*. Read through the questions and check difficult words, e.g. *deal*. Students read, listen and answer the questions. Ask students to underline the answers in the texts. Students compare answers with a partner before checking in class.

TAPESCRIPT

See the reading texts on page 62 of the Student's Book.

Answers

1   a Doctor Jekyll   b Dorian Gray   c Dr Faust
    d Victor Frankenstein
2   It has become older.
3   He drinks a special drink he has invented.
4   Faust will get what he wants on earth and the devil will get his soul.
5   Bits of dead bodies

OPTIONAL ACTIVITY

Students can discuss the following questions in pairs or small groups. Check answers.

1   *What idea connects the stories?* (**They all involve characters who want more than they have at the moment**)
2   *What stories do you know or have you read?*
3   *Would you like to read any of them?*

2 Grammar
Verbs + gerunds

(a) **Weaker classes:** Books closed. Write two sentences about yourself on the board using the following models:
I enjoy going to the cinema.
I dislike cleaning the house.
Check students understand there are two verbs in each sentence and that the second verb is in the –*ing* form. Elicit the name of this second verb form (*gerund*). Ask some students for examples of their own using *I enjoy …* and *I dislike …* . Tell students that after some verbs we can use a gerund form of a verb but not an infinitive form. Check students understand that this is only necessary when we are using a second verb and so sentences such as *I enjoy films* are correct but if you want to include a verb the sentence is *I enjoy watching films* not **I enjoy to watch films*.

Stronger classes: Books closed. Write these sentence beginnings on the board:
I enjoy …
I dislike …
Give students a minute to make as many sentences as possible using the words. Ask students to read out their sentences and encourage them to use the gerund after *enjoy* and *dislike* when appropriate. When you have enough examples, ask students what they notice about the verbs in the sentences. Elicit the rule that when we use a verb after *enjoy* and *dislike* we use a gerund rather than the infinitive form. Ask students if they know any other verbs that behave like this.

Students now open their books at page 63 and complete the sentences using the correct verbs from the texts on page 62. Check answers and point out that the four verbs used in these sentences are followed by gerunds.

Answers
1 detests   2 enjoys   3 suggests   4 imagines

(b) Students read about verbs with gerunds. Check students understand the meaning of the verbs and ask them to write an example sentence if necessary.

(c) Ask students to read the text through once before they complete it with the words in the box. Ask students who they think Jacob is (*possibly a friend or a pet*). Students complete the story by using the gerund form of the verbs in the box and then check answers in pairs before feedback.

Answers
2 going   3 seeing   4 crossing   5 shouting
6 hearing   7 having   8 singing

Verbs + infinitives

(d) Books closed. Write on the board:
One day I want to …
I often forget to …
Ask students to complete the sentences for themselves. If necessary give students examples of your own. Ask students for a few examples of their sentences and check that they are using the infinitive form after each verb correctly. Tell students that, like the group of verbs that are followed by a gerund, there is also a group of verbs that are followed by an infinitive.

Students now open their books at page 63 and underline the verbs in each sentence. Check answers and elicit the difference in the form between the two verbs (*the second is in the infinitive form*).

Answers
1 wants, to stay   2 promises, to give
3 decides, to build

(e) Students read the list of verbs followed by an infinitive form. Check students understand the meaning of the verbs and ask them to write an example sentence if necessary. Point out that when *hope* and *expect* are used in present simple and are followed by an infinitive they express a future meaning.

(f) Students complete each sentence using a verb from box A followed by a verb from box B. Point out that students will need to think about the correct tense for the verbs from box A. Go through the first sentence as an example. Check answers in class.

Answers
2 decided to go   3 hope to live   4 offered to help
5 is learning to play   6 didn't expect to do

3 Speak

(a) Look at the pictures with students. Elicit sentences about the people using the verb *want* + infinitive (*the couple want to go to the moon on holiday, the girl doesn't want to get a jumper for her birthday*). Students write sentences about what their partner would say for the three different sentences. Make sure students use either the –*ing* or the infinitive form as appropriate.

(b) Students compare their predictions. Encourage students to correct each other's sentences if necessary. Ask a few pairs to tell the class about their partner's answers. For example,
Elma hopes to get a computer for her next birthday.
Boris enjoys going shopping at the weekend.

Weaker classes: Students can read their sentences to their partners.

Stronger classes: Encourage students not to read their sentences but to practise saying them from memory.

4 Speak and listen

If you set the background information as a homework research task, ask students to tell the class what they found out.

BACKGROUND INFORMATION

Tomb Raider: was originally a computer game developed in 1996. It was one of the first games to combine action and puzzle-solving. It became very popular and over 25 million copies of the games have been sold. It made a computer heroine of its main character, Lara Croft, and there are many fan sites on the Internet dedicated to her. There have been six Lara Croft computer games in total and the most recent is *The Angel of Darkness*. There have also been two films, both starring Angelina Jolie as Lara Croft.

Warm up

a Ask students to look at the pictures and read the questions. Students discuss the questions in pairs. Ask a few pairs for their answers and help with vocabulary as necessary. Elicit the names of a few popular computer games that your students play.

Answers
1 The woman is Lara Croft, the female heroine from the Tomb Raider video games.
2 Students' own answers

b 🔊 Tell students they are going to listen to a dialogue between two people about a Lara Croft computer game. Students listen and choose the name of the game. Play the recording and check answers.

TAPESCRIPT

Jessica ... Yes, Charlotte, but I hate stories where there's always one person who's the goodie, and the goodie fights all the baddies. It doesn't take much imagination to figure out who wins in the end, does it?

Charlotte No, listen Jessica. There's a new game out, *The Angel of Darkness*. You should play it!

Jessica I know, I know. The superwoman fighting the bad ones. Whatever she does is right, and whatever the others do is wrong.

Charlotte No, this one's different, honestly.

Jessica Different? How?

Charlotte Well, in *The Angel of Darkness* she's both the hunter and the hunted. It's not a clear-cut case of good versus evil any more. It's much more complex. It all starts with a phone call from her friend, Werner von Croy. He's in Paris, and he's been asked by a criminal called Eckhardt to get him a painting from the 14th century that he

badly wants to own. So, Lara goes to Paris, and starts looking for von Croy. But all of a sudden she finds herself in the middle of a horror scene. Her friend von Croy gets killed by a serial killer, and the police want to arrest her as his murderer.

Jessica Wow. So all of a sudden she's the bad one.

Charlotte Right, at least in the eyes of the police. Anyway, she escapes from the police, and follows Eckhardt to Prague.

Jessica Eckhardt? Hang on a minute, Charlotte. Who—

Charlotte He's the guy who wants to have the painting, remember? And he's in Prague now, and he threatens to attack the world, and so she—

Jessica Sounds great. I'd love to play it! Can I borrow it?

Charlotte I'm afraid I've lent it to someone. But if I remember to ask ...

Answer
4 The Angel of Darkness

c 🔊 Ask students to read through the questions. Check any difficult vocabulary: *hunt, serial killer, threaten*. Then play the recording again. Students check answers with a partner before repeating the recording, pausing if necessary.

Answers
1 b   2 a   3 a   4 d

5 Vocabulary
Noun suffixes

a Books closed. Write this table on the board:

verb	noun
relax arrange	
adjective	**noun**
weak popular	

Ask students if they can complete the noun form of the verbs and the adjectives. Check answers and underline the suffix of the noun form in each case (see Answers). Tell students that we can often form nouns from verbs or adjectives by adding a suffix.

Answers
relax**ation**   arrange**ment**   weak**ness**   popular**ity**

Weaker classes: You could give alternative forms for the nouns and ask student to choose the correct answer.

Stronger classes: Ask students if they can add any more words to each table.
Students now open their books at page 64 and identify the underlined words in each sentence.

(b) Read through the different suffixes that are used to make nouns from verbs and adjectives. Check students understand the meaning of each word and ask them to write an example sentence if necessary. Point out that *–ation, –ment, –ion*, are added to verbs to make nouns, *–ness* and *–ity* are added to adjectives to make nouns and *–ence* is added to verbs and adjectives to make nouns.

Language note
You may want to make students aware of some general spelling rules for the formation of nouns. When a suffix is added to words ending in a consonant and then *e*, e.g. *imagine*, then the *e* is usually dropped. Remind students that the same thing happens with gerunds, e.g. *take/taking*. The exception to this is with the suffix *–ment*, where the *e* is <u>not</u> dropped, e.g. *manage/management*. The suffix *–ence* is often used for adjectives ending in *–ent*. In this case the *–ent* changes to *–ence*, e.g. *intelligent/intelligence*.

(c) In pairs, students add other examples to the table. Encourage students to try and think of words ending in each suffix and then to work out the verb or adjective form. Check students' answers or provide dictionaries for students to check their own work. Each pair can then take it in turns to read a verb or adjective to another pair and see if they can add the correct suffix to make a noun. Each pair scores a point for a correct answer. Check answers and write new examples on the board for students to copy. Finally, drill the words and make sure students mark the correctly stressed syllable on each word. Point out that sometimes the stress changes position: i'magine/imagi'nation. Students practise this feature of word stress in Exercise 6.

Possible answers
–ation: 'educate/edu'cation, in'form/infor'mation
–ment: im'prove/im'provement, manage/'management
–ion: e'lect/e'lection, dis'cuss/dis'cussion
–ence: pre'fer/'preference, re'fer/'reference
–ness: 'happy/'happiness, ill/'illness
–ity: 'stupid/stu'pidity, 'similar/simi'larity

┌─ OPTIONAL ACTIVITY ─────────
Weaker classes
Write a list of verbs and adjectives for students to make nouns from. Encourage students to say nouns aloud in order to see if they sound correct. When you have checked answers, make sure students close their books before quizzing another pair. They can use the list on the board as a prompt for their quiz.

(d) **Weaker classes:** Do this exercise in class.

Stronger classes: Set this exercise for homework.

Students make nouns from the verbs and adjectives in the box. Check students understand the words in the box. Go through another example if necessary. Check that students are stressing the correct syllables in their answers.

Answers
2 popularity   3 preparation   4 agreement
5 reaction   6 entertainment   7 preference

Vocabulary notebook
Encourage students to start a section called *Noun suffixes* and to note down the words from this exercise. They may find it useful to note down translations of the words too.

6 Pronunciation
Stress in nouns, adjectives and verbs

(a) ◁)) Write the word *record* on the board. Ask students to tell you where the stress is on the word. Elicit the stress on the noun *record* (record) and the verb *record* (record). Tell students that some words in English have stress on different syllables according to whether they are verbs, adjectives or nouns. Students turn to page 120, read the words and underline where they think the stressed syllables are. Play the recording for students to check.

TAPESCRIPT/ANSWERS
1 im<u>a</u>gine   2 imagin<u>a</u>tion
3 re<u>fer</u>   4 <u>re</u>ference
5 <u>po</u>pular   6 popul<u>a</u>rity
7 <u>po</u>ssible   8 possib<u>i</u>lity
9 re<u>lax</u>   10 relax<u>a</u>tion

(b) ◁)) Play the recording again, pausing after each word for students to repeat. Encourage students to mark the stressed syllable when they write words in their vocabulary notebook.

7 Grammar
Verbs with gerunds or infinitives

(a) Books closed. Write the following sentence on the board:
I started .... the piano when I was 10.

Ask students to complete the sentence with the verb *play* (*to play* or *playing*). Point out that some verbs can be followed by either a gerund or an infinitive without a change in meaning. Students now open their books at page 65 and read the explanation. Tell students that there are some verbs that can be followed by either form but there is a change of meaning. Read the explanation about *remember* and *stop*. Point out the illustrations which make the difference in meaning for *stop* clear. It might help for students to think about how to say this in their own language.

(**b**) Students read through the sentences and choose the correct form of the verb. Go through the first sentence as an example. Check answers and ask students to give reasons for their choices.

Answers
1 meeting (past reference)
2 to give (future reference)
3 making (refers to stopping something after that time)
4 to buy (refers to an interrupted action – to do something else)

(**c**) Students complete the sentences with the correct form of the verbs. Ask students to check answers with a partner before checking in class. Encourage students to give reasons for their answers.

Answers
1 telling (past reference)
2 talking
3 to phone (future reference – when I get home)
4 to say (refers to an interrupted action)
5 locking (past reference)
6 to get (refers to an interrupted action)
7 to post (future reference)
8 shouting

Grammar notebook
Remind students to note down the rules for verbs + gerunds and infinitives and to write a few examples of their own.

8 Speak

(**a**) Write on the board a series of things you hate doing: *getting up early at weekends, doing the washing up,* etc. Ask students to guess what this list of things is about (*things you hate doing*) and continue writing examples until students guess. Tell students they are going to play a similar guessing game. Students work with a partner. Student A follows the instructions on page 65. Student B follows the instructions on page 122. Remind students not to include the verb, e.g. *remember, start,* etc, and just write their answers beginning with an infinitive or gerund.

(**b**) Students take it in turns to guess their partner's answers. Read the example dialogue with students as an example. Monitor and help with vocabulary as necessary.

Look
Read through the Look box with students. Ask students to write short examples using each verb.

Culture in mind

9 Read

If you set the background information as a homework research task, ask students to tell the class what they found out.

BACKGROUND INFORMATION

Temper: was born in Wolverhampton, England in November, 1971 and his real name is Arron Bird. He started painting in 1982 and has had his work commissioned from companies such as Lee jeans, Airwalk skate brand, Kickers shoes and Coca-Cola where he was asked to create imagery for a limited edition Sprite can. In 2004 he complted a 12 metre mural in the bay of Torquay.

Hip-hop: is a cultural movement that began amongst urban and primarily African American young people in New York in the early 1970s. The four main elements of hip-hop are MC-ing (rapping), DJ-ing (see below), graffiti art, and break dancing (see body popping). Hip-hop music is related to West African travelling singers and poets whose musical style is similar to hip-hop. As a style of music, hip-hop is now common throughout the world.

Beat-boxing: is the art of vocal percussion, which is making drum sounds and beats using your lips, tongue and voice.

Body popping: is a dance style that became popular alongside hip-hop culture. It probably originates from mime dancing, and a good early example is given by a young Michael Jackson, who appeared on American TV in 1974 doing a robotic dance to the Jackson Five's song *Dancin' Machine.*

Break dancing: refers to the movements of dancers between 'breaks' in music, for example when a record is being changed. The dancing commonly includes spinning on the knees, head, hands and elbows and can be quite dangerous.

DJ-ing: is short for disc-jockeying and refers to playing records, commonly using a record player and vinyl records. From the late 1960s disc-jockeys (DJs), in particular hip-hop DJs, developed various tricks and techniques with records for making new music using turntable record players.

Warm up

Ask students to look at the pictures. Discuss the following questions:

1 Can you see a difference between the two types of graffiti? (*one is a* mural – *a large picture painted on a wall or side of a building, the other is a* tag)
2 Where do you usually see graffiti?
3 Is there a lot of graffiti in students' own towns?

Use the discussion and the pictures to pre-teach *vandalism, spray, legal/illegal* and *tagging* (spraying or marking one's name or initials on a surface).

(a) Ask students to read the titles and check any difficult words. Then they read the article quickly to match the headings to the paragraphs. Encourage students not to look up every new word but just to read and get the general idea of the paragraphs. Check answers in class.

Answers
1 D   2 A   3 B   4 E
Unused title: C But is it music?

(b) Ask students to read through the questions. Check any difficult vocabulary. Then students read the text again and decide if the sentences are true or false. Students correct false sentences and check answers in pairs before feedback.

Answers
1 T   2 F – The scheme is for people of all ages
3 T   4 F – There has been a fall in the amount of vandalism   5 F – His teacher thought he was very good at art 6 T   7 T   8 F – A burner is a technical and stylish piece of graffiti

Discussion box
Weaker classes: Students can choose one question to discuss.

Stronger classes: In pairs or small groups, students go through the questions in the box and discuss them.
Monitor and help as necessary, encouraging students to express themselves in English and to use any vocabulary they have learned from the text. Ask pairs or groups to feedback to the class and discuss any interesting points further.

10 Vocabulary
Belonging to a group

(a) Tell students that sentences 1 to 5 are from the text but part of each sentence has been replaced with the underlined words. Ask students to replace the underlined words with the appropriate form of the verbs in the box. Students can check their answers with the text on page 66.

Answers
1 hanging out   2 looked up to   3 hooked up with
4 felt left out by   5 relate to

(b) Students work in small groups and write questions using the vocabulary in Exercise 10a. Students then discuss the questions. Monitor and help with vocabulary where necessary.

Vocabulary notebook
Encourage students to add these words to *Friends* from Unit 1. They may find it useful to note down translations of the words too.

11 Write

The planning for this exercise can be done in class and the writing can be set as homework.

(a) Ask students to look at the title of the composition. Elicit a few possible advantages and disadvantages of organised graffiti walls. Students answer the questions. Check answers and point out the structure of the composition: introduction (outlining the problem), advantages, disadvantages, and conclusion.

Answers
1 Second paragraph – help bring teenagers together, encourage creativity, encourage artists to use art constructively rather than destructively, reduce illegal graffiti
2 Third paragraph – graffiti walls make the crime of vandalism seem more acceptable
3 The writer is generally positive about graffiti walls in the conclusion.

(b) Students look at the underlined words in the text and answer the questions. Check answers and explain that these phrases are very important in compositions. Point out that they give a signal to the reader of what to expect in the next sentence and paragraph.

Answers
1 To sum up   2 In addition   3 On the other hand
4 Because of

(c) Explain that students are going to write a composition about the advantages and disadvantages of one of the two topics. Encourage students to:
• make a list of the advantages and disadvantages before they start
• use the phrases from Exercise 10b in their composition
• be clear about their opinion in the conclusion.

In a subsequent lesson, encourage students to read each other's compositions and vote on the most convincing arguments.

10 Getting into trouble

Unit overview

TOPICS: Teenage crime and doing things wrong

TEXTS
Listening: a dialogue about doing something wrong
Reading: a questionnaire about honesty
Listening: radio interviews about teenage crime
Reading and listening: Story: *A problem for Matt*
Writing: a formal letter of opinion

SPEAKING AND FUNCTIONS
Talking about getting into trouble
Discussing a questionnaire about honesty
Describing hypothetical situations
Describing something you wish could be different
Discussing doing something wrong

LANGUAGE
Grammar: Second conditional review; *I wish / If only +* past simple
Vocabulary: Crime; Phrasal verbs with *down*
Pronunciation: *I wish ...* and *If only ...*
Everyday English: *the way I see it; and besides; that's a good point; you never know*

1 Speak and listen

Warm up

Ask students what kind of things they normally get into trouble for at home. Ask students what kind of punishments they get for the things they do. Discuss interesting stories in class, helping with vocabulary as necessary.

a Using the pictures, pre-teach *fruit bowl, pieces, stone, damage* and also *stick, glue* (verb and noun), *get caught* and *get away with (something)*. Ask students to describe the situations in each picture (*in story 1 a girl has broken a fruit bowl and in story 2 a boy has kicked a stone into a car*). Students work in pairs and discuss how the stories might end. Do not comment at this stage.

b 🔊 Play the recording. Students check answers to Exercise 1a with a partner. Ask if they got caught or got away with what they did. Play the recording again if necessary

TAPESCRIPT

Steve Did you ever get into trouble when you were younger, Megan?

Megan Who, me? Umm, well, there was this one time, when I was about ten, I think, and I was playing in the living room in our house and there

was a fruit bowl on the table. It was my mother's favourite thing, a present from my grandmother, I think. Anyway, while I was playing, I knocked the bowl off the table and it broke!

Steve So what did you do?

Megan Panicked! I knew Mum would be really angry when she came in. Anyway, I picked the bowl up, and I saw it was broken in two pieces, so I got some glue and I stuck them back together, really quickly.

Steve So did she notice?

Megan Well, not to start with but then when she went to use it, she couldn't lift the bowl off the table!

Steve What?

Megan Yeah, I'd glued the bowl to the table as well. It was a really expensive table too. She was so angry.

Steve Well, when I was about nine, and I was walking to school with a friend of mine, kicking stones, like boys do, pretending we were playing for England and, anyway, I kicked one of the stones really hard – Goal! – only, the stone hit the headteacher's car and damaged the door.

Megan Oh, no!

Steve That's right. Well, the headteacher found out and he called me to his office and asked me if I had damaged his car. And you know what I did? This is so embarrassing.

Megan No, go on.

Steve Well, I said that it was my friend who had kicked the stone. Isn't that awful?

Megan Well, yes, basically!

Steve And of course my friend never spoke to me again, or not for a few weeks anyway, and of course the headteacher found out, and he was really angry because I'd told him a lie.

Megan Did you get into big trouble?

Steve Oh, sure! The next day, he called me into his office ...

Answers
Megan stuck the pieces together with some glue. Unfortunately she glued the bowl to the table. She didn't get away with it.
Steve kicked the stone into his headteacher's car and he had to go and see him. Steve blamed his friend and the friend got into trouble. Eventually the headteacher found out and Steve was in more trouble for lying. He didn't get away with it.

c Students work in pairs and discuss the questions. Encourage students to use *remember +* gerund from Unit 9. After a few minutes, ask the class for their opinions. Discuss anything that the students remember doing at junior school.

2 Read

Students work in pairs. Check difficult vocabulary in the questionnaire: *change, by mistake, charity box, lend, take something back (to a shop)*. Students ask their partners the questions in the questionnaire and add up the scores. Then students turn to page 128 to find the results. Ask students if they agree with them.

> **Language note**
> *Borrow* and *lend* are often confused. You may like to point out the differences to your students:
> If you borrow something <u>from</u> someone, you take it, with or without their permission. You intend to return it. *Can I borrow your car?*
> If you lend something <u>to</u> someone, you allow them to have it or use it for a period of time. *I never lend anyone money*.
> Compare: *Can I borrow a pencil (from you)?* and *Can you lend me a pencil?*

3 Grammar

Second conditional review

Students covered the second conditional in SB2, Unit 14.

Weaker classes: Write this sentence on the board: *If I became the prime minister / president of my country, I would ...*
Ask students to complete the sentence for themselves. Elicit a few examples and check students are using an infinitive without *to*. Ask students if we are talking about a present or a future situation (*future*). Ask students if it is likely they will become prime minister or president (*no*). Elicit the name of the second conditional and point out the structure (*If + past tense, would + infinitive without to*). Now follow the procedure for stronger classes.

Stronger classes: Students read the example sentence. Ask students if this situation is imaginary or real (*imaginary*). Remind students of the construction of the second conditional.

(**b**) Ask students to read through the rule and complete it with the verbs. Check answers.

Answers
past, would; could, might

> **Language note**
> You might want to point out question 3 of the questionnaire: *Suppose you **were doing** ...* Ask students which tense it uses in the *if* clause (*past continuous*).

Look
Read through the Look box with students. Point out that when the *if* clause comes first, then there is a comma before the main clause.

(**c**) Students complete the sentences using the correct form of the verbs in brackets. Remind students that there is probably more than one choice for the verb in the main clause depending on the meaning you want to give. Do the first sentence as an example if necessary. Check answers and point out that there is no difference in the meaning if the clauses are reversed.

Answers
1 found   2 would/could/might send
3 would/could/might go out   4 didn't go
5 would, do   6 lived   7 wouldn't tell
8 went

> **Language notes**
> 1 Students may produce statements like: **If I would be rich, I would buy a new car*. Remind them that we can't use *would* in the *if* clause in the second conditional.
> 2 Explain to students that after *If I* in the second conditional we can use *was* or *were*, e.g. *If I were you, I'd ...* or *If I was you, I'd ...* Explain too that *were* can also be used with the third person.
> 3 Remind them that the *if* clause can go at the beginning or at the end of the conditional sentence.

First and second conditional review

(**d**) Students read the two sentences and identify which is first conditional and which is second conditional. Elicit the construction of the first conditional (*If + present tense, will + infinitive without to*). Ask students whether the main clause refers to the present or the future (*the future for both conditionals*). Then ask students which conditional talks about more likely situations.

Answers
Sentence 1 – second conditional;
Sentence 2 – first conditional
Situation 2 (first conditional) is more likely to happen.

(**e**) Students match and complete the sentences with their own ideas. Check answers and make sure students are using the correct construction.

Answers
2 If I go out this weekend, I'll ...
   (students' own answers)
   If I went out this weekend, I'd ...
   (students' own answers)
3 If I get a good job when I leave school, I'll ...
   (students' own answers)
   If I got a good job when I left school, I'd ...
   (students' own answers)

(f) Students read the questions in the questionnaire in Exercise 2 and find the other words used to introduce the situations. Tell students that the words have similar meanings and are used when considering a possible situation and then thinking about what effects it would have.

Answers
imagine, suppose, say

Grammar notebook
Remind students to note down the rules to compare first and second conditionals and to write a few examples of their own.

4 Speak

Students complete the questions and then add two more. Encourage students to use *imagine*, *suppose* and *say* to introduce a possible situation. Monitor and check students are using the correct form. Students then ask a partner the questions. Discuss any interesting answers in class.

Possible answers
1 where would you go?
2 who would you meet?
3 what would you say?
4 what would you change?

5 Listening and vocabulary
Crime

If you set the background information as a homework research task, ask students to tell the class what they found out.

BACKGROUND INFORMATION

Young people and crime: In Britain the age of criminal responsibility is 10. At this age a child can be convicted of a crime but cannot be sent to an adult prison before they are 17. In a recent survey of 5,000 schoolchildren, 25% of children admitted to committing a crime in the past year. The top three crimes were: fare-dodging (not paying for tickets on public transport), graffiti and shoplifting. The survey also reported that over 80% of children committing crimes have been caught at some point and that they had received some form of punishment.

Community service: Sometimes people who have committed minor crimes receive community service when a prison sentence would be too serious for the crime. Then a person might do something to benefit their local community such as helping old people or picking up litter.

Prison: There are 139 prisons in England and Wales and they hold approximately 75,000

people. In the early nineties the average prison population was approximately 45,000.

(a) 🔊 Students match the words with the pictures. Encourage students to make a guess by using clues in the word, e.g. *shop* in *shoplifting*, *riding* in *joyriding*, etc. Play the recording to check answers and make sure students understand the meaning of the words.

TAPESCRIPT/ANSWERS
a 6 vandalism
b 4 shoplifting
c 2 joyriding
d 5 pick-pocketing
e 1 burglary
f 3 arson

(b) 🔊 Explain that students are going to listen to a radio show about teenage crime and tick the crimes mentioned. Tell students not to worry about any unknown vocabulary at this stage and encourage them to listen for the words in the box. Play the recording and check answers.

TAPESCRIPT
Presenter   Hello and welcome to Talking Point. Now, teenagers have been getting into trouble for as long as ... well, as long as there have been teenagers, I suppose, but a frightening new survey into UK teenage crime has found out that almost 50% of schoolchildren aged 11 to 17 have broken the law. In the studio today we have three teenage ex-law-breakers, who have agreed to tell us about some of the reasons they got caught up in crime at such an early age. So, Chloe, what sort of things did you do?

Chloe   Well, vandalism – graffiti mainly. I had a competition with a few of my friends – who could spray paint their name in the craziest place. I painted mine at the top of the church. No one could beat that so I won. Now when I pass the church and I see my name I feel really terrible.

Presenter   Why did you do that?

Chloe   Just for fun really.

Presenter   For fun? But you knew it was wrong?

Chloe   Yeah, of course I did. But I mean this town's really boring. I wish there was more to do in this town then maybe kids wouldn't get into so much trouble.

Presenter   Ian, what kind of things did you do?

Ian   Well, I did a lot of shoplifting when I was younger, and then I started breaking into houses.

Presenter   Burglary! – that's very serious. Why did you start doing that?

Ian   I often sold the things I stole to get money.

Presenter   But you stopped, didn't you? What made you do that?

Ian   Yeah, burglary was a big mistake. I got caught and had to do 500 hours of community service, picking up litter from the park every day. But it made me see that I was messing up my life. Now

I've got a Saturday job. It doesn't pay as much as burglary but at least it's honest.

Presenter Would you like things to be different?

Ian Yeah, I wish I was a millionaire, if only I had more money, then I wouldn't have to worry about anything.

Presenter Anything more realistic?

Ian Well, I wish I could leave school and get a real job. I really want to buy a car.

Presenter And finally, Liam, you say you regularly broke the law. What sort of things did you do?

Liam Well, me and my mates stole cars a lot.

Presenter Joyriding? How often?

Liam At least one a week – usually on a Saturday night. There were lots of cars parked in town. The police chased us sometimes. That was what I enjoyed – the excitement.

Presenter And what happened?

Liam Well, we had a really serious accident and my mate had to go to hospital. I realised how stupid it was. I mean, someone could have been killed! The police organised a course for us and I'm training to become a mechanic.

Presenter So now you fix cars instead of stealing them?

Liam Yeah! The mechanics course has really changed me. I feel much more positive about life now.

Presenter Well, thank you all for coming in to speak to us. Next week on Talking Point …

Answers
vandalism (destroying public property)
shoplifting (stealing from a shop)
burglary
joyriding (stealing cars and riding around in them for fun)

(c) 🔊 You may want to explain some difficult vocabulary: *fines, community service, (car) accident*. Play the recording again and students use the words in the box to complete the table with the crimes and the reasons for committing them. Check answers.

	crime	reason
Chloe	vandalism	fun
Ian	shoplifting	money
	burglary	
Liam	joyriding	excitement

(d) Read the questions with students and check difficult vocabulary: *spray*. Students answer the questions in pairs, then play the recording again for students to check their answers. Check answers and, if necessary, play the recording again, pausing after each answer.

Answers
1 At the top of a church   2 Really terrible
3 He got caught   4 He's got a Saturday job
5 On Saturday nights   6 The police organised a mechanics course for them

6 Speaking and vocabulary
Crime

(a) Ask students what usually happens to people who are caught committing a crime. Elicit *punishment*. You might like to elicit some forms of punishment in L1.

Students complete the text with correct forms of the verbs in the box. If students are finding the text difficult, encourage them to use dictionaries to look up a noun and then find the verb most commonly used with it. Students check answers in pairs before feedback in class.

Answers
1 get   2 doing   3 committing   4 breaks
5 gets   6 gets   7 Sending   8 pay   9 put
10 do

(b) Ask students to read the text again and find the four types of punishment.

Answers
send them to prison
pay a fine
put them on probation
do community service

(c) Read through the questions with students and check any difficult vocabulary: *drop litter, offender*. Students work with a partner and discuss the questions. In open class discuss the answers and ask students how they would punish each of the crimes in Exercise 5a.

Answers
1 Students' own answers
2 Students' own answers
3 Not buying tickets on public transport, downloading music, copying CDs
4 Students' own answers

Vocabulary notebook
Encourage students to start a section entitled *Crime* with the categories *crimes, verbs, punishments* and to note down the words from this exercise. They may find it useful to note down translations of the words.

7 Grammar
I wish / If only for present situations

(a) **Weaker classes:** Write these sentences on the board:
I'm poor. I wish I had more ....
I live in a boring village. I wish I lived ....
Ask students to suggest ways of ending each sentence, e.g. *I wish I had more money* and *I wish I lived in a town*. Point out the tense of the verb used after *wish* (*past simple*). Check students understand that we are not talking about the past.

Stronger classes: Ask students to complete the sentence *I wish …* with their own words. Elicit a few examples and rephrase the students' wishes such that they have a past tense after *I wish*, e.g. *I wish I had* *more money, I wish I <u>was</u> rich, I wish I <u>could speak</u> better English*. Tell students that after this structure we use the past simple to refer to wishes about a present situation.

Open books at page 71. Students look at the example sentences. Tell students that *If only* is used in a similar way to *I wish* (see Language note). Read the questions with students and elicit the answers. Point out that this use of the past tense is similar to the use of a past tense in the second conditional.

Answers
1 The speaker (Chloe) thinks there isn't enough to do in the town. She wants to have more to do.
2 The speaker (Ian) thinks that he doesn't have enough money. He wants to have more money.
3 past simple

Language notes
1 *If only* is a stronger phrase than *I wish* and is also commonly used with the past perfect to talk about regrets. (Student's will cover this in Unit 14)
2 It is also possible to use the past continuous after *I wish* and *If only*. This often refers to a wish for the future. eg. *I wish I was going to the cinema tonight.*
3 It is common to use were instead of *was* after *I wish* / *If only*, e.g. *I wish I was/were rich* and *If only he was/were here now* are all correct.

b Ask students to look at the pictures. Tell students that the boy on the left is Tom and the boy on the right is Ryan. Students complete the sentences using the verbs in the box. If necessary, go through the first sentence as an example. Check answers and quickly elicit the present situation that is relevant to each case.

Answers
1 understood – Ryan doesn't understand maths
2 was – Ryan isn't as intelligent as Tom
3 didn't have – Ryan has a lot of homework tonight
4 knew – Tom doesn't know how to talk to girls
5 was – Tom isn't as good looking as Ryan
6 played – Tom doesn't play football as well as Ryan

Grammar notebook
Remind students to note down the rules for this structure and to write a few examples of their own.

8 # Speak

BACKGROUND INFORMATION

Work by Ford Madox Brown: Although born to British parents, Brown (1821–1893) was always an outsider to the British art establishment. He studied art in the great schools of Antwerp and

Paris. His pictures are now much in demand, but his contemporaries largely ignored his work and he never made much money out of painting. He was never able to leave a work alone and would continually retouch it, even though sometimes the painting had already been sold. *Work* took him 13 years to finish and is an interpretation of Heath Street, Hampstead, London.

a Ask students to look at the painting. Discuss anything that the students know about the picture. Students work with a partner to think of three thoughts beginning with *I wish* or *If only*. Ask a few pairs for their answers and encourage students to give reasons. Check students are using the past simple after *I wish* / *If only*.

Possible answers
If only it wasn't so hot.
I wish I didn't have to work so much.
I wish I had some shoes.
If only I had another dress.
I wish these children went to school.

b Read the topics in the box and check students understand possessions. Ask students to discuss the topics using *I wish* / *If only*. Monitor and check students are using the correct tense.

9

Pronunciation
I wish ... and *If only ...*

a 🔊 Students turn to page 120 and read the sentences. Play the recording and ask students to listen to the underlined words. Ask students how the underlined parts are pronounced. *If only* and *I wish I ...* are examples of linking between a consonant at the end
of one word immediately followed by a vowel at the beginning of the next. In *I wish they ...* the sounds at the end of *wish* and *they* are also linked so that one word is pronounced together with the next.

TAPESCRIPT
1 If <u>on</u>ly there was something to do.
2 If <u>on</u>ly she liked me.
3 If <u>on</u>ly they'd ask me.
4 If <u>on</u>ly he knew.
5 I wish <u>I</u> knew his name.
6 I wi<u>sh I</u> could go home.
7 I wi<u>sh you</u> weren't so noisy.

b 🔊 Play the recording again, pausing for students to repeat each sentence. Encourage students to link the sounds at the ends and beginnings of words in the same way as the recording.

A problem for Matt

10 Read and listen

Warm up

Ask students what they can remember about the last episode of the story (*Ben called Caroline to see if she was going to the party and Caroline told him about Matt's problem. She thinks it's about money.*)

(a) 🔊 Pre-teach *second-hand, interest, break down*. Ask students to read the questions and predict the answers but do not comment at this stage. Play the recording while students read and check their predictions. Check answers in open class. If students ask questions about vocabulary, write the words on the board but do not explain their meaning at this stage.

TAPESCRIPT

See the story on page 72 of the Student's Book.

Answers

Matt owes someone some money for a second-hand motorbike he bought. He's going to talk to the guy he bought the bike from.

(b) Read through the sentence halves and check difficult vocabulary: *used*. Students match parts of the sentences and compare their answers with a partner. Check answers.

Answers

1 d   2 c   3 f   4 b   5 a   6 e

11 Everyday English

(a) Ask students to locate expressions 1 to 4 in the story on page 72 and decide who says them.

Weaker classes: Check answers at this stage.

Answers

1 Ben   2 Ben   3 Matt   4 Ben

Students then match the expressions with the situations. Go through the first item with them as an example if necessary. Check answers.

Answers

a 3   b 4   c 1   d 2

(b) Ask students to read through the sentences and complete the answers. Go through the first sentence with them as an example if necessary.

Answers

1 and besides
2 the way I see it
3 that's a good point
4 You never know

OPTIONAL ACTIVITIES

See Unit 2, Exercise 11: Everyday English, Optional Activities.

12 Vocabulary

Phrasal verbs with *down*

(a) Students match the underlined verbs with their meanings. Encourage students to find the verbs in the text and use the context to help them decide.

Answers

1 b   2 c   3 a   4 d

(b) Students complete the sentences with the appropriate phrasal verbs. Remind students to use the correct form of the verb. Check answers by asking students to say the sentences aloud.

Answers

1 Slow down   2 broke down   3 gets, down
4 turned, down

Vocabulary notebook

Encourage students to add these to the section *Phrasal verbs* from Unit 2 and to note down the words from this exercise under the heading *down*. They may find it useful to note down translations of the words too.

13 Write

Students can do the preparation in class and the writing for homework.

(a) Students read the text quickly to find the problem and the action Peter suggests. Encourage students not to look up every new word but just to read quickly and find the answers.

Answers

He is writing about the increase in teenage crime. He suggests a town meeting where the public try and work out a solution to the problem.

Check any difficult vocabulary before moving onto the next stage: *convict someone of* (a crime), *compared to, work out*.

(b) Tell students they are going to write a letter about the problem from the point of view of a teenager. Elicit how a formal letter is started (*Dear Sir/Madam*) and finished (*Yours faithfully*). Encourage students to plan their letter in three paragraphs:
- their reason for writing
- their opinion on the problem
- their suggestions for a solution

11 Two sides to every story

1 Read

If you set the background information as a homework research task, ask students to tell the class what they found out.

BACKGROUND INFORMATION

Thailand: is in south-east Asia. It has borders with Burma, Laos, Cambodia and Malaysia. The capital is Bangkok and its population is about 65 million (July 2003). The monsoon season in Thailand and lasts from about June to October. It does not rain every day but the humidity makes it feel hot and sticky.

The Beach: was originally a book by Alex Garland, published in 1996. It was made into a film in 2000 and is about a young American traveller, Richard, in Thailand. Richard is given a hand-drawn map by a strange man at a cheap hotel in Bangkok and with two French travellers, sets off to find the island on the map. There were many problems during the filming of *The Beach*. These are mentioned in the texts in the Student's Book. Soon the newspapers became aware of the problems and many people decided not to see the film as a protest against the film company's actions.

Phi Phi Lei: is a very small island off the south-west coast of Thailand near the large popular holiday island of Phuket. *The Beach* was filmed on Maya beach on the island.

Leonardo Wilhelm DiCaprio (1974–): was born on 11 November in Los Angeles, California. He has an Italian-born father and a German-born mother. Leonardo has appeared in over 20 films and TV series including *Romeo and Juliet* (1996), *Titanic* (1997) and *Alexander the Great* (2005). In *The Beach*, Leonardo plays Richard.

Virginie LeDoyen (1976–): is a French actress who appeared in *The Beach* as French traveller Françoise. She has appeared in over 25 films, mostly in her home country.

a) Students work in small groups and discuss what they know about *The Beach*. After a few minutes, ask for their ideas. Use the pictures to elicit the main actors (*Leonardo DiCaprio and Virginie LeDoyen*), and where the film was made (*Thailand*), and pre-teach *palm trees*, *sand* and *bulldozer*.

b) Tell students they are going to read two versions of the filming of *The Beach*. In pairs, Student A reads the text and answers the questions on page 74. Student B turns to page 122 and reads the text and answers the questions there. Monitor and help students with vocabulary as necessary.

Answers (Student A)
1 They made the beach flatter to make filming easier and they planted some coconut trees.
2 The beach looked even more beautiful.
3 They put wooden poles on the beach but it didn't work.
4 Yes, there was some heavy rain during the filming.
5 Yes, they paid the local people $100,000.
6 Tourists thought it looked like paradise.

Answers (Student B)
1 They took away the natural plants (vegetation) and they put in coconut trees.
2 The trees killed other plant life.
3 They put wooden poles in the sand but it didn't work.
4 No, the rain was normal monsoon rain.
5 No, it wasn't enough to help.
6 They were shocked because they thought the beach looked bad.

c) In pairs, students discuss the answers to their questions. Encourage students to present their answers as if they are either a member of the film crew or an inhabitant of Phi Phi Lei. Students should not argue about the answers but present their views politely.

Weaker classes: Students can do the activity in groups of four, with two members of the film crew and two inhabitants of the island.

If your class enjoy the activity on *The Beach*, then they could discuss the issue in a debate. Divide the class into two halves (one half representing the film crew and the other half representing the inhabitants). You might also ask one student to be neutral and lead the debate. Students represent their views of what happened during the filming and decide on a solution to the problem.

2 Grammar

Linkers of contrast: *however / although / even though / in spite of / despite*

(a) Books closed. Write the following sentences on the board:

The film crew paid $100,000 for the damage.
The islanders were not happy.

Ask students if they can join the sentences with a connecting word. Elicit *but* and point out that this word links the sentences.

Now write these sentences on the board:

1 *The film crew paid $100,000 for the damage.*
.... *, the islanders were not happy.*
2 .... *the film crew paid $100,000 for the damage, the islanders were not happy.*
3 .... *paying $100,000 for the damage, the islanders were not happy.*
4 .... *the money, the islands were not happy.*

Write the different linkers of contrast on the board and tell students that these words are also used to link contrasting sentences. Ask students to match the linkers with each sentence. Encourage them to read the sentences aloud to see if they sound correct.

Answers

1 However – Point out the comma that follows *however*. Tell students that this has a similar meaning to *but*. Point out that it is usually used at the beginning of a sentence and not in the middle.
2 *Although / Even though* – Tell students that *even though* is a stronger form of *although*. Point out that we do not say **even although*.
3 *In spite of / Despite* – Tell students that these phrases have the same meaning. Point out that we do not say **despite of*.
4 *In spite of / Despite* – Tell students that we use these phrases in front of a noun group or an *–ing* form.

Students open their books at page 75 and choose the correct options. Encourage them to choose the words they think sound right before checking on pages 74 and 122. Check answers in open class.

Answers

1 Although   2 Despite   3 However
4 In spite of   5 Even though

(b) Students look at the sentences in Exercise 2a, and complete the rule and the examples in the rule box.

Answers

although, even though, Although / Even though;
despite, in spite of, Despite / In spite of;
however, However, however

(c) Students combine the two sentences using the linker given. If necessary go through a few sentences as an example. Point out that there is often more than one way to say these sentences.

Answers

2 I'm going for a run, even though it's raining.
   Even though it's raining, I'm going for a run.
3 Although the bus was late, we arrived on time.
   We arrived on time, although the bus was late.
4 The garden isn't very nice. However, I like the house.
   The garden isn't very nice. I like the house, however.
5 In spite of having lots of money, they aren't happy.
   They aren't happy, in spite of having lots of money.
6 People have skin. However, animals have fur.
   People have skin. Animals have fur, however.
7 She went to see the film, despite having seen it before.
   Despite having seen it before, she went to see the film.
8 Even though he didn't study, he passed the exam.
   He passed the exam, even though he didn't study,
9 Although I didn't like the book, I enjoyed the film.
   I enjoyed the film, although I didn't like the book.
10 Despite being cold, she didn't wear a jacket.
   She didn't wear a jacket, despite being cold.

Grammar notebook

Remind students to note down the rules for linkers of contrast and to write a few examples of their own.

3 Pronunciation

/əʊ/ *though*

(a) ◁») Students turn to page 120 and read through the words. Play the recording, pausing after each word for students to repeat. Tell students that /əʊ/ is a long vowel sound, and make sure students are pronouncing the sound correctly.

TAPESCRIPT

1 so   2 go   3 don't   4 slow   5 nobody
6 though   7 although   8 won't

(b) ◁») Students read through the sentences and underline the /əʊ/ sound. Go through the first one with them as an example, if necessary. Play the recording again, pausing after each sentence for students to check and repeat.

TAPESCRIPT/ANSWERS

1 <u>D</u>on't <u>g</u>o <u>so</u> <u>s</u>lowly.
2 I <u>w</u>on't watch the game sh<u>ow</u>.
3 Although I <u>k</u>now Alex, I <u>d</u>on't <u>k</u>now his brother.
4 <u>N</u>obody likes him, even th<u>ough</u> he's friendly.

Look

Read through the Look box with students. Point out that in the negative form *not* separates *despite / in spite of* from the noun phrase or *–ing* form.

 # **4** Listen

If you set the background information as a homework research task, ask students to tell the class what they found out.

BACKGROUND INFORMATION

The first moon landing: was on 20 July, 1969. The Apollo 11 had taken off from the Kennedy Space Center four days earlier. There were three astronauts on board: Neil Armstrong, Michael Collins and Edwin 'Buzz' Aldrin. A camera on the spaceship provided live television coverage as Neil Armstrong climbed down the ladder to the surface of the moon. The astronauts spent over two hours on the moon's surface and returned to earth on 24 July. Some people think that they were filmed in a television studio because the Americans wanted to beat the Russians in the 'Space Race'. In 2001 a TV programme in America interviewed many people who believe the conspiracy theory. The North American Space Agency (NASA) received so many emails that it put an article on their website which answers all the theories.

a Students answer the questions with a partner. Discuss answers in open class but do not comment at this stage.

b Students listen to the start of a radio programme and check their answers to Exercise 4a. Play the recording and, if necessary, repeat with pauses.

TAPESCRIPT

Armstrong 'That's one small step for man, one giant leap for mankind,'

Presenter When Neil Armstrong said these famous words as he stepped from his spaceship, the Eagle, onto the moon, the whole world listened in amazement. It was the 20th of July 1969 and the Americans had put the first man on the moon.
Since then, of course, space travel has become quite common. But whenever we hear that broadcast or see those photos of the first

mission to the moon we are always reminded of the magic of that moment when science fiction came true. So why does Professor John Hartson now want us to believe that it never really happened? He's here with me in the studio to explain his theory. Professor, welcome to the programme ...

Answers
1 Commander Neil Armstrong 2 On 20 July, 1969
3 American

c Ask students to find the words in the box in the photos. If necessary, give students dictionaries.

Answers

d Tell students that they are going to listen to the next part of the radio programme where the professor talks about why he believes the moon landings didn't happen. Pre-teach *studio* and *fake*. Ask students if they have heard about this before and if they can predict anything he will say. Play the recording and ask students to tick the words in Exercise 4c the professor mentions.

TAPESCRIPT

Presenter ... He's here with me in the studio to explain his theory. Professor, welcome to the programme.

Professor Thank you. Now I know people could be shocked to hear that the moon landing never happened so I'd like to show you some photos so that you can understand my theories. Look carefully at this first photo. What do you notice about the shadows of the astronauts?

Presenter They are pointing in different directions.

Professor Exactly. Now the light in this photo supposedly comes from the sun. Therefore the shadows should be pointing in the same direction. The fact the shadows point in different directions means that there must be two light sources – studio lights.

Presenter So you're saying that this photo was taken in a studio?

Professor Exactly, because of the shadows, this photo must be a fake.

Presenter You can't be serious.

Professor Well, look at this second photo. Where is the sun?

Presenter Behind the astronaut.

Professor So if the light is behind the astronaut, why is the front of him not in darkness. Why? Because they used a studio light to shine on the astronaut.

Presenter Uh huh.

Professor Now, look at the sky in the background. What can you see?

Presenter Nothing.

Professor Exactly. Where are the stars? This can't be a photo of the moon because there are no stars!

Presenter But why would the Americans want to do something like this?

Professor Well, you have to remember that back in the sixties the US was in the middle of the Cold War with the Russians. It was very important for both countries to show their advanced technology. Space travel was the greatest challenge. The Russians were the first to put a man into space, in 1959. The US needed to do something better. I believe the American government produced these photos so that the world would think they were winning the race.

Presenter Thank you for your fascinating theories, Professor. After the break we'll be talking to Janet Hargreaves, a spokeswoman for NASA, who will be trying to explain that the moon landing really did happen.

Answers

shadow   astronaut   light source   sky

(**e**) Students work in pairs and think of arguments against the professor's theories. Ask the class if anyone believes the moon landings didn't happen.

(**f**) 🔊)) Tell students they are going to listen to a NASA spokeswoman answering the professor's theories. Read through the sentences with students and check any difficult vocabulary: *hoax, mirror, flash (photography)*. Play the recording and ask students to listen and decide if the sentences are true or false. Students check answers with a partner. Play the recording again, pausing if necessary. Students correct the false statements.

Weaker classes: It might help students if they predict whether the answers are true or false first and then listen to check.

TAPESCRIPT

Presenter Welcome back. Next in the studio we have Janet Hargreaves, a spokeswoman for NASA. Janet, welcome to the programme.

Janet Thank you.

Presenter Now, Professor Hartson used these photos to explain why he felt the moon landing was a hoax.

We were wondering if you could comment on some of his ideas?

Janet Well, I think the professor has a very good imagination – but he has no idea about either physics or space travel. Let's look at the shadows in the first picture.

Presenter Yes, he said it was because there were two light sources – studio lights.

Janet Well, if there were two light sources then each astronaut would have two shadows.

Presenter But why do the shadows point in different directions?

Janet Well, the surface of the moon is very uneven. It isn't flat at all. This means the shadows seem to be pointing in different directions.

Presenter I see. Well, what about this photo? The professor explained that because the sun is behind the astronaut the front of him should be in darkness.

Janet Well, from samples brought back to earth we know that the surface of the moon contains hundreds of small bits of mineral – it's like lots of little bits of glass. The surface of the moon is reflecting the sun's light back up at the astronaut, which is why he is not in darkness.

Presenter Ok, so finally how do you explain the fact that there are no stars in the sky?

Janet Well, anyone who's ever taken a photo at night using a flash knows the answer to this one. The stars are trillions of kilometres away and when you take a photo at night there isn't enough time for their light to hit the film. To take a photo of stars, you have to keep the camera open for a long, long time. That makes the image of the person very unclear. It's almost impossible to do both things. If you want a good image of the person, you won't see any stars in the background.

Answers

1 F – Two light sources would result in two sets of shadows.   2 F – It isn't flat.   3 T   4 F – The stars are trillions of kilometres away.   5 F – It's almost impossible to do both things.

5 # Speak

You may want to set the preparation for this for homework.

BACKGROUND INFORMATION

Conspiracy theories: are the beliefs that historical or current events are the result of planning by secretive powers, usually government organisations. The moon landings are a common conspiracy theory.

Princess Diana (1961–1997): was born Lady Diana Frances Spencer. She married Charles, Prince of Wales, in 1981, but the couple divorced in 1996. She and her companion Dodi Al Fayed were killed in a car accident in Paris. Some people believe that Diana was killed by the British secret service because she was a threat to the monarchy.

John Fitzgerald Kennedy (1917–1963): was the 35th president of the USA (1961–1963). He was shot in his car in Dallas, Texas. A man was charged with his murder but he was also shot and died before he went to court. There are theories that Kennedy was killed by many different people including the Russian secret service, the Italian mafia, the American government and the Cuban government.

The Roswell Incident: in July 1947 in Roswell, New Mexico, USA, the American Air Force supposedly found the wreck of some kind of aircraft. Some people claimed that they had also found the bodies of some aliens and that the government kept their findings secret to avoid panic.

Read through the information about conspiracy theories with students. Ask students if they recognise any of the conspiracy theories from the photos. Students work in groups of four and choose a conspiracy theory they know. Ask them to prepare a small presentation about the theory and the theories about it. Give each group 10 minutes to prepare their mini presentations and then ask them to report to the class. Discuss interesting theories and ask the class to vote on whether they believe the conspiracy theory or not.

6 Grammar
Modal verbs of deduction (present)

a Books closed. Write these sentences on the board:

The moon landings didn't happen.
J.F.K. was murdered by the American secret service.
Princess Diana was killed by the British government.
The governments of the world know that there is life on other planets.

Ask students if they believe any of the conspiracy theories. Ask if they think any of them *could/might be* true. Ask if they think any of them *must be* false. Elicit the sentences *It could/might be true* and *It must be true/false.*

Students open their books at page 77 and read the examples and answer the questions. Check answers.

Answers
1 This can't be a photo of the moon because there are no stars.

Because of the shadows this photo must be a fake.
2 I know people could be shocked to hear that the moon landing never happened.
3 can't be

Remind students that modal verbs are followed by an infinitive without *to* and that the opposite of *must be* when making deductions is *can't be* and that *could* and *might* have similar meanings in this context.

b Students complete the sentences. Check answers and make sure students are pronouncing *must be* as /mʌsbi/.

Answers
1 must be   2 can't be   3 might be   4 can't be
5 must be   6 might be   7 can't be

c 🔊 Ask students to look at the four pictures and elicit what is going on in them. (*In various combinations: there is a baby crying, someone singing, someone vacuuming, the TV is on and a dog is barking.*) Play the recording and, with a partner, students discuss which picture it is. Do the first one with them as an example if necessary, eliciting phrases like: *It can't be picture a because there isn't a dog barking. It might be picture b because ....*, and finally deduce which picture it is with the phrase: *It must be picture ... because ...*

Answers
1 picture c   2 picture d   3 picture a
Unused picture: b

Grammar notebook
Remind students to note down the rules for modal verbs of deduction and to write a few examples of their own.

7 Vocabulary
Problems

a Ask students to read through once before they match the underlined words with the definitions, to get a general idea of the text. Point out several of the underlined words are phrasal verbs and that the main verb will give them a clue to its meaning, e.g. *think it over = think about it*. Encourage students to guess the meanings of other words. Students check answers in pairs before feedback in open class.

Answers
1 sort it out   2 talk it over   3 sleep on it
4 think it over   5 make up my mind   6 ignore it
7 comes up   8 go away   9 come up with
10 come back to it

┌─ **OPTIONAL ACTIVITY** ────────────
Depending on the sensitivity of your class, you might want to ask students if they have a similar approach to problems at school and at home. Encourage them to use suitable vocabulary.

b Students complete the sentences with words from the text in the correct form. If necessary go through the first example with them. Monitor that students are using the correct form.

Answers
1 sort (everything) out   2 comes up
3 making up my mind   4 talk over, comes up with
5 ignore, go away

c You might want to choose partners carefully for this exercise. Students tell their partner which sentences are true for them. If necessary, give an example for yourself.

Vocabulary notebook
Encourage students to start a section called *Problems* and to note down the words from this exercise. They may find it useful to note down translations of the words too.

Fiction in mind

8 Read

> **BACKGROUND INFORMATION**
>
> **Hypnotism:** is the art of putting someone in a sleep-like state, in which a person's thoughts can be easily influenced by someone else. From the beginning of the 20th century, hypnotism started to appear as a form of entertainment. Now, hypnotism is used in medicine, psychology and even dentistry.
>
> **The Real Aunt Molly:** is a short story from *The Fruitcake Special and Other Stories,* published as part of the Cambridge English Readers series.

a Ask students if they have ever seen a hypnotist's show (either live or on television). Students discuss what happened or what they think happens. Then students read the extract from the short story and compare what they discussed with what happened in *The Real Aunt Molly*. Encourage students not to look up every new word or to worry about the gaps in the text, but just to read and get the general idea.

Answer
In the story, Aunt Molly is hypnotised. The hypnotist tells her that she will be a confident person but then he has a heart attack.

┌─ OPTIONAL ACTIVITY ─────────────
│ You may like to do a small comprehension activity on the extract of the story before students do Exercise 8b. Write these questions on the board and give students a minute to find the answers:
│ 1 *What is the name of the person being hypnotised?* (Molly)

2 *What is the name of the hypnotist?* (Maxwell)
3 *What happens to the hypnotist?* (He has a heart attack)

b Students read through sentences 1 to 8. Point out that there are two extra sentences. Students insert the sentences in the gaps and check with partner before class feedback.
Check answers. You may like to read the completed text aloud with the class or alternatively, the extract is recorded on track 34 of the Workbook CD/CD ROM.

Answers
b 4   c 2   d 6   e 5   f 8
Unused sentences: 3 and 7

c Read the questions with students and check any difficult vocabulary: *evidence*. Encourage students to answer the questions from memory before reading the text again to check. Check answers and ask students to give reasons.

Answers
1 Winston was her son. (line 12)
2 She needed more confidence and to be more decisive. (lines 12–15)
3 Yes, he hypnotised her. It worked because the first thing Molly did was shout at a man in the audience. (line 45–49)
4 He wanted to know how to get Aunt Molly back to normal without Maxwell Marvel. (line 57)

Discussion box
Weaker classes: Students can choose one question to discuss.

Stronger classes: In pairs or small groups, students go through the questions in the box and discuss them.
Monitor and help as necessary, encouraging students to express themselves in English and to use any vocabulary they have learned from the text. Ask pairs or groups to feedback to the class and discuss any interesting points further.

Possible answers
1 *The Real Aunt Molly* might refer to the personality that Aunt Molly has after being hypnotised.
2 She might become too confident and stay that way forever.

9 Write

Students can do the preparation for this in class and the writing for homework.

a Ask students to look at the photos. Ask which photo shows the negative effects of tourism. Elicit some of the negative effects, e.g. *pollution*. Then use the other photo to elicit some positive effects of tourism, e.g. *more money and jobs for local people*. Students read the text and find the negative points made about tourism.

Answer
The writer expresses three negative points about tourism.

(**b**) Students find the words that introduce each negative point.

Answers
First of all, Secondly, And finally

(**c**) Students match the underlined words with phrases 1 to 4 in the box. Remind students that all the underlined phrases and the phrases in the box are suitable for use in compositions.

Answers
1 However   2 To conclude   3 As a result
4 Moreover

(**d**) Tell students they are going to write a composition about one of the topics given. Students should choose a topic and then make notes about each side of the argument. Encourage students to use:
- linkers of contrast
- the words and phrases in the example composition and in Exercise 9c.

12 Mysterious places

1 Read and listen

If you set the background information as a homework research task, ask students to tell the class what they found out.

BACKGROUND INFORMATION

Peru: is in western South America and borders the South Pacific Ocean, Chile, Ecuador, Colombia, Brazil and Bolivia. The population is about 27,544,305 (July 2004) and the main language is Spanish.

The Nazca lines: are drawings of birds, spiders, fish, and even a monkey. There are also rectangular shapes and a large number of straight lines. The area is dry and the climate is stable so the lines have not changed for many centuries. There are several theories, but the main explanation is that the lines were religiously significant to the people who lived in the desert.

Easter Island: is called Rapa Nui by local people and is part of Chile. Only 2,000 people live on the island. The official language is Spanish, but many islanders speak Rapa Nui. The island has had a violent history and the most of the Moai

(the stone statues of faces) were destroyed by the islanders themselves.

Erich von Däniken: has spent many years developing theories about ancient wonders of the world such as the pyramids and the Moai on Easter Island. He has written several best-selling books.

Warm up

Books closed. Write these mysterious places on the board:
The Nazca Desert
Easter Island
Ask students if they know anything about them and pre-teach *mysterious*. Discuss what students know about each place and ask if they know any other places in the world that are mysterious.

(a) Students open their books at page 80. Ask students to look at the photos and elicit *desert, lines, island, statues*. Students read the text to find two questions about each place that we don't know the answers to. Encourage students not to look up every new word but just to find the answers. You could give them a 2 minute time limit, to encourage them to read the text quickly.

Answers
The Nazca Desert: When and why were the lines drawn?
Easter Island: Why were the statues built and who made them?

(b) 🔊 Read through the questions with students. Pre-teach any difficult words in the text, e.g. *figures, runways*. Students read and listen to the text and answer the questions. Play the recording. Students check answers with a partner before repeating the recording, pausing if necessary.

TAPESCRIPT
See the reading text on page 80 of the Student's Book.

Answers
1 In the 20th century, people flew over the lines.
2 The lines form pictures of enormous animals, people and plants and also runways (similar to those at airports).
3 Moai are strange statues of faces made from volcanic rock.
4 He suggested that the Moai were built and moved by aliens.

2 Grammar

Indirect questions

(a) Books closed. Write on the board:
We want to know …
Ask students if they can finish the sentence with any of the questions we can't answer about the Nazca lines and Easter Island. Elicit the indirect question form of each question from Exercise 1a and write them on the board:
We want to know …

when the lines were drawn
why the lines were drawn
why the statues are there
who made the statues.

Tell students that these are indirect questions. Ask students what differences there are between the direct and indirect question form (*in indirect questions you do not use an interrogative word order and, in these examples, there is no question mark*). Students open their books at page 81. Check students can identify the indirect and direct question examples.

Answers
The questions on the left are indirect.
The questions on the right are direct.

(b) Students work out the word order of each type of question.

Weaker classes: You might want to write these prompts on the board for students to put in order: *subject, question word, verb.*

Answers
1 In direct questions, there is a verb after the question word: question word, verb, subject.
2 In indirect questions, the subject (the lines, the statues, etc.) comes after the question word: question word, subject, verb.

Point out that transforming a direct question into an indirect question is done by using the same structure as a normal sentence after the question word.

(c) Students choose the correct options in the indirect questions. If necessary do the first item as an

example. Students will often instinctively choose the phrase which sounds correct and so encourage them to use instinct rather than formulas. Check answers and ask students to read their answers aloud.

Answers
1 why you are angry 2 what he's doing
3 where he is 4 where she has gone
5 who he is

(d) Students put the words in the correct order. Check answers and make sure students are using the correct word order after the question word. As a check, ask students if they can give you the direct question for each indirect question.

Answers
2 I wonder who that man is.
3 I can't tell you where they are.
4 We don't understand what she is saying.

Indirect questions and auxiliaries

(e) Ask students to look at the pictures and match them to the questions. Check answers and ask students what is different about these direct questions and the direct questions in Exercise 2a (*these questions include the auxiliary verb do/did*).

Answers
a 2 b 4 c 1 d 3

(f) 🔊 Tell students that they are going to hear the indirect forms of the questions in Exercise 2e. Ask students to write the questions they hear. Play the recording and repeat, with pauses, if necessary. Check answers and ask students what differences they notice between the direct and indirect question forms. Point out that in these examples the indirect question is still a question and so there is a question mark at the end.

TAPESCRIPT/ANSWERS
1 Can you tell me what time you close?
2 Do you know when it finishes?
3 Can you tell me where you got that cold drink?
4 Do you know if they won?

(g) Ask students to summarise what happens to auxiliary verbs after the question words in the examples in Exercise 2f. Check answers and point out the language notes below.

Answers
The auxiliary *do/does* is not used in the indirect question form. The word order after the question word is the same as a normal sentence.

Language notes
1 Without the auxiliary *do*, the subject must agree with the main verb, e.g. *When **does** it finish?* becomes *Do you know when it finish**es**?*

2   Remind students that the tenses must agree,
    e.g. *Did they win?* becomes *Do you know if they won?*
3   Tell students that when the question starts with an auxiliary, e.g. *Did they win?*, we replace the auxiliary with *if*.

(h) Students rewrite the questions in the indirect question form. Monitor that students are using the correct word order and that the subject agrees with the verb. Check answers.

Answers
2   where they went   3   if he lives around here
4   what time the plane leaves   5   if he speaks English

Grammar notebook
Remind students to note down the rules for indirect questions and to write a few examples of their own.

3 Speak

Tell students that indirect questions are useful as they often make a normal question more polite. Ask students to write four questions using the indirect question beginnings *Do you know …* and *Can you tell me …* . Students work in pairs and ask and answer the questions. Monitor and check that students are using the correct word order.

Weaker classes: Students can prepare their questions in pairs and then ask them individually to someone from a different pair.

4 Speak and listen

BACKGROUND INFORMATION

Stonehenge: is a unique monument in Wiltshire, England. It consists of a circle of very large stones and was probably built between 3000 BC and 1500 BC. Theories about who built it have included the Druids (religious groups from Roman times), Greeks and aliens. Reasons include human sacrifice, a monument to King Arthur or a tool to help astronomy.

Seahenge: See tapescript for Exercise 4c.

(a) Students look at picture 1. Ask students what they know about the place (*Stonehenge*).

(b) Use picture 2 to pre-teach *wooden posts*, *sand*, *coast*, *upside down*. Then students answer the questions in pairs or small groups. Ask students for their ideas but do not comment at this stage.

(c) ◁)) Tell students they are going to listen to an interview with an archaeologist. Play the recording while students listen and complete the notes. Check answers.

TAPESCRIPT

Interviewer   Tonight we're talking to Richard Kirk, who is one of the archaeologists involved in the discovery of Seahenge. Richard, can we begin by asking you what is Seahenge?

Richard   Seahenge is an ancient site that was found a few years ago on the coast of Norfolk, in the east of England.

Interviewer   The name Seahenge, of course, makes us think of Stonehenge – so is Seahenge basically the same thing?

Richard   No, not at all. Seahenge is a circle of 55 wooden posts, in the sand on the beach, and each post, is about 3 metres high. In the middle of the circle there is an upside down oak tree. All this was found in shallow water on the beach.

Interviewer   But they can't have built Seahenge in the water.

Richard   No, they probably didn't. The wood is about 4,000 years old. We think that they must have built the circle about a kilometre or more from the coast, and then throughout the years the sea has moved inland and covered it.

Interviewer   Do we know what it was used for?

Richard   Well, it's a bit too early to tell. We think that people might have put the bodies of the dead on the tree in the middle. That way, they would have decayed very fast.

Interviewer   Seahenge must be a fascinating place. Is it open to visitors?

Richard   Not at the moment, unfortunately. The wooden posts have been carefully removed and transported to a place called Flag Fen, where they are kept in water tanks.

Interviewer   Water tanks? What for?

Richard   Well, scientists want to do more research. They want to use the posts to find out more about people's lives 4,000 years ago.

Interviewer   And how do they do that? …

Answers
Shape: circle
Made of: 55 wooden posts
Height: 3 metres
Age: About 4,000 years old
Possible use of the site: To put dead people there so their bodies decayed quickly.

(d) ◁)) Read the statements with students and check difficult vocabulary: *protect*. Then play the recording again. Check answers and play the recording again, pausing if necessary.

Answers
1 F – Seahenge is a circle of wooden posts in the sea.
2 F – Seahenge was probably built about a kilometre from the coast but the sea has moved in since that time.

3 F – It's a bit to early to tell.
4 F – The wooden posts have been removed.
5 T

5 Grammar
Modals of deduction (past)

Students covered modals of deduction in Unit 11.

a Books closed. Tell students you are going to revise a few modal verbs. Think of a picture to draw on the board, e.g. a car or a house. Draw a line of the picture on the board and ask students to guess what the drawing is. Encourage them to use the modals of deduction *might, could, must*. Complete a little more of the drawing and ask them to comment again. Continue until you have nearly finished the drawing and invite them to comment again. Point out that *might* and *could* have similar meanings in this context but *must* indicates you are sure about something.

Students open their books at page 82. Ask them to read the examples in Exercise 5a. Ask students what the difference is between these examples and the ones they gave when you were drawing (*these examples are about the past*). Point out the difference in the structures of modals in the present and the past (in the present we use modal + infinitive, in the past we use modal + *have* + past participle). Students match meanings 1 to 3 with sentences a to c. Check answers.

Answers
a 3   b 1   c 2

b Students complete the rule. Remind students there is a table of past participles on page 123.

Answer
past, past participle

c Students complete the sentences using a modal of deduction and the correct form of the verb. Point out that there is more than one answer for most sentences. Go through the first sentence as an example and ask students if there are any alternatives to the answer given (*might/could have been* are also correct but indicate the speaker is less sure that Jane was angry). Check answers and that students understand the meaning of using a different verb.

Answers
2 can't/couldn't have brought (no difference in meaning)
3 might have been
4 might/must have left (*must* indicates the speaker is sure)
5 can't/couldn't have got (no difference in meaning)
6 might/must have taken (*must* indicates the speaker is sure)

Grammar notebook
Remind students to note down the rules for modals of deduction and to write a few examples of their own.

6 Pronunciation
have in *must have / might have / can't have / couldn't have*

a Students turn to page 120 and read the sentences. Tell students that there are two main ways of pronouncing *have*, a strong form /hæv/ and a weak form /əv/ or /həv/. Play the recording and ask students to circle the weak forms and underline the strong forms.

TAPESCRIPT/ANSWERS
1 She must (have) been very happy.
2 Yes, she must <u>have</u>. She was smiling a lot.
3 I might (have) passed the exam.
4 You can't <u>have</u>. You didn't study.
5 They must (have) walked here.
6 Well, they can't (have) come by car – they haven't got one!
7 Oh no! I can't (have) lost my keys again!
8 You must (have) left them in the car.
9 He couldn't (have) known the answers.
10 He must <u>have</u>. He passed the test.

b Ask students if they can work out when *have* is pronounced in its strong and weak forms (have *is pronounced in its weak form except when in a final position*). Point out that when *have* is at the start of a sentence, e.g. *Have you got a car?*, it is pronounced in a weak form but with an initial /h/, that is /həv/. Play the recording again, pausing after each sentence for students to check their answers and repeat.

7 Vocabulary
Phrasal verbs

If you set the background information as a homework research task, ask students to tell the class what they found out.

BACKGROUND INFORMATION
The ancient Egyptians: thought of their Pharaohs as gods. The Egyptians preserved the bodies of the dead by cleaning, drying and wrapping them in about 20 layers of cloth. These are called mummies and were buried in the pyramids along with many valuable items.

The pyramids were designed to stop thieves from breaking into them and in some cases, a curse was placed on the entrance. This meant that if anyone broke into the tomb, they would soon die.

Tutankhamen: was a Pharaoh of Egypt and he died in 1352BC in his late teens. Little is known about the period when he ruled and he is famous because his tomb was found in its original state. His mummified body was inside three coffins, one of which was made from solid gold.

Howard Carter (1874–1939): See text on page 83 of the Student's Book.

Warm up

Ask students if they know anything about Tutankhamen. Elicit *Egypt, Egyptian, pyramids, Pharaoh, curse*. Ask students if they know anything about the curse of Tutankhamen.

(**a**) Students read the text quickly and answer the question. Encourage students not to look up every new word but just read quickly to find the answer.

Answer
On 4 November 1922

(**b**) Students read the article again and match the phrasal verbs with definitions 1 to 8. Check answers and encourage students to write an example of their own for each verb in their vocabulary notebooks.

Answers
1 talked (him) into   2 call off   3 came across
4 passed away   5 tied in with   6 started out
7 went out   8 paid off

┌─ OPTIONAL ACTIVITY ─────────────────
│ Write these questions on the board. Students read the
│ text again and answer them:
│ 1 *Why did Carter first go to the pyramids?* (To paint
│   the pyramids)
│ 2 *Who paid for the search to find Tutankhamen's
│   tomb?* (Carnarvon)
│ 3 *How did Carnarvon die?* (He was bitten by an
│   insect)
│ 4 *What happened in Cairo at the same time?*
│   (The lights went out)

(**c**) Students complete the dialogue using the correct form of three of the phrasal verbs in the text.

Answers
passed away   came across   went out

(**d**) In pairs, students write a short dialogue using three of the phrasal verbs from the text. You could ask pairs to act out their dialogue to the class and vote on the most interesting.

Unit 12   87

8 Speak and listen

BACKGROUND INFORMATION

World Party: was a pop group formed by Karl Wallinger in 1986. Their first album was recorded in Wallinger's home studio in 1987 (*Private Revolution*). The song *The Curse of the Mummy's Tomb* was on an album called *Egyptology* (1997) which also included the song *She's the One.*

Robbie Williams: is an English singer and songwriter who was born on 13 February, 1974. From 1990 to 1995 he was a member of *Take That* and, when the group split up, Robbie started a solo career. In 1999, he released a cover version of *She's the One,* which reached number one in the UK charts.

(**a**) Read through the sentences with students and ask them to match the underlined words with their definitions. Encourage students to use the meaning in the sentence to help them.

Answers
1 c   2 f   3 a   4 b   5 d   6 e

(**b**) Ask students to look at the underlined words in Exercise 9a. Tell them that they are all words in a song called *The Curse of the Mummy's Tomb.* Check the meaning of *mummy.* In pairs or small groups, students try to predict the content of the song. Encourage students to use suitable modals of deduction such as *could/might* or *must.*

(**c**) 🔊 Students read through the sentences. Play the recording and students write the numbers of the missing lines in the spaces. Check answers and play the recording again, pausing if necessary.

TAPESCRIPT
See the song on page 84 of the Student's Book.

Answers
b 4   c 1   d 6   e 3   f 5

Did you know …?

Read the information in the box with students. Ask students if they know the song *She's the One.* Elicit *cover.* Ask students if they know any other famous covers of songs.

9 Vocabulary

Expressions with *be* + preposition

(**a**) Ask students to choose the best explanation of the phrase *It's up to you.*

Answer 2

(**b**) Ask students to match sentences 1 to 4 with their replies. Check answers and elicit possible meanings of the underlined expressions with *be.*

Answers

1 b   2 c   3 d   4 a

(c) Students match the underlined expressions in Exercise 9b with their meanings (1–4). Check answers and encourage students to write the expressions in their vocabulary notebooks.

Answers

a be against – 4
b be off (something) – 2
c be onto (something/someone) – 3
d be about to – 1

10 Write

Students covered story writing in SB2, Unit 15. Students can do the preparation in class and the writing for homework.

(a) Read the instructions with students. Point out that a useful way of developing a story (or narrative) and adding details is to ask and answer questions.

Tell students they are going to read part of a story. Students look at the picture. Ask them to imagine

what has happened in the room. Encourage students to speculate using modals of deduction such as *might have, could/can't have* and *must have*. Students then answer the questions using the text.

Answers

1 It was large and empty. There was hardly anything in it. The only piece of furniture was a large mirror. It was broken and there was glass on the floor. There was a window at the end of the room and a curtain in front of it.
2 A body was behind the curtain.
3 It was the noise of police cars. You panicked.
4 There was a knife in your hands.

(b) Students work in pairs. Tell them they are going to write a story. Ask students to decide on a simple theme, e.g. a mystery story, and write four questions about it. Students swap and answer their partner's questions adding as much detail as possible. Students then use their partner's answers to develop a short story. Encourage students to use:
● new vocabulary they have learned in the unit
● Modals of deduction in the present and the past.

Module 3 Check your progress

1 Grammar

(a) 2 to be   3 to travel   4 to study   5 going
6 to give   7 getting   8 to have   9 drinking

(b) 1 I wish I was/were taller.   2 I wish I understood physics.   3 I wish my football team were top of the league.

(c) 2 had, wouldn't share   3 would be, did
4 wouldn't be, had   5 didn't talk, would understand
6 Would, travel, won

(d) 2 Despite not being very tall, he plays basketball really well.
3 I look like my mother. However, my brother looks like my father.
4 I continued working even though I was really tired.
5 Although the exam was difficult, I think I passed.

(e) 2 where they went   3 if she left her phone number
4 if she likes me   5 who won the game

(f) 2 can't have gone   3 might be   4 might have gone
5 can't be   6 could be

2 Vocabulary

(a) 2 hang   3 turned   4 look   5 hook   6 come
7 let   8 get

(b) 1 slow down – the other words are associated with friends
2 excitement – the other words are crimes
3 law – the other words are punishments
4 call off – the other words are associated with problems
5 kind – the other words are verbs (and in the noun form end in –*ment* and the noun of *kind* is *kindness*.)

(c) 2 imagination   3 entertainment   4 popularity
5 kindness   6 reaction   7 possibility
8 relaxation

(d) *Across*
1 shoplifting   6 prison   7 community service
8 burglary

Down
2 pick-pocketing   3 vandalism   4 joyriding
5 arson   9 fine

Module 4
Emotions

YOU WILL LEARN ABOUT ...

Ask students to look at the pictures on the page. Ask students to read through the topics in the box and check that they understand each item. You can ask them the following questions, in L1 if appropriate:

1 *Why do you think the girl is happy?*
2 *Do you know which film this is?*
3 *What are the women doing?*
4 *What do you know about this actor?*
5 *What do you think they are celebrating?*
6 *What do you think is happening?*

In pairs or small groups students discuss which topic area they think each picture matches. Check answers.

Answers
1 What makes people happy
2 Scary films
3 Getting angry
4 *The Lord of the Rings*
5 A love story from 1906
6 Different wedding ceremonies

YOU WILL LEARN HOW TO ...

Use grammar

Students read through the grammar points and the examples. Go through the first item with students as an example. In pairs, students now match the grammar items in their book. Check answers.

Answers
Reporting verbs: She offered to pay, but I told her not to worry about it.
Third conditional: If you hadn't told me, I would have forgotten.
I wish / if only + past perfect simple: I wish I had got up earlier this morning.
should/shouldn't have: We shouldn't have spent all the money.
Non-defining relative clauses: James Bond is a secret agent whose codename is 007.
Defining relative clauses: Elijah, who played Frodo, was only 18 at the time.
be used to + gerund vs. *used to* + infinitive: I used to live in Tokyo, so I'm used to speaking Japanese.
Grammar of phrasal verbs: Why don't you sort the problem out?

Use vocabulary

Write the headings on the board. Go through the items in the Student's Book and check understanding. Now ask students if they can think of one more item for *Appearance*. Elicit some responses and add them to the list on the board. Students now do the same for the other headings. Some possibilities are:

Appearance: *tall/short, well-dressed, good-looking*

Personality: *generous, (un)friendly, ambitious*

Phrasal verbs with *out*: *find out, point out, eat out*

Adjectives with prefixes: *friendly/unfriendly, possible/impossible, common/uncommon*

13 Love

1 Read and listen

If you set the background information as a homework research task, ask students to tell the class what they found out.

BACKGROUND INFORMATION

O. Henry: is a pseudonym (writing name) of William Sydney Porter (1862–1910), an American short story writer. In 1896 he was charged with stealing money from the bank where he worked. He escaped to Honduras, Central America, but when he returned he was sentenced to three years in prison. While he was there, he started writing short stories and his most famous collection is *The Four Million* (1906), which included *The Gift of the Magi*.

The Magi: are the wise men who, in the Bible, came to Bethlehem to give Jesus presents.

Warm up

Ask students to give you examples of famous love stories. Make a list of their suggestions on the board and discuss their favourites briefly. Tell students to choose a love story they have read or watched and liked/disliked. Then students find a partner who does not know that story.

Possible answers
Romeo and Juliet, Antony and Cleopatra

a In pairs, students tell their partners about the love story they liked/disliked. Ask a few students to tell the class about their partner's story.

b Use the pictures to pre-teach *silver hair clasp* /klɑːsp/ and *gold watch chain*. Tell students that the pictures are all connected with the story *The Gift of the Magi*. In pairs, students predict the content of the story. Ask a few pairs to tell the class their predictions. Students read the text quickly to check their ideas. Encourage students not to look up every new word but just to read and get the general idea of the text.

c 🔊 Read through the questions with students and check difficult vocabulary: *deep breath, gasp*. Then students read the text and listen. Play the recording and give students a few minutes to answer the questions. Check answers and remind students about the causative (used when people do things for you, e.g. *I've had my hair cut*).

TAPESCRIPT
See the reading text on page 90 of the Student's Book.

Answers
1 They live in a tiny flat. He works but she doesn't. They are poor but in love.
2 She was probably nervous.
3 He was surprised that Della had had her hair cut.
4 She was too excited to wait.
5 He liked the present but he also smiled because he had bought a hair clasp for Della and she now had short hair.
6 He sold his gold watch.

Discussion box
Weaker classes: Students can choose one question to discuss.

Stronger classes: In pairs or small groups, students go through the questions in the box and discuss them.
Monitor and help as necessary, encouraging students to express themselves in English and to use any vocabulary they have learned from the text. Ask pairs or groups to feedback to the class and discuss any interesting presents students have received or given.

Grammar

Reported statements review

Students covered reported statements in SB2, Unit 16.

BACKGROUND INFORMATION

Christopher Columbus: (Cristobal Colón) was an Italian born Spanish explorer. In 1492, he became the first European to reach the New World (various Caribbean islands).

Neil Armstrong: see background information on page 78.

William Shakespeare (1564–1616): was an English playwright whose plays have been translated and performed throughout the world. He wrote comedies (*A Midsummer Night's Dream*), historical plays (*Richard III*), romances (*Romeo and Juliet*) and tragedies (*Hamlet*).

Walt Disney (1901–1966): was an American animator and film producer. He created Mickey Mouse in 1927 and many other characters including Goofy, Pluto and Donald Duck.

Ellen McArthur: see background information on page 38.

(a) **Weaker classes:** Follow the procedure for stronger classes but just ask three questions. Tell students they can takes notes while you are talking.

Stronger classes: Ask a student to come to the front of the class and interview him/her for a minute or two about one of his/her hobbies. Try to ask questions in a variety of tenses so you get different tenses in the answers. Tell other students to listen and try to remember as much as possible. After the interview, ask students to work in pairs and write down, in reported speech, everything they can remember of what the student said. Help students with the first few examples, e.g. *Paola said her favourite hobby was shopping. She said that yesterday she had bought …* etc. After a few minutes, ask pairs to swap their work with other students and check for mistakes. Monitor and help with obvious mistakes.

Students open their books at page 91 and match the parts of the sentences. Students check answers by finding the sentences in the text.

Answers

1 c   2 a   3 b

(b) Students look at the examples and answer the question. Elicit the tense names in each sentence (*past simple, past perfect*). Students answer the question.

Answer

The verb changes from the past simple tense to the past perfect tense.

OPTIONAL ACTIVITY

Ask students for the names of other tenses and elicit *present simple, present continuous, present perfect, is going to,* and *will.* Students decide what happens to the verb in each case and summarise the changes in a table:

Direct speech	→	Reported speech
Present simple	→	Past simple
Past simple	→	Past perfect
Present perfect	→	Past perfect
am/is/are going to	→	*was/was/were going to*
will/won't	→	*would/wouldn't*

(c) Students write the reported speech for each sentence. Remind students that quotes are not used in reported speech and tell them *that* is optional after the reporting verb with *say* and *tell.* Check answers and that students are using the correct tense in the reported sentences. Point out that the past form of *must* is *had to.*

Answers

2 Della said that she had sold her hair.
3 She said that she had to give it to him immediately.
4 Jim said that he had bought a present for her.
5 She said that she could grow her hair again.
6 He said that he wouldn't stop loving her.

Language notes

1 Students may not change the tenses in reported speech and produce statements like: *He said they want to leave at 8 o'clock.* Tell them that this is only correct if the fact is still true or hasn't happened yet. For example in the above sentence the student may be talking about the future, in which case it is correct and the past simple would also be correct. However, if the student is referring to what has already happened he/she will need to use the past simple.

2 Remind students that pronouns may also need changing in reported speech and some time words, e.g. *this – that; here – there,* etc.

Reported questions review

(d) Read through the examples with students. Remind students that when we use reported questions we also use the word order of a statement not a question, e.g. *Could you tell me what the time is?*

OPTIONAL ACTIVITY

You may like to do the following exercise before Exercise 2e to remind students about the word order of reported questions. Write these reported questions on the board:

1 *We asked how old was he.*
2 *She asked where does he live.*
3 *I asked what were her hobbies.*
4 *They asked if I needed help?*
5 *He asked where was I going.*
6 *You asked if would I go.*

Ask students to decide what the mistake is in each sentence. Students correct the sentences. Check answers and encourage students to explain their reasons.

Answers
1 We asked how old he was. (word order)
2 She asked where he lives. (no auxiliary *do*)
3 I asked what her hobbies were. (word order)
4 They asked if I needed help. (no question mark)
5 He asked where I was going. (word order)
6 You asked if I would go. (word order)

(e) Ask students if they remember anything about Neil Armstrong. Tell students to imagine what Neil might have said to the other astronaut in the spacecraft that landed on the moon. Write suggestions on the board. Then write *Neil Armstrong asked ...* and ask students to report the suggested questions. Students complete the other questions that famous people might have asked.

Answers
2 Neil Armstrong asked if he could go first.
3 William Shakespeare asked where his pen was.
4 Walt Disney asked what name he could give to that mouse.
5 Ellen McArthur asked when she would sail around the world again.

┌─ OPTIONAL ACTIVITY ───────────────
In pairs students write down more questions that famous people might have asked. Then they write the reported speech form of the questions. Each pair joins another pair and takes it in turns to read out their reported question without saying who said it. The other pair must try and guess the famous person. For example:
A: *He asked if I enjoyed his film Titanic.*
B: *Leonardo DiCaprio.*
A: *Yes!*

Grammar notebook
Remind students to note down the rules for reported speech and to write a few examples of their own.

3 Vocabulary and speaking
Appearance

(a) Ask students if they remember anything about Della and Jim's appearance from the story in Exercise 1. Write what they remember on the board: e.g. *Della had long hair.* Then tell students to turn to page 90 and underline the descriptions of Della's and Jim's physical appearance in the text. Check answers and make sure students understand the words. Elicit other common words connected with hair, e.g. *curly, highlights,* and also height and build, e.g. *slim, thin, fat.*

Answers
Della: long, straight brown hair; her hair, cropped and spiky

Jim: not broad-shouldered or good looking; kind of short and plump

(b) Tell students that all the words in the box describe aspects of physical appearance connected with the face, hair, height/build and other special features. Ask them to look at the first picture and elicit *wavy hair, centre parting, rosy cheeks* and *wrinkles.* Students decide which column the words should go in. Then students work in pairs to identify the other words and categorise them in the table. Check answers by asking students to talk about each picture using *She's got a double chin, wrinkles,* etc.

Answers
face – a moustache, a double chin, wrinkles, spots, long eyelashes, a beard, rosy cheeks, freckles, bushy eyebrows
hair – straight, cropped, a ponytail, highlights, long, an afro, a centre parting, a fringe, short, spiky
height and build – broad-shouldered, short, medium height, tall, plump, well-built
special features – a tattoo, a mole

(c) Describe a famous person to the class without using his/her name. Invite students to guess who it is. Then ask students to do the same exercise in pairs. Encourage them to use as many of the words in Exercise 3b as possible. Monitor and help as necessary.

Personality

(d) This exercise is listed as a warm up activity in Unit 3. However, it can be repeated in a slightly different form here as now students will have a much wider vocabulary. Show students a picture of your husband/wife/boyfriend/girlfriend and write on the board:
I love my husband/wife/boyfriend/girlfriend because he's/she's ...
a
b
c
etc. (list the alphabet until z)
Ask students to work with a partner and write an adjective for as many letters as possible of the alphabet. For example, *ambitious, bossy, considerate,* etc. Give students a time limit, say 2 minutes. Check answers quickly in class and see which pair has completed adjectives for the most letters.

(e) Students complete the definitions with the adjectives in the box. Encourage students to use dictionaries for difficult words. Check answers by asking a different student to read out each sentence. Point out that you can form the opposite of some words by adding a prefix, e.g. *sensitive/insensitive.*

Answers
2 insensitive   3 sensitive   4 independent
5 imaginative   6 sensible   7 determined
8 bad-tempered   9 bossy   10 considerate

Vocabulary notebook

Encourage students to start a wordmap called *Describing people* with the categories *appearance* and *personality* and to note down the words from this exercise. They may find it useful to note down translations of the words too.

4 Speak

In pairs or small groups students answer the questions. Give examples of your own if necessary and encourage students to use as many words as possible from Exercises 3b and 3e.

5 Listening

If you set the background information as a homework research task, ask students to tell the class what they found out.

BACKGROUND INFORMATION

The English Patient: was originally a book by Michael Ondaatje and published in 1992. It won the Booker Prize in the same year and was made into a film starring Ralph Fiennes and Kristin Scott Thomas in 1996. It is about a Hungarian map maker who is exploring the Sahara Desert in Africa. His plane is shot down during the 2nd World War and he is badly burned. He tells the story of his life to a Canadian nurse.

2nd World War: see background information on page 25.

a 🔊 Ask students if they have seen the film (or read the book) *The English Patient*. Use the pictures to elicit/pre-teach *desert*, *cave*, *army*, *soldier*, *spy*. Students listen to the dialogue and put the pictures in the correct order.

TAPESCRIPT

Woman My favourite romantic film of all time has to be *The English Patient*. It's set at the time of the Second World War. It's the story of a Hungarian count and a British woman called Katharine Clifton, who meet in North Africa and fall in love. Katharine is involved in a plane crash in the middle of the desert and the count finds her. Unfortunately she is badly hurt and she can't walk. He tells her that he has to leave her to get help.

Count I have to leave you and get help.

Woman But he can't leave her where she is, because of the sun. He knows the area well, so he suggests taking her to a cave that he knows.

Count I know a cave near here. Why don't I take you there?

Woman She is able to stay there while he gets some help. He explains that it will be at least three days before he'll be back.

Count I'm afraid it's going to take me three days to get help, but I will be back.

Woman Katharine agrees to stay in the cave.

Katharine Yes, my darling. I'll stay here and wait for your return.

Woman He walks across the desert, and he finds a British Army camp. He begs them to help him.

Count Please, please, please. You have to help me!

Woman But they refuse.

Soldier No, I'm sorry but we can't help you.

Woman Although he speaks excellent English he has a slight accent, so the British soldiers think he is a spy and they arrest him. Eventually he manages to escape. He finally gets back to the cave but it's too late – Katharine is dead.

Answers
1 c   2 a   3 e   4 d   5 b

b 🔊 Tell students that the words in the box are reporting verbs. They are similar to *say* and *tell* but give more idea about the meaning of what someone said or how they said it. Check the meaning of each verb carefully by asking students to match a verb to an imaginary situation, e.g. *You want to go to a party but your parents want to know how you will get home – what do you need to do?* (*explain*). Students complete the sentences with a reporting verb in the correct form. Play the recording for students to check, pausing if necessary.

Answers
1 tells   2 suggests   3 explains   4 agrees
5 begs

6 Grammar
Reporting verbs

a Remind students that reporting verbs are very useful in reported speech as the information they give makes texts sound more interesting. Tell students that reporting verbs have different patterns of grammar, e.g. *tell* is always followed by an object. Students use the sentences in Exercise 5b to help them complete the rules about the verbs in the box. Check answers and the meaning of the other verbs in the rule box.

Answers
1 agree   2 explain   3 suggest   4 beg, persuade

b Students rewrite the sentences using the reporting verbs in the rule box. Point out that students can use any of the reporting verbs in the rule box and that they still need to use the normal rules of reported speech. Check answers and make sure students are changing the tenses and the pronouns of the original sentence appropriately.

Weaker classes: Before students rewrite the sentences, read each one, eliciting the reporting verb in each case.

Answers
2 She apologised for breaking a glass.
3 He begged her to write to him.
4 I offered to help you with your e-mails.
5 The student explained that he/she hadn't got his/her homework because the dog had eaten it.
6 She ordered the boys to go out into the garden.
7 He refused to help him/her.

Grammar notebook
Remind students to note down the rules for reporting verb patterns and to write a few examples of their own.

7 Pronunciation
Intonation in reported questions

a 🔊 Write these two sentences on the board:

Did you park the car?
Where did you park the car?

Point out the difference in intonation between these two questions (*in the first, intonation rises at the end [it can also fall], in the second it commonly falls*). Students turn to page 120 and read the sentences. Play the recording and ask students to identify whether the intonation falls or rises at the end of each question.

TAPESCRIPT/ANSWERS
1 Have you got a girlfriend? (↑)
2 She asked me if I had a girlfriend. (↓)
3 Did you finish the homework? (↓)
4 She asked me if I had finished the homework. (↓)
5 Do you live near here? (↓)
6 She asked me if I lived near here.(↓)
7 Are you enjoying the party? (↑)
8 He asked me if I was enjoying the party. (↓)
9 Do you want a cup of tea? (↓)
10 She asked if I wanted a cup of tea. (↓)

b 🔊 Play the recording again, pausing after each sentence for students to repeat. Encourage students to mimic the recording.

Culture in mind

8 Read

If you set the background information as a homework research task, ask students to tell the class what they found out.

BACKGROUND INFORMATION
Hinduism: is a system of religious beliefs and social customs. There are an estimated 705 million Hindus in the world.
Islam: is the religion of Muslims. It was founded by the Prophet Muhammad in the 7th century AD and is now the religion of nearly 1000 million people worldwide.
The Qur'an: or Koran is the book of the Islamic religion. Muslims believe that the Qur'an is the word of God told to his messenger Muhammad. It is written in classical Arabic.

a Ask students to think of a wedding that they have been to. Ask who the two main participants were and elicit *bride* and *groom*. Students use dictionaries to find the definitions of the words in the box. If you are using monolingual dictionaries point out that these definitions may be for traditional Western weddings.

Answers
The bride is the woman who is getting married.
The bridegroom or groom is the man who is getting married.
The best man is a male friend or relative of the bridegroom. He usually gives the priest the rings at a wedding. He might also make a speech about the bridegroom at the wedding reception (the meal or party after the ceremony).
The priest leads the wedding ceremony.
Witnesses are friends or relatives of the bride and bridegroom. They witness that the wedding has been conducted properly and sign their names in a book as proof.

b Read the questions with students and check difficult vocabulary: *fire, powder*. Ask students to read the text quickly to find the answers and encourage them not to look up every new word. It may help to give students two minutes to find the answers.

Answers
1 Islamic wedding   2 Hindu wedding
3 Hindu wedding

OPTIONAL ACTIVITY
Pre-teach difficult words in the text: *ceremony, mosque, headscarf, cap, grand occasion, canopy, yogurt, token, purity, sweetness, turmeric, sacred, prayer*. Use the photos to elicit as many of the words as possible. Then ask students to find definitions of other words in a dictionary. Emphasise that not all the words are needed to understand the text.

c Students read the text and write six questions to test their partner. Give students an example, e.g. *At a Hindu wedding, what does the bride give the groom?* Ask students to check the questions for grammar before exchanging them with a partner. When students have finished, they should give their answers to their partner for marking. Ask a few pairs about how many they got correct and find out if there were any questions that students could not answer.

9 Vocabulary

Relationships

a Ask students to read the text through once quickly before matching the phrases with the pictures. Check answers and encourage students to write the infinitive form of each verb for future reference.

Answers

a 3 broke up with – break up with
b 1 going out – go out
c 5 got divorced – get divorced
d 6 has fallen in love – fall in love
e 4 got back together and got married – get back together, get married
f 2 broke up with – break up with

You might like to point out picture f. In many Western cultures, it is common for the man to kneel on one knee and put a ring on the finger of the woman when asking her to marry him. In Britain, we wear the engagement and wedding rings on the left hand.

OPTIONAL ACTIVITY

Ask students to put the events in the order they might happen. Discuss differences between their answers.

Possible answer

go out, fall in love, break up, get back together, fall in love (again), get engaged, get married, get divorced

b Students complete the sentences with the phrases in the box.

Answers

1 going out   2 fell in love   3 are getting divorced
4 got engaged, get married   5 broken up, get back together

Vocabulary notebook

Encourage students to start a section called *Relationships* and to note down the words from this exercise. Students could sort the words into positive and negative phrases. They may find it useful to note down translations of the words too.

10 Write

a The planning for this exercise can be done in class and the writing can be set as homework. Ask students read the composition quickly and answer the questions.

Answers

1 third paragraph
2 first paragraph
3 fourth paragraph
4 second paragraph

OPTIONAL ACTIVITY

Weaker classes

Write these sentences on the board and ask students to decide if they are true or false. Students correct the false sentences:

The writer says her grandmother …

1 *did a lot of travelling when she was younger.* (F – The writer's parents did)
2 *died a long time ago.* (F – Her grandmother died a few years ago)
3 *looked younger than she was.* (T)
4 *read her lots of stories from books* (F – Her grandmother told her stories she had made up)
5 *her grandmother taught her to be patient.* (T)
6 *her grandmother was a pessimistic person.* (F – Her grandmother looked for the good in things)

b Students think of someone who has taught them something important in their life. Encourage students to plan their composition using the same structure as the example. Tell students to use the vocabulary of appearance and personality they learned in the unit.

14 Anger

1 Read and listen

If you set the background information as a homework research task, ask students to tell the class what they found out.

BACKGROUND INFORMATION

Barry Cadish: is an American author who discovered that thousands of people, via the Internet, were willing to answer his question: What is your biggest regret in life? He published a book of everyone's regrets called *DAMN! Reflections on Life's Biggest Regrets.*

Warm up

Tell students about a few regrets that you have using the form *I regret + –ing*, e.g. *I regret buying my car. It breaks down all the time.* Check the meaning of *regret* and ask students to write down a few regrets of their own. Students share their regrets in open class and explain them to each other.

(a) Students read the blue text and answer the question.

Answer
He is an author and he also started his own website to publish people's regrets.

(b) Read the titles and check any difficult vocabulary: *missed opportunity, know best, strangers* and *'Beauty is only skin deep'*. Students read the text quickly and match a title to each text. Encourage students not to

look up every new word but just to read and get the general idea of each text. Remind students there is one extra title. Check answers.

Answers
CJ's text 4   Mia's text 1   Ben's text 2
Unused title: 3 Never talk to strangers

(c) 🔊 Check students understand the questions. Play the recording and ask students to check their answers with a partner.

TAPESCRIPT
See the reading text on page 96 of the Student's Book.

Answers
1 CJ   2 Mia   3 Ben   4 Mia   5 Mia

Discussion box
Weaker classes: Students can choose one question to discuss.

Stronger classes: In pairs or small groups, students go through the questions in the box and discuss them.
Monitor and help as necessary, encouraging students to express themselves in English and to use any vocabulary they have learned from the text. Ask pairs or groups to feedback to the class and discuss any interesting points further.

2 Grammar
Third conditional review

BACKGROUND INFORMATION
Norwich City Football Club: was formed by two school teachers in 1902. They are known as The Canaries because they play in bright yellow and green football clothes. Their biggest success was in 2004 when they won the First Division and were promoted to the Premiership (the top league of English football).

Students covered the third conditional in SB2, Unit 16.

(a) Ask students to read the example. Ask them the questions in 1 and confirm the answers (*No, for both*). Ask them to imagine that she <u>did</u> shoot, and elicit *she would have scored*. Ask students about Ben and elicit the answers to the questions. Then tell students to imagine that Ben had listened to his parents. Elicit *If he had listened to his parents, he would have made some better decisions.*

Ask students to find a similar sentence in the text about Ben (*If I had listened to them, I might have made some better decisions in my life*). Point out that *might* is similar to *would* but less certain.

Elicit the construction of the third conditional (*if* + past perfect tense, *would/might* + *have* + past participle). Tell students that the third conditional talks about imagined events in the past and their past result. Point out the comma between the clauses and remind students that the main clause of the past participle has the same construction as modals of deduction in the past. Students complete the rules.

Answers

1   She didn't shoot and she didn't score.
2   He didn't listen and he doesn't think he made the best decisions.

Rule: past perfect, *have* + past participle; *might*

Language notes

1   Student may produce statements like **If I looked at my watch I'd have been on time*. Remind them of the form of the third conditional if necessary.
2   Remind them (as in all conditional sentences) that the *if* clause can go at the beginning or the end.

(b) Explain that Norwich City is a football club. Ask students to look at the pictures and make predictions about how they met. Write their suggestions on the board. Read through the sentences with students and check difficult vocabulary: *final* (the last game in a competition), *roof, aerial*. Students read the first two sentences and the third conditional sentence. Point out that all these events happened in the past so we are imagining that they didn't happen.

Students read the second and third sentences again and try to complete the conditional (Tom wouldn't have turned on the TV). Then, ask students to construct more third conditional sentences linking each sentence in the story. Check answers.

Answers

3   If he hadn't wanted to watch the game on TV, he wouldn't have found out it wasn't working.
4   If he hadn't found out the TV wasn't working, he wouldn't have climbed on the roof to check the aerial.
5   If he hadn't climbed on the roof to check the aerial, he wouldn't have fallen off.
6   If he hadn't fallen off the roof, his friends wouldn't have taken him to hospital.
7   If his friends hadn't taken him to hospital, he wouldn't have met a doctor called Josie.
8   If he hadn't met a doctor called Josie, he wouldn't have fallen in love with her and got married.

(c) Students think of five things in the past that they did or didn't do which had a past result. Give students an example of your own, e.g. *If I hadn't started teaching at this school, ...* and ask them to guess the result, e.g.

I wouldn't have met this wonderful class. Point out that students should think of things that had a past result and not a present one. Students write the *if* clause for each sentence and then swap with a partner, who tries to guess how they finish. Make sure students are using tenses correctly and encourage students to contract the past perfect and *would* + *have* /wʊdəv/ appropriately.

Grammar notebook

Remind students to note down the rules for the third conditional and to write a few examples of their own.

3 # Grammar

I wish / If only for past situations

Students covered *I wish / If only* for present situations in Unit 10.

(a) Books closed. Tell students that another way of expressing regrets about the past is using *I wish / If only*. Remind students about *I wish / If only* about present situations by giving them a simple example to complete, e.g. *I am poor. I wish I ...* (*was rich*). Ask students to guess which tense is used after *I wish / If only* when talking about past events (*past perfect*). Students open their books at page 97, read the examples, answer the questions and complete the rules.

Answers

1   The answer to all questions is *no*.
2   sad; the sentences are expressing regrets they had
Rule: past perfect

(b) Students write regrets that have resulted in the situations. Point out that students have to imagine what happened in the past that led to this present situation. Go through the example and establish that the speaker probably went to bed late last night so is tired today. Elicit ideas for the second sentence, e.g. *I missed lunch, I left my lunch at home*, etc. Then elicit the sentence with *I wish*, e.g. *I wish I hadn't missed lunch* or *If only I hadn't left my lunch at home*.

Possible answers

2   I wish I hadn't missed lunch
3   I wish I hadn't broken up with her
4   I wish the music had been quieter
5   If only I hadn't failed the exam
6   If only I hadn't lost the ticket

Language note

See page 74 for an explanation of the difference between *I wish* and *If only*.

Grammar notebook

Remind students to note down the rules for this structure and to write a few examples of their own.

4 Listen

(a) Students look at the illustrations. Elicit *frozen turkey, argue, repair man, to point, unconscious, soft drink.* Tell students that the pictures are connected with two stories. In pairs students predict the stories. Students tell their stories to another pair.

(b) 🔊 Tell students that one picture will be used twice. Play the recording while the students check their ideas and put the pictures in the correct order. Check answers and play the recording again, pausing if necessary. Compare the stories briefly with the students' predictions.

TAPESCRIPT

Woman This crazy thing happened at my supermarket just before Christmas. I was getting a bit of last minute shopping when I heard two women having an argument. They were arguing about a turkey. It was the last one in the freezer, and they'd both grabbed it at the same time, and they were arguing about who should have it. Well, then they really started to get angry. They were pushing each other around and eventually, one woman got hold of the turkey and walked to the checkout with it. Of course, this didn't stop the other one, and she ran behind her shouting all sorts of things.

Anyway, the woman with the turkey paid for it, and walked out of the shop towards her car – the other woman was still following, still shouting, and everyone inside the shop was watching. I know I shouldn't have, but I was laughing, like everyone else. If I'd thought, I would've tried to stop her.

Suddenly the woman with the turkey turned round and shouted, 'Do you want it? Do you want it? Well, come and get it.' So, the other woman looked a bit surprised, but she reached for the turkey. Then, just as she was putting her hands on it, the first woman lifted the bird into the air and hit her in the face. I couldn't believe it! She then got into her car and drove off, leaving the other woman unconscious on the ground. Someone should have stopped her, but it was just so unbelievable. Talk about Happy Christmas, eh?

Man I've got an embarrassing story, something that happened to me in the Natural History Museum in London. It was a really hot day and I wanted a drink, so, I went to the machine, put in my money, pressed the button and … nothing. I pressed again and again, but it was clear that nothing was coming out.

Now, if I'd had another coin then I'm sure I'd have tried again, but I didn't, so I resorted to more violent methods. First, I tried hitting the machine, gently at first, but still nothing, so I started hitting it harder and harder. Still no can. By now, I was getting really angry, so I kicked the side of the machine as hard as I could. Yes, I know what you're thinking – I shouldn't have done that. But it worked, would you believe! Something dropped. I bent down to get the drink, but there was nothing there! So I put my hand up the hole to see if the can had got stuck somewhere. Well, I don't know why I did that, I should've just walked away, but no – I pushed my arm all the way up inside the machine. But I still couldn't feel anything, so I tried to pull my arm out and – you've guessed it – it was stuck. I don't know how, but it just wouldn't come out.

So there I was, knees on the ground with my arm stuck in a machine. Of course, by this time there was quite a crowd of people there, most of them laughing. Eventually, after about half an hour, a repair man arrived with his tool box and took the front of the machine off. What an idiot I felt. And he didn't even give me my can!

Answers
a 2   b 1   c 7   d 3,6   e 4   f 5

(c) 🔊 Read the questions with students and check difficult vocabulary: *horrified, amused, pay attention.* Play the first story again. Students choose the correct answers. Check answers and play the recording again, pausing if necessary.

Answers
1 a   2 c   3 a   4 b   5 c   6 a

┌─ OPTIONAL ACTIVITY ──────────────
Weaker classes

🔊 Write the sentences about the second story on the board. Play the recording and ask students to decide if they are true/false:
The speaker …
1 *was in a museum in Liverpool.* (F – It was a museum in London)
2 *put his money in the drinks machine.* (T)
3 *started hitting the machine hard.* (T)
4 *was laughing at the time.* (F – The speaker was embarrassed)

5 Speak

Students read the items in the box. Check difficult vocabulary: *to queue.* In pairs, students answer the questions. Monitor and help with vocabulary if necessary.

6 Grammar

should have / shouldn't have (done)

(a) Books closed. Ask students if they can remember what Mia and Ben, from the texts on page 96, regretted (*Mia didn't shoot in a football game and Ben didn't listen to his parents*). Ask students if they can give any advice to Mia or Ben using *should.* Elicit *Mia should*

have shot and Ben *should have listened to his parents*.
Point out that *should have* can be contracted to
should've /ʃʊdəv/.
Students open their books at page 99 and read the
first sentence. Ask students what the speaker is
referring to (*laughing at the women arguing*). Then
students decide if he <u>did</u> laugh or he <u>didn't</u> laugh.
Ask students to read the second sentence and decide
if he did or didn't buy another drink. Students
complete the rule. Point out the pronunciation of
shouldn't have /ʃʊdntəv/

Answers
1 She did it (she laughed)   2 He didn't go
Rule: past participle

(b) Students match the parts of the sentences. Check
answers and elicit the difference between *should go*
and *should have gone* (*the first has a present meaning
– the speaker thinks that it's a good idea for him/her
to go to the shop; the second has a past meaning –
the speaker didn't go to the shop but now thinks it
would have been a good idea to do so*).

Answers
1 d   2 b   3 a   4 c

(c) Students work with a partner and write responses to
the sentences using *should've* or *shouldn't have*. Go
through the example and point out the use of *Well*
to introduce the phrase with *should've/shouldn't have*.
Encourage students to practise reading their dialogues.
In feedback, ask different pairs to give examples of
their suggestions or criticisms.

Possible answers
1 Well, you should've saved some money.
   Well, you shouldn't have spent all your money.
2 Well, you should've spent more time on it.
   Well, you shouldn't have copied.
3 Well, you should've have set a timer.
   Well, you shouldn't have gone out.
4 Well, you should've remember his/her birthday.
   Well, you shouldn't have told everyone his/her
   secrets.
5 She should've lent him only €50.
   She shouldn't have been so kind.
6 Well, you should've looked after your teeth more.
   Well, you shouldn't have eaten so many sweets.

Grammar notebook
Remind students to note down the rules for this
structure and to write a few examples of their own.

7 Pronunciation
should have / shouldn't have

(a) 🔊 Students turn to page 120 and read the
sentences. Play the recording and ask students to
listen to the underlined words. Ask students how the
underlined parts are pronounced. Point out that *have*
is pronounced in its weak form /əv/ in each sentence.

Ask students how the two words *should have /
shouldn't have* are pronounced (*there is linking
between them so that the /d/ or /t/ sound is linked
with /əv/*).

TAPESCRIPT
1 I'm sorry – I shouldn'<u>t have</u> done that.
2 He shoul<u>d have</u> left earlier.
3 You shouldn'<u>t have</u> forgotten her birthday.
4 They shouldn'<u>t have</u> driven so fast.
5 Your brother shouldn'<u>t have</u> hit me.
6 I shoul<u>d have</u> asked more questions.

(b) 🔊 Play the recording again, pausing for students
to repeat each sentence. Encourage students to link
the sounds between *should have* and *shouldn't have*
in the same way as the recording.

8 Vocabulary
Anger

(a) Ask students to remember what kind of things they
discussed in Exercise 5 that make them angry. Elicit
any synonyms for *angry* that students know, e.g.
furious, *cross*, etc. Students read the text and
complete the definitions. Point out that students
should use the infinitive form of verbs where
necessary.

Answers
2 hot-headed   3 temper   4 tantrum   5 head off
6 cool   7 furious   8 calm

(b) Students work in pairs and discuss the questions. In
feedback ask a few pairs for the answers to their
questions and see what the most common reasons
are for students' parents being cross with them.

Vocabulary notebook
Encourage students to start a section called *Anger*
and to note down the words from this exercise. They
may find it useful to note down translations of the
words too.

Working things out
9 Read and listen
Warm up

Ask students what they can remember about the last
episode of the story. (*Matt had a party. He told the
others that he had bought a motorbike from someone
in his street and he doesn't have enough to pay him
the rest of the money.*)

(a) 🔊 Ask students to read the questions and predict
the answers but do not comment at this stage. Play
the recording while students read and listen to check
their predictions. Check answers in open class.

See the story on page 100 of the Student's Book.

TAPESCRIPT

Answers

Yes, he still owes Tony the money and he hasn't got it. Ben offers to pay Tony the money if Matt can't get it by next month.

(b) Read through the questions. Students read the text again and answer the questions.

Answers

1 He hopes Matt is going to pay him the rest of the money he owes him.
2 He wants to pay him next month.
3 She knows that Matt is really honest.
4 They agree that Matt will pay him the money next month and, if he doesn't, Ben will pay him.
5 Because she missed him when he was in Hong Kong. It's good to have friends like him.

10 Everyday English

(a) Ask students to locate expressions 1 to 4 in the story on page 100 and decide who says them.

Weaker classes: Check answers at this stage.

Answers

1 Matt   2 Matt   3 Ben   4 Tony

Students then match the expressions with the situations. Go through the first item with them as an example if necessary. Check answers.

Answers

a 2   b 1   c 4   d 3

(b) Ask students to read through the sentences and complete the answers. Go through the first sentence with them as an example if necessary.

Answers

1 In that case   2 The thing is   3 what I mean is
4 There's something I want to say

┌ OPTIONAL ACTIVITIES ══════════════
See Unit 2, Exercise 11: Everyday English, Optional Activities.

11 Write

Students covered story-writing and setting a scene in Unit 12.

BACKGROUND INFORMATION

New York City: is a city in the US state of New York on the Atlantic Ocean. Its population is approximately 7.5 million. It is the richest city in the USA and contains the financial centre Wall Street, several universities, and the headquarters of the United Nations.

Central Park: was the first urban landscaped park in the USA. It was started in 1857, took almost ten years to complete and cost about $10 million. In the winter of 1858, the park's first area was opened to the public. At first, because of its location, the park was generally only visited by rich people. However, these days, there are many events in the park including free performances of Shakespeare and many pop concerts.

(a) Students can do the preparation in class and the writing for homework. Elicit/pre-teach *jogger/jog, muggers, bump into* and *grab*. Ask students to read the story quickly and answer the question.

Answer

His wife told him that he had left the money on the table.

┌ OPTIONAL ACTIVITY ══════════════

Weaker classes

Write these sentences on the board. Students decide if they're true or false and correct false sentences:

1 *The writer lives in New York.* (F – He and his wife were living in New York a few years ago)
2 *The writer took his wallet with him.* (F – He took just $10 with him)
3 *The other jogger said sorry for bumping into the man.* (T)
4 *The writer gets angry easily.* (F – He says he isn't usually a hot-headed person)
5 *The other jogger gave the writer $10.* (T)
6 *The writer forgot to buy the bread.* (F – He bought the bread)

(b) Tell students they are going to write a story about a time when they got angry. Ask students to plan their writing and practise setting the scene (see Unit 12). Encourage students to use:
- the vocabulary they learned in Exercise 8
- *should have / shouldn't have* if appropriate

In a subsequent lesson, encourage students to read each other's stories and vote on the funniest or most interesting.

15 Fear

TOPIC: Fear and frightening stories

TEXTS:

Reading and listening: an article about *The Lord of the Rings* and its author
Listening: a dialogue about *The Blair Witch Project*
Reading: an extract from a ghost story
Writing: a film review

SPEAKING AND FUNCTIONS

Discussing scary films
Discussing a ghost story
Talking about things that make you angry

LANGUAGE

Grammar: Non-defining relative clauses; Defining vs. non-defining relative clauses; Definite, indefinite and zero article
Vocabulary: Adjectives with prefixes; Phrasal verbs with *sit*
Pronunciation: Pausing in non-defining relative clauses

1 Read and listen

If you set the background information as a homework research task, ask students to tell the class what they found out.

BACKGROUND INFORMATION

Charlie's Angels: was one of the most successful TV series of the 1970s. It was about three female detectives who worked for the Charles Townsend Detective Agency. Charlie, who was their boss, gave them assignments via a telephone. It started in 1976 and finished in 1981. In 2000, there was a film of the series, starring Drew Barrymore, Lucy Liu and Cameron Diaz as the new Angels and in 2003 there was a second film called *Charlie's Angels: Full Throttle.*

James Bond: was created by the author Ian Fleming and is one of the most famous secret agents in modern fiction. The popular Bond movie series began in 1962 with *Dr. No* and a new Bond film, the twenty-first, will be released in 2005. Bond has been played by a series of actors including Sean Connery, Roger Moore and Pierce Brosnan.

Indiana Jones: is the fictional archaeologist played by Harrison Ford in the action films

The Raiders of the Lost Ark (1981), *Indiana Jones and the Temple of Doom* (1984) and *Indiana Jones and the Last Crusade* (1989).

J.R.R. Tolkien (1892–1973): was a British writer and academic. He was a professor of English language and literature at Oxford University and is most famous for his fantasy adventure books *The Hobbit* (1937) and *The Lord of the Rings* (1954–55).

The Lord of the Rings: was a series of three books written by J.R.R. Tolkien, *The Fellowship of the Ring, The Two Towers* and *The Return of the King,* published from 1954 to 1955. Tolkien actually wanted the story to be published as a single book but there was a shortage of paper after the second world war. The film version was made by Peter Jackson, a New Zealand film director. In total the films won 17 Oscars.

Hobbits: are a fictional race of people, related to humans. Their most distinguishing feature is that they are rarely taller than 120 centimetres. *The Hobbit* was Tolkien's first novel and was about a hobbit called Bilbo Baggins.

Frodo Baggins: is a hobbit and the hero of *The Lord of the Rings* story. In the films by Peter Jackson, Frodo was played by Elijah Wood.

Middle Earth: is the imaginary land in *The Lord of the Rings.*

Sauron: is the evil ruler of a place called Mordor, in Middle Earth.

Elves: are mythical creatures and are often shown as beautiful, young and small men and women who live in forests.

Dwarves: are mythical people and are generally shorter than humans but live at least four times as long.

New Zealand: is a country approximately 2,000 kilometres south-east of Australia. Its population is approximately 3.8 million (1995) and the capital is Wellington.

Elijah Wood: is an actor who played the hobbit Frodo Baggins in Peter Jackson's film versions of *The Lord of the Rings.* He was born in America on 28 January 1981.

Warm up

Write the title of the unit on the board: *Fear.* Check students understand its meaning and ask them what kind of thing they are afraid of. Discuss interesting answers further, helping students with vocabulary as necessary.

(a) Ask students if they recognise any of the people in the photos (*Harrison Ford as Indiana Jones, Elijah Wood as Frodo Baggins, Pierce Brosnan as James Bond, and Lucy Liu, Cameron Diaz and Drew Barrymore as Charlie's Angels*). Check if students have seen any of the films shown and ask them who their favourite character is and why. Encourage students to use relevant adjectives of personality from Unit 14 as appropriate. Make sure students know who the characters are before reading the text.

(b) Read through the titles with the students and check difficult vocabulary: *endless*. Students read the article and match the titles with the paragraphs. Remind students there is one extra title. At this stage, encourage students to ignore unknown vocabulary.

Answers
1 B   2 E   3 C   4 A   Unused title: D

(c) 🔊 Read the questions with students and check any difficult vocabulary: *real*. Then pre-teach/elicit important vocabulary in the text: *survive, unrealistic, invent, audition*. Students read, listen and answer the questions. Play the recording and ask students to check answers in pairs before feedback. In class, encourage students to justify their answers.

TAPESCRIPT
See the reading text on page 102 of the Student's Book.

Answers
1 b (Tolkien invented the land)   2 c   3 c

2 Grammar
Non-defining relative clauses (giving extra information)

(a) Weaker classes: Write two sentences on the board:

Tolkien wrote 'The Lord of the Rings'.
Tolkien died in 1973.

Tell students that you can combine the two sentences into one using a relative pronoun, *who*. Elicit *Tolkien, who died in 1973, wrote 'The Lord of the Rings'*. Ask students in pairs to do the same thing for two more sentences:

Indiana Jones is an archaeologist.
Indiana Jones is the hero of 'The Raiders of the Lost Ark'.

Help students to produce *Indiana Jones, who is the hero of 'The Raiders of the Lost Ark', is an archaeologist*. Point out that the relative clause in each case adds extra information to the sentence. Tell students that the relative pronoun we use depends on whether we are adding information about a person, thing or place. Now follow the procedure for stronger classes.

Stronger classes: Students complete the sentences by looking at the text. Check answers and make sure students understand that the relative clause adds extra information to the sentence but it isn't necessary in order to understand the rest of the sentence. Point out the commas around the clause and tell students that these are an important part of non-defining relative clauses. Make sure students understand the meaning of *whose* (see Language note).

Answers
1 who   2 which   3 where   4 whose

> **Language note**
> You use *whose* at the beginning of a relative clause to show who or what something belongs to or is connected with. In modern English it is acceptable to use *whose* to refer to people or things, e.g. *The writer, whose first book was published in 1937, died in 1973. The book, whose story was about a small man called Bilbo Baggins, became a huge success. Whose* is used in questions when we are asking who something belongs to, e.g. *Whose pen is this?*

(b) Students complete the rule.

Answers
who; which; where; whose

> **Language note**
> Students may produce statements like: **She is the woman which works in the library*. Remind them we can only use *who/that* for people.

(c) Students join the two sentences using the word at the end of the sentence. Remind students to use commas around the non-defining relative clause. Go through the first sentence as an example. Check answers and make sure students are using commas where appropriate.

Answers
2 Elijah Wood, whose career began when he was a child, became a big star after *The Lord of the Rings*.
3 He had to stay away from home for 18 months, which was difficult for him.
4 Tolkien, who wrote the books in the 1950s, couldn't find anyone to publish his books at first.
5 Frodo has to go to Sauron's kingdom, where the final battle takes place.

3 Pronunciation
Pausing in non-defining relative clauses

(a) 🔊 Students turn to page 120 and read the explanation about pausing in non-defining relative clauses. Play the recording and ask students to put a comma at the points in the sentence where there is a pause.

TAPESCRIPT/ANSWERS

1   Peter Jackson, who was born in New Zealand, directed *The Lord of the Rings*.
2   J.R.R. Tolkien, who was a very shy man, wrote many books.
3   My sister, who lives in Hong Kong, writes stories for children.
4   Manchester, which is in the north of England, gets a lot of rain every year.
5   My best friend, whose father is a doctor, wants to study medicine at university.
6   Elijah Wood, whose career began when he was a child, became a big star after *The Lord of the Rings*.

b 🔊 Play the recording again, pausing for students to repeat each sentence. Encourage students to pause at the beginning and end of the relative clause and to lower the tone of their voice for the relative clause.

4 Grammar
Defining vs. non-defining relative clauses

Students covered defining relative clauses in SB2, Unit 13.

a Books closed. Write these sentences on the board:
Jenny, who lives opposite me, is having a baby.
The woman who lives opposite me is having a baby.
Ask students who is having a baby in each sentence (*in 1 Jenny and in 2 the woman who lives opposite me*). Then erase the relative clause (*who lives opposite me*) in each sentence. Ask students if they know who is having a baby now (*in 1 Jenny and in 2 the woman*). Tell students that the relative clause in sentence 2 defines the woman and without it we don't know which woman is having a baby. Point out that in this case we do not use commas around the relative clause as it is not adding extra information. Tell students that with defining relative clauses we can use *that* instead of *who/which* and there is no difference in meaning.

Students open their books at page 103 and complete the sentences with a relative pronoun. Ask students to check their answers in the text. Point out that you can also use *which* in sentence 2 and *that* in sentence 4.

Answers
1 whose   2 that/which   3 where   4 who

Look
Read through the Look box with students. Ask students which sentence could use *that* instead of *who* (*the second, defining relative clause*).

Language note
You may want to summarise which relative pronouns you can use in non-defining and defining relative clauses with the following table:

relative causes	Example	people	things
non-defining	My brother, who is a doctor, lives in London.	who	which
defining	My brother who is a doctor lives in London.	who/ that	which/ that

b Students decide if the sentences contain defining or non-defining relative clauses and insert commas where appropriate. Check answers and encourage students to give reasons.

Answers
1   New Zealand, where the films were made, is a popular tourist destination. (there is only one New Zealand and so it is not defined by the relative clause)
2   No comma (the film is defined by being the best I've ever seen)
3   Sally Campion, whose brother wrote the story, spent three years making the film. (There is only one Sally Campion and so the rest is extra information.)
4   No comma (the hotel is defined by being the one we always stay in)

Grammar notebook
Remind students to note down the rules for relative clauses and to write a few examples of their own.

5 Speak

BACKGROUND INFORMATION

The Shining: is a film made in 1980 by Stanley Kubrick and based on a story by Stephen King about a writer and his family who are looking after a hotel in the mountains in Colorado, USA. However, the hotel has ghosts and they start talking to the writer and his son.

Jaws: is a film made in 1975 by Steven Spielberg and is about a huge shark that is killing people at a beach in New England, USA.

Alien: is a film made in 1979 by Ridley Scott and is about a spaceship that investigates a call for help on a nearby planet.

The Blair Witch Project: is a film made in 1999 and is about a group of students who go into the forest to make a documentary about a local legend: the Blair Witch. The film was made in a documentary style and when it was released it was advertised to sound like a true story. The film makers, created a website, on which there was a long story about the Blair Witch and lots of photos and drawings. Many people thought the story was true at first and this made it more frightening.

(a) Ask students to look at the photos and film titles and match them with the descriptions. Check answers and ask if students have seen any of the films. If they have, briefly discuss what they thought about them.

Answers
1 D   2 A   3 B   4 C

(b) Students work with a partner and discuss the questions. Check difficult vocabulary: *creepy*, *gore* (thick blood), *sudden shocks*. In feedback discuss the questions further and find out the scariest film that the class have seen.

6 Listen

(a) 🔊 Ask students if anyone has seen *The Blair Witch Project*. Briefly discuss the story and what the students thought of the film. Students listen to the person talking about the film and tick the items in Exercise 5b which the film uses to frighten its audience. Point out that some of the items might be mentioned but they are not necessarily used in the film. Play the recording.

TAPESCRIPT
The Blair Witch Project was one of the biggest films surprises of 1999. The film cost less than $100,000 to make and earned more than a $100,000,000 at the box office. A lot of the film's success was because of the way it was publicised. Before it was released, rumours appeared on the Internet which talked about a film which had been discovered in woods in Maryland in the USA. The rumours suggested the film was true. The film had been shot by three young film makers, who were making a documentary about a mythical witch who lived in the woods. After a while, there are a few screams, the camera falls to the ground and the filming stops. The film makers were never seen again. When *The Blair Witch Project* arrived at the cinema many people didn't know if they were seeing something real or not. Even now that everyone knows the film is fiction, it continues to frighten new audiences. Perhaps the cleverest thing about the film is that it doesn't use the traditional techniques usually used in horror films. There is no music to create a creepy atmosphere. There are no special effects or blood and gore. There are no sudden shocks to make the audience jump. There isn't even a monster because

we never meet the witch. *The Blair Witch Project* is frightening because it plays on our own fears, the kind of fears we might meet in our worst dreams, getting lost in a wood, getting hungry and tired, being followed by something strange and slowly losing control of our own destiny.

Answer
The film doesn't use any of the items mentioned in Exercise 5b.

(b) 🔊 Students read through the summary of *The Blair Witch Project*. Tell students to listen and try to complete the text. Play the recording and then give students time to check their answers and complete more of the text. If necessary, play the recording again, pausing to check answers.

Answers
1 1999   2 £1,000,000   3 Internet   4 true
5 three   6 documentary   7 woods   8 fears

7 Vocabulary
Adjectives with prefixes

(a) Books closed. Tell students that one of the reasons for the success of *The Blair Witch Project* was that it was realistic. Check the meaning of the word and ask students for the opposite (*unrealistic*). Elicit some films that are unrealistic.

Point out that the opposite of many adjectives can be formed by adding a prefix. Ask students, in pairs, to write down other examples they know. After about two minutes, write students' examples on the board. Point out the different prefixes they use.

Students open their books at page 104 and read the adjectives in the box. Check their meaning by asking, e.g. *If someone is able to wait a long time for things, they are ... (patient)*. Then ask students to put the adjective in the correct column. Encourage students to say the opposites aloud to see if they sound correct. Check answers in class or ask students to use a dictionary.

Answers
un – uncomfortable, unhelpful
im – impatient, impossible, impolite
in – informal, inexpensive
ir – irresponsible, irregular
il – illogical, illegal

> **Language notes**
> You may want to point out some of the following about noun prefixes:
> *un–* is the most common prefix, e.g. *unusual*
> *im–* is used before some words beginning with 'p' or 'm', e.g. *impatient*, *immoral*
> *in–* is often used before words with a Latin origin, e.g. *invisible*
> *ir–* is only used before a few words beginning with 'r', e.g. *irrational*
> *il–* is used before 'l', e.g. *illegible*

(b) Students complete the sentences with adjectives from the table in Exercise 7a. Check answers by asking student to read the sentences aloud and make sure students are putting the correct stress on the adjectives. Point out that prefixes of one syllable are never the main stressed syllable in adjectives.

Answers
2 uncomfortable   3 unhelpful   4 impatient
5 irresponsible   6 irregular

(c) Students work in pairs and answer the questions. Ask a few pairs to give you their answers. Discuss interesting points further.

Vocabulary notebook
Encourage students to start a section called *Prefixes* and to note down the words from this exercise under the different prefix headings. They may find it useful to note down translations of the words too.

8 Grammar
Definite, indefinite and zero article

(a) Students read the examples and match them with the rules. Point out that there are many rules in English about articles and that students will need a lot of practice before the can use them perfectly.

Answers
2 b   3 a   4 g   5 d   6 f   7 c   8 h

(b) Students complete the sentences with the correct article or no article. Check answers and encourage students to give reasons from the rule box.

Answers
1   an
2   the
3   nothing
4   the
5   a
6   the
7   nothing
8   the

(c) Ask students to look at the text and tell them that some lines are correct and some have an extra word. Students identify the correct sentences and cross out the extra words in the incorrect sentences. Tell students that all the mistakes are an inappropriate use of articles. Check answers and encourage students to give reasons.

Answers
3   the   8   ✓
4   ✓   9   ✓
5   the (home)   10 ✓
6   the (tickets)   11 the
7   ✓

Grammar notebook
Remind students to note down the rules for articles and to write a few examples of their own.

Fiction in mind

9 Read and listen

If you set the background information as a homework research task, ask students to tell the class what they found out.

BACKGROUND INFORMATION

Inishbofin: is an island off the west coast of Ireland. The name means 'The Island of the White Cow'. The island now has a population of about 200 people.

Ireland: is an island which is west of Great Britain. It is split into the Republic of Ireland and Northern Ireland, which is part of the United Kingdom. The population of the Republic of Ireland is about 4 million (2004) and of Northern Ireland about 1.5 million (2004).

The Lady in White: is a book published as part of the Cambridge English Readers series.

(a) Tell students they are going to read part of a horror story set in Inishbofin, Ireland. Students look at the photo of the island and imagine what life is like there. Discuss students' ideas and help with vocabulary as necessary.

Possible answers
With only 200 people, the island is very peaceful. The landscape is hilly with sandy beaches. The climate can be very windy in western Ireland. It is ideal for tourists who like outdoor activities such as hill-walking, rock-climbing, cycling or fishing.

(b) Ask students to read through the extract. Tell them not to worry about difficult vocabulary. You may like to read it aloud with them or alternatively, the extract is recorded on track 35 of the Workbook CD/ROM.

Students read through the questions. Check difficult vocabulary: missing. Ask students to read the extract again and answer the questions. They can compare with a partner before feedback. In feedback, ask students if they found the story frightening and, if so, what frightened them.

Answers
1   It was probably the middle of the night because he had been asleep and it was dark.
2   Two men on the beach pushing their boat into the Atlantic.
3   The room was too quiet.
4   He tried to call her name.
5   He screamed her name.
6   The wardrobe door opened and someone stepped out.

10 Vocabulary
Phrasal verbs with *sit*

a Students read the sentence and decide on the meaning of *sit up*. Students match the phrasal verbs and their definitions. Encourage students to use dictionaries if necessary. Check answers and encourage students to write the verbs in their vocabulary notebooks with an example sentence.

Answers
1 d   2 a   3 b   4 c

b Students complete the sentences with phrasal verbs from Exercise 10a. Remind students that they will need to put the verbs in the correct form.

Answers
1 sit for   2 sat out   3 sit back   4 sit through

Vocabulary notebook
Encourage students to add these to the section *Phrasal verbs* from Unit 2 and to note down the words from this exercise under the heading *sit*. They may find it useful to note down translations of the words too.

11 Write

BACKGROUND INFORMATION
Psycho: is a film made in 1960 by Alfred Hitchcock and is about a lonely motel owner and the people who stay in his house. The film was remade in 1998.

Alfred Hitchcock (1899–1980): was a British film director who made many films and was particularly famous for thrillers.

Anthony Perkins (1932–1992): was an American actor whose most famous role was in *Psycho*.

a Students can do the preparation in class and the writing for homework. Ask if they have seen the film *Psycho*. Students read the film review and answer the question (*yes, the writer thinks the film is an all-time classic*).

b Students read the text and answer the questions. In feedback, deal with difficult vocabulary in the text: *deposit, tempted, put off* (discourage).

Answers
1 a third paragraph
  b second paragraph
  c first paragraph
2 The writer doesn't tell the whole story because it's a film review. He/she doesn't want to spoil the film for people who haven't seen it.
3 The writer likes the story and that it keeps you guessing until the end. He/she also thinks the film is one of the scariest he/she has ever seen and that Anthony Perkins' performance is very good.

OPTIONAL ACTIVITY
Write these definitions on the board. Ask students to match them with words or phrases in the film review on page 107:
1 *an unusual piece of action in a film often made by computer* (special effects)
2 *the people who watch a film* (audience)
3 *acting* (performance)
4 *not in colour* (black and white)
5 *a piece of writing or a film that is famous and very good quality* (a classic)

b Tell students they are going to write a review of a film they really like or dislike. Encourage students to:
• plan their writing in the same way as the example review
• use new vocabulary, e.g. if the film is a horror film use the vocabulary in Exercise 5b on page 104
• use relevant vocabulary about films
• use defining and non-defining relative clauses where relevant
• tell some of the story but not to spoil it!

In a subsequent lesson, encourage students to read each other's film reviews and vote on which review makes them most want to see the film.

16 Happiness

Unit overview

TOPIC: Happiness and good days

TEXTS
Reading and listening: an article about happiness
Listening: dialogues about being happy
Reading and listening: Song: *Thank You*
Writing: a poem

SPEAKING AND FUNCTIONS
Talking about the flow of happiness
Talking about your idea of happiness

LANGUAGE
Grammar: *be used to (doing)*; *be used to doing* vs. *used to do*; Phrasal verbs
Vocabulary: Expressions with *feel*; Expressions with prepositions
Pronunciation: Stress in phrasal verbs

1 Read and listen

If you set the background information as a homework research task, ask students to tell the class what they found out.

BACKGROUND INFORMATION

Professor Mihaly Csikszentmihalyi: was born in Hungary but during the 2nd World War he moved to Italy, where he went to school. In the 1950s he moved to America and became a student at the University of Chicago in Illinois. He was a professor at the same university from 1971 to 1999. He then moved to Claremont Graduate University, where he is now a professor in the School of Management.

Warm up

Write the sentence *What makes me happy is ...* on the board. Give students an example of your own, e.g. *a sunny day and no work* or *having a meal with my family*. Ask students to write down three things that make them happy and discuss them with a partner.

a Ask students to look at the pictures and elicit why people are happy or unhappy in each photo (*the laughing teenagers are with their friends, the man has a lot of money, it is raining, the teenager is bored*

watching TV). Read the captions under each photograph and ask students which things affect how happy they are.

b 🔊 Students read the article and answer the questions. Encourage them to ignore unknown vocabulary at this stage.

Answers
1 He started thinking about happiness when he was a child. He saw many people who were very upset by the war but others who were always helpful and happy.
2 Flow is when people get involved in a challenging task and they don't notice time passing.

c 🔊 Read through the statements with the students. Pre-teach *well-defined* and *challenging* from the text. Play the recording and ask students to read and listen to the text, and decide if the statements are true or false. Students correct the false statements. Play the recording again pausing if necessary.

TAPESCRIPT
See the reading text on page 108 of the Student's Book.

Answers
1 T 2 F – The professor thinks that many people waste their free time 3 T 4 F – We experience flow when we do tasks that are challenging, not impossible 5 T 6 F – Pleasure is an experience that we enjoy, e.g. eating ice cream. Enjoyment is about doing something, achieving something and feeling positive about it.

Discussion box
Weaker classes: Students can choose one question to discuss.

Stronger classes: In pairs or small groups, students go through the questions in the box and discuss them.
Monitor and help as necessary, encouraging students to express themselves in English and to use any vocabulary they have learned from the text. Ask pairs or groups to feedback to the class and discuss any interesting points further.

2 Grammar

be used to (doing) something

BACKGROUND INFORMATION

Spain: is a country in south-west Europe that borders Portugal, France, the Mediterranean Sea and the North Atlantic Ocean. Its capital is Madrid and its population is approximately 40 million (July 2004).

A siesta: is a short sleep after lunch that is common in some hot countries.

a Books closed. Ask students if they like speaking to large groups of people. Elicit a few answers and then tell them that, because you are a teacher, you've spoken in front of an audience lots of times. Tell them *I'm a teacher. I'm used to speaking to large groups of people.* Write the sentence on the board. Then write on the board: *I'm a student. I'm used to …* Ask students if they can complete the sentence with examples of their own. Point out that students can put a noun after *(be) used* to, e.g. *I'm used to homework every night,* but if they want to put a verb after the structure they must use the *–ing* form: *I'm used to doing homework every night.*

Students open their books at page 109 and complete the sentences with a word. Encourage students to guess the answers before reading the text to check their answers. Finally, make sure that students understand that when you are used to doing something you have done it lots of times. Point out that this is different from the structure *used to* that talks about the past.

Answers
1 doing   2 happiness

b Students read through the examples. Point out the negative form and ask students if they are used to getting up early. In the second example, ask if the speaker finds the person's accent easy or difficult to understand now (*he/she finds it easy but they didn't in the past*).

c Students read the examples in Exercises 2a and 2b and circle the correct words in the rule.

Answer
a noun, a gerund

d Ask students to look at the picture and tell them that Irene is Spanish but at the moment she is living in London. Ask them to predict the kind of things she isn't used to because they are different from her home country, e.g. no siesta, British money, British food. Go through the example with students and

then ask them to complete the sentences with the words in the box. Students check their answers with a partner before feedback.

Answers
2 weather, sunshine   3 working, having
4 British money, going   5 speaking   6 laughing

┌─ **OPTIONAL ACTIVITY** ─────────────
Ask students to imagine in pairs they are living in another country. Students write down a series of things they are and aren't used to doing because it's different in their home country. Then each pair read their sentences to another pair, who should try and guess where they are living. In feedback ask some students to read their sentences and the whole class can guess where they are living. For example:
A: *I'm not used to the long nights. And I'm not used to wearing a spacesuit.*
B: *You're living on the moon!*

3 Grammar

be used to doing vs. *used to do*

Students covered *used to* in SB2, Unit 13.

a **Weaker classes:** Follow the procedure for stronger classes but students can just read their complete sentences to a partner.

Stronger classes: Books closed. Ask students to think back to a time when they were five years younger. Students write three sentences that contrast the past with the present. Give students an example of your own, e.g. *Five years ago, I used to walk to school, but now I drive.* Then ask students to form pairs and read the first half of their sentence to their partner, who should try and guess the second half. For example:

A: *Five years ago, I used to use the computer at school but now …*
B: *You have a computer at home.*
A: *Yes.*

Students then read through the examples with *used to* talking about habits/situations in the past that are not true any more. Point out that *be used to (doing)* talks about the present.

b Students complete the sentences using the correct from of *be used to* or *used to.* Go through the example and ask whether the speaker eats vegetables now (*no*). Check answers and make sure students are pronouncing *used to* as /juːstə/.

Answers
2 'm used to sleeping   3 's not used to speaking
4 didn't use to like   5 'm not used to walking
6 used to live   7 didn't use to wear   8 'm used to speaking

Grammar notebook
Remind students to note down the rules for *used to* and *be used to* and to write a few examples of their own.

4 **Listen**

a **Weaker classes:** Follow the procedure for stronger classes but discuss the pictures as a class.

Stronger classes: Students look at the pictures and in pairs, decide what happiness means for each person. Do the first picture as an example and give students the structure *Happiness for him/her/them is … .* Monitor and help with vocabulary.

Possible answers
Happiness is:
a playing with her baby
b lying on a beach
c eating a bar of chocolate
d flying
e walking his dog
f driving his taxi

b Students listen and number the pictures in the order that they hear them. Play the recording and ask students to check answers with a partner.

TAPESCRIPT
Joanna   Excuse me, we're doing a survey for our school magazine. Have you got a minute for us?
Man   Go right ahead, love.
Joanna   We're trying to find out about happiness. What is happiness for you?
Man   Well, when I was young, I used to think that you can get happiness by travelling to other countries. But I discovered that it doesn't matter where you live or what you do: happiness comes from inside you. You can be happy wherever you are.
Joanna   So can you give us an example of when you are really happy?
Man   Erm, let me think. Yes. When I see my dog, and he's waiting for me to take him for a walk. That's it. That's happiness.

Philip   When are you happy?
Woman   That's easy, really. We have a little boy, Benjamin. He's two. Looking after him, playing with him – being with my family and my friends, that's happiness!
Philip   That's nice. Thank you.

Joanna   Can you tell us what happiness is for you?
Woman   Umm, that's not an easy one, really. Happiness? Umm, well, for me it's the beginning of a holiday. When I'm sitting on the plane, and I'm waiting for it to take off. And then the plane takes off, and it's that moment, that feeling of freedom. That's happiness.

Philip   We're doing this survey about happiness. Can we ask you a few questions?
Man   Err, All right.
Philip   Can you tell us what happiness means for you? When are you happy?
Man   Easy. It's when I drive my taxi. I feel I'm doing an important job. So I try to do it right, because, you know, what I do is important for other people. And most of my passengers are really thankful. That's a great satisfaction, you know.

Joanna   Hi, can we ask you a question for our school magazine?
Boy   Err, yeah.
Joanna   When are you happy?
Boy   Well, when I can lie in the sun. It just rains here far too often. I'd love to live in a warm climate, you know, where you can get a nice suntan, and lie in the sun for an hour or so every day. That would be great.

Philip   What's happiness for you?
Woman   Happiness? Well, I don't know really. Erm, chocolate!
Philip   Chocolate?
Woman   Yes! I absolutely love chocolate. I'm a real chocoholic. When I get home from work, there's nothing better than putting my feet up, reading the paper, and enjoying a bar of chocolate! I eat it very slowly, bit by bit. And I feel great. I don't think I could ever give up chocolate!

Answers
1 e   2 a   3 d   4 f   5 b   6 c

c Read through the sentences with students and encourage them to guess the missing words. Play the recording again and check answers.

Answers
1 wherever   2 family, friends   3 takes, feeling
4 important   5 climate, suntan   6 bit, bit

5 Speak

In pairs students discuss the questions. In feedback ask a few pairs to share their answer with the class. For question 1, encourage students to choose a person whose idea of happiness is closest to their own. For question 2, encourage students to use *used to* when expressing their answers, e.g. *Sweets used to make me very happy but now I don't really eat them.* or *Friday nights now make me happy but I didn't use to like them.*

6 Vocabulary
Expressions with *feel*

a Ask students to read the last item in Exercise 4c again and elicit *I feel great.*

b Check difficult words in the box, e.g. *weird, feel up to doing something* (usually negative – when you don't feel capable of doing something because you don't feel well enough). Students complete the sentences with the words in the box. Point out that *feel* is often followed by an adjective.

Answers
2 strange   3 sorry for   4 up to   5 confident
6 the need   7 lonely   8 stupid

7 Grammar
Phrasal verbs

a Books closed. Ask students what you do if you need to find the meaning of a new word. Elicit *look it up in a dictionary*. Ask students what you do if you've lost something. Elicit *look for it*. Write the examples on the board:

A: *What does this word mean?*   B: *Look it up in a dictionary.*

A: *I've lost my coat.*   B: *Look for it.*

Ask students what the phrasal verb is in each sentence (*look up, look for*). Ask students if they notice a difference between the phrasal verbs (*look* and *up* are separated by *it* in the first sentence). Tell students that some phrasal verbs are separable and the object can be put between the two parts. Students open their books at page 111 and underline the two parts of each phrasal verbs in the sentences.

Answers
1 bumped into   2 broke down   3 sorted out
4 looked up

b Students compare sentences 1 and 2 with sentences 3 and 4. Elicit that the phrasal verbs in sentences 3 and 4 can be separated. Students read the rules about separable and inseparable phrasal verbs. Point out that when a verb is separable the object can come between the parts of the verb or after it, e.g. *Look up the word.* or *Look the word up.* However, emphasise

that when we use a pronoun with separable phrasal verbs the pronoun must come between the two parts of the verb, e.g. *Look it up* not **Look up it.*

Look
Point out that there is no rule that tells students if the verb is separable or not. Students need to note the information down whenever they record a phrasal verb. Read through the Look box with students and tell them that dictionaries usually tell you if a verb is separable or inseparable. Check students understand that *sb/sth* is short for *somebody/something*. Then point out that phrasal verbs with three or more parts are not separable.

> **Language note**
> A few phrasal verbs with three words are separable but not necessarily something you want to teach students at this level. For example:
> *take (somebody) up on (something)* – *I'll take you up on that offer.* (*I'll accept that offer.*)
> *let (somebody) in on (something)* – *I'll let you in on a secret.* (*I'll share a secret with you.*)

c Students put the words in order to make sentences. Go through the example and point out the alternative answer. Ask students whether *made up* is separable or inseparable (*separable*). Check answers and elicit other possibilities where relevant. Finally ask students whether each verb is separable or inseparable.

Answers
2 He takes after his father. (inseparable)
3 They can't put us up tonight. (separable)
4 I picked Italian up on holiday. (separable) or I picked up Italian on holiday.
5 How do you put up with that noise? (inseparable)

OPTIONAL ACTIVITY
Ask students to replace the object in sentences 1, 2, 4 and 5 in Exercise 7c with a pronoun.

Answers
1 You made it up.   2 He takes after him.
4 I picked it up on holiday.   5 How do you put up with it?

Grammar notebook
Remind students to note down the rules for the grammar of phrasal verbs and to write a few examples of their own.

8 Pronunciation
Stress in phrasal verbs

a 🔊 Remind students that phrasal verbs consist of a verb and one (or more) prepositions. Play the recording and ask students to circle the prepositions that are weak and underline the prepositions that are stressed.

TAPESCRIPT/ANSWERS

1 You made that story <u>up</u>.
2 Did you just make (up) that story?
3 We can work the problem <u>out</u>.
4 We can work (out) the problem.
5 Please take (off) your shoes when you arrive.
6 Take your jacket <u>off</u> and have a cup of tea.
7 I looked (up) my old friends on the Internet.
8 I looked it <u>up</u> in the dictionary.

b 🔊 Check answers and ask students to give reasons. If necessary, write the example sentence *Put away your books* on the board. Check the meaning and then ask students if the sentence can be written in any different ways (*Put your books away* or *Put them away*). Point out that these sentences have the preposition at the end of a sentence or clause. Say each sentence and ask students in which sentences *away* is stressed (*the sentences with away in final position*). Play the recording again, pausing for students to repeat each sentence.

9 Speak and listen

BACKGROUND INFORMATION

Dido /daɪdəʊ/: is a pop singer who was born in England on 21 December, 1971. Her first album *No Angel* was released in 1999 and in 2001 it became the biggest-ever-selling debut album from a British female artist. The single *Thank You* reached number 3 in the UK charts in 2001. Her second album was called *Life for Rent* (2003).

Eminem: is the recording name of the controversial rapper Marshall Mathers, who was born in Missouri, USA on 17 October 1973. His records include *The Slim Shady LP* (1999) and *The Eminem Show* (2002). He was also the main actor in the film *8 Mile* (2002) about a young rapper.

Warm up

Ask students to turn back to page 7 in Unit 1 and find what teenagers do on a bad day in Britain (watch TV). Ask students what they do on good days and bad days. Discuss interesting ideas further and write new vocabulary on the board.

a In pairs, students ask and answer questions about good days and bad days. Student A asks the questions on page 112 and Student B asks the questions on page 123. Ask a few students to tell the class about their partner's good or bad day habits.

b Read the statements and check any difficult vocabulary, e.g. *soaked*. Ask students to decide which statements are illustrated by the pictures (*5, 7 and 8*). Students decide which of the items put them in a bad mood and which items don't bother them. In feedback encourage students to rephrase the sentences

appropriately, e.g. *Making a hot drink and forgetting about it doesn't bother me.* or *Missing the bus into town puts me in a bad mood*.

c 🔊 Tell students that they are going to listen to a song that is about someone's bad day. Ask students if they recognise the singer in the picture (*Dido*). Students listen and tick the things in Exercise 9b that she mentions. Play the recording and check answers.

TAPESCRIPT
See the song on page 112 of the Student's Book.

Answers
1 2 4 5 7

d 🔊 Students read the song and guess any of the missing words. Help students with difficult vocabulary: *imply* (suggest). Play the recording for students to check and complete the rest of the song.

Answers
1 tea   2 window   3 picture   4 bills   5 bus
6 day   7 home   8 towel   9 down

Did you know ...?

Read the information in the box with students. Ask students if they know the song *Stan*. You may like to ask if a student can bring the song into class in a later lesson.

e In pairs, students discuss the questions. In feedback ask a few students to tell the class about the people in their partner's life that make them happy.

Possible answers
1 She's having a bad day for many reasons: her tea's gone cold, it's raining, she's got bills to pay, she's got a headache, she missed the bus and is late for work again.
2 Because she is in love with her partner.
3 She has his picture on her wall and he calls her at work.

10 Vocabulary
Expressions with prepositions

a Students answer the question. Give students other examples of sentences using *through and through* (see answers).

Answer
Through and through means 'completely'.
For example: My mother is Irish through and through.

b In pairs, students decide what the expressions mean. In feedback encourage students to write other example sentences using the expressions (see answers). Point out that the expressions are generally informal.

Answers
1 *up and about* means 'well enough to be able to get out of bed and move around again after a period of illness'.

2 *up and down* means 'sometimes good and sometimes bad'.

3 *on the up and up* means 'continually improving'.

4 *on and on* means 'continuing or not stopping'.

5 *in and out* means 'to be frequently staying in a particular place, e.g. a hospital or prison'.

(c) Students complete the sentences with the expressions in Exercise 10b. In feedback check students understand the sentences.

Answers
1 on and on   2 in and out   3 up and about
4 on the up and up   5 up and down

11 Write

(a) Ask students if they have any favourite poems and whether they've ever written a poem before. Ask students to complete the poem using the words in the box. Point out that the pictures illustrate different lines in the poem and will help them decide. Check answers and ask a different student to read each line of the poem.

Answers
2 Always   3 Parties   4 Perfect   5 Icy
6 Never   7 Eating   8 Staying   9 Sleeping

(b) Finally, ask students if they can think of a title for the poem. Write suggestions on the board. Ask students to write down the first letter of each word. Ask what they spell.

Answer
HAPPINESS

(c) Tell students that they are going to write a poem called *A Perfect Day* about what they think perfect day is. Point out that each line of the poem should spell the title. Help students to start the poem. For example:

*A*lways smiling
*P*rofessor's theory:
*E*njoyment not just pleasure
etc.

Encourage students to use new vocabulary they have learned in the unit. In a subsequent lesson, encourage students to read each other's poems and vote on the best.

Module 4 Check your progress

1 Grammar

(a) 2 if I was hungry   3 they would come to my party
4 where the hotel was   5 she had lived in Paris for three years   6 if he could help me   7 she had to leave at 7 o'clock   8 what my favourite film was
9 how old I was

(b) 2 apologised   3 told   4 offered   5 asked
6 explained   7 suggested   8 invited   9 refused
10 begged

(c) 2 If I'd had time, I would've finished my homework.
3 If Ben hadn't given me the money, I wouldn't have bought the motorbike.
4 If I hadn't seen the film before, I wouldn't have gone to see it.
5 If we hadn't arrived at the restaurant late, we would've got a table.
6 If I'd had enough money, I would've got a taxi.
7 If I hadn't got up late, I wouldn't have missed the bus.

(d) 2 , which started in the USA, is increasing.
3 whose car had broken down.
4 his next holiday in Florida, where he was born.

5 in a café that/which sells Italian food.
6 on holiday to Spain, where her family live.

(e) 2 the   3 an, a   4 nothing, nothing
5 nothing   6 the, the

(f) 2 didn't use to do   3 aren't used to staying up
4 used to send   5 'm used to driving   6 used to play   7 Did, use to live   8 'm used to getting

(g) 2 takes after her father   3 pick you up
4 look up to him   5 put us up   6 look after my little brother   7 Both are correct

2 Vocabulary

(a) 1 determined   2 ambitious   3 bad-tempered
4 imaginative   5 independent

(b) *Across*
4 centre parting   7 highlights   8 wrinkles
11 moustache

Down
1 double chin   2 tattoo   3 slim   5 ponytail
6 eyelashes   9 scar   10 plump

Project 1
A class survey: who we are

Divide the class into groups of three or four.

1 Prepare the survey

(a) Students read the instructions. Explain that students will ask everyone in the class the same questions so that they can produce statistics about their topic. Groups choose a topic from the box and appoint someone to take notes at this stage.

Students think of four or five questions about the topic they have chosen. Give example questions for each topic to help them start. For example:

1 Free time activities: What is your favourite free time activity?
2 Technology we have in our homes: How many televisions are there in your house?
3 Earning money: Do you have a part-time job?
4 Spending money: What percentage of your pocket money do you spend each week?

(b) Read the example questionnaires with students and point out the different ways of asking a question in each one. Ask students to adapt their questions from Exercise 1a to use a variety of question forms.

(c) Students divide the questions between them so that each member of the group has a question to ask the rest of the class. Each student asks the rest of their group his/her question and notes down their answers. Then students ask all the other students their question and note down the answers.

2 Write up the results

(a) Back in their groups, students discuss and work out the answers for the whole class to each question.

(b) Ask groups to think about how they are going to write up their results. Students covered report writing in Unit 1. Point out the bar chart that illustrates part of the results and elicit other types of charts students might know, e.g. pie charts. Remind students of the structure of a report: *Introduction, Findings, Conclusion*. Students now write short paragraphs to describe their results. Encourage students to make any drawings large so they can be seen by the whole class.

3 Present your report

Ask students to decide which students are going to present each part of the report. Encourage them to use charts and make sure students include a conclusion about their findings. Monitor and give students time to rehearse their presentations. Students present their reports to the class. At the end of each report discuss any interesting findings further.

Project 2
A group presentation

Divide the class into groups of three or four.

1 The situation

Read through the situation with the class and check difficult vocabulary: *survivor, destroyed, buildings, insects.*

2 To help you survive

Read through the list of items in the box and check students understand each of them. Explain that they need to choose six of the items that they think will be most useful on the island. Encourage students to think about why the items might or might not be useful and go through a few items with them. Monitor groups, helping with vocabulary and answering questions as necessary. Reminds students that there is no correct answer but just that some items may be more useful than others.

3 Prepare the presentation

Read the next part of the situation and check difficult vocabulary in the questions: *manage.* Ask each group to answer the questions. Students should all take notes so that they can take part in the presentation. Monitor and help with vocabulary as necessary. Remind students that their story will be published so it needs to be as interesting as possible.

4 Presentation

(a) Students divide the questions between them so that each student answers two or three questions. Encourage students to make notes about their question to help them during their presentation.

(b) Give students time to rehearse their presentation. Remind students to speak clearly and encourage them to use their notes rather than just read their answers.

(c) Ask students to present their answers. You could do this as a roleplay, with other class members acting as reporters asking the questions.

Project 3
A poster: a mystery

Divide the class into pairs. Exercise 1b could be set as a homework research task, giving students more time to research their mystery.

1 Do your research

a Look at the pictures and elicit a little information about each mystery. Students choose a mystery to research. Encourage stronger classes to think of their own ideas. Make sure the class chooses a variety of mysteries.

b If you set this exercise as a homework research task, ask students to share information with their partner about their mystery.

2 Make the poster

a Explain that students are going to make a poster that explains the history and some theories about their mystery.

b Read the instruction with students and ask them to plan the two texts about their mystery. Remind students that Unit 12 has several texts about other world mysteries that might help them. Encourage students to use modals of deduction (present and past) as appropriate in their writing. Monitor and, if there is time, encourage students to swap their texts with another pair for correction.

c Students think of a question to ask the class about their mystery. Read the examples and monitor, helping with vocabulary as necessary. Make sure students are going to ask questions whose answers can be expressed in the form of a pie chart. Each pair asks their question to other members in the class and records the answers. Encourage students to record the number of people they ask as they will need the information in Exercise 2e.

d Give students a large piece of paper to make their poster. Students read the instructions and prepare part of the poster. Tell students to leave space at the bottom of the paper to summarise the results of their class survey.

e Point out the pie chart and make sure students understand how it works. Ask students to prepare a pie chart to summarise the results of their class survey and include it at the end of their poster.

3 Presentation

Students put their posters on the wall around the classroom. Ask each pair to prepare to present their poster. Encourage them to make a few notes about each area of the poster so they do not need to read from their texts. Give time at the end of each presentation for students to ask the presenters questions about their mystery. When all pairs have presented their poster, give students time to walk around the classroom looking at each poster. Students can then vote on the most interesting poster presentation.

Project 4
Designing a website

Divide the class into groups of three or four.

1 Prepare your website

a Remind students about Barry Cadish's website about regrets. Ask them what they remember about the website (see SB page 96).

b Pre-teach *links* and ask students to find the links on the website www.famouspeopleregrets.com (*Sport, Literature, Politics, Music*). Ask students to think of famous people they might find in each link. Students read the example of William Shakespeare. Ask them what he thinks he should have done *(he should have given Romeo and Juliet a different ending so that everyone lived happily at the end)*.

c Groups think of one person in each category that they would like to include on their website.

d Groups make notes on what their famous people in Exercise 1c have achieved. Encourage them to think of ideas why people might have regretted the things they did. Point out that their ideas do not have to be serious but should be entertaining and fun to read.

2 Make your website

a Each student in the group writes a text about one of the people they have chosen. Encourage students to use structures such as *I wish / If only, should/ shouldn't have* + past participle, and the third conditional. Monitor and help as necessary.

b When students have completed their texts ask them to swap their work with other students in the group and make corrections as necessary. Ask students to make other suggestions that might make the text more interesting. Students should then rewrite their texts as necessary.

c Students find pictures to illustrate their texts. Give students a large piece of paper to put their texts and their pictures on. Ask students to think about how they want to arrange their pictures and texts to make it clear which relate to each link.

d Students put their websites on the wall and then walk around the classroom reading each other's websites. Students can vote on the funniest or most interesting regrets.

Workbook key

① Best of British

1 **a** 2 'm not doing 3 work 4 is getting
5 need 6 'm starting 7 get 8 are getting
9 use / are using 10 prefer

b 2 d Are you eating a lot of fast food these days?
3 c What kind of music do you and your friends listen to?
4 a Are you doing much sport or exercise at the moment?
5 b Do you or any of your friends ever do online gaming?
6 e Do you think people your age are spending too much money?

2 **a** 2 c 3 c 4 a 5 a

b 2 prefer 3 tend, more 4 lot, think
5 majority 6 common

3 **a** TAPESCRIPT
1 Almost half of British teenagers have cable or satellite TV at home.
2 Most teenagers prefer seeing friends to watching TV.
3 Boys tend to play sport more often than girls.
4 A lot of teenagers think that going to the cinema is better than playing sport.
5 On a 'boring day', the majority of teenagers say they watch TV or a video.
6 It is quite common for teenagers to have a part-time job.

b TAPESCRIPT
1 Most of my friends tend to listen to rap.
2 A lot of my friends prefer basketball to football.
3 It's quite common for me to send text messages to my friends.
4 More and more teenagers are starting to use the Internet at home.

4 **a** 1 for 2 since 3 for 4 since 5 since
6 for

b 2 How long has she had a car? Since January 2005. / For … years
3 How long have you supported Newcastle United? Since I was a baby. / For a long time.
4 How long have you had your watch? Since my birthday. / For … months.

c 2 c 3 c 4 a 5 a 6 c

d 2 I've already seen this film.
3 I've been doing this course since last week.
4 Joy still hasn't used her new mobile.
5 I've just told you that!
6 You've had that computer for … months/years.
7 Your friends haven't called you yet.

5 **a** 2 A, 3 C, 4 G, 5 B, 6 F Unused question: E

b 1 F 2 F 3 N 4 F 5 F 6 T

6 2 join in 3 settled in 4 fit in 5 feel left out

7 2 d 3 a 4 c 5 d 6 d 7 c 8 c
9 b 10 b

Unit check

1 2 settled 3 life 4 watching 5 immigrant
6 culture 7 for 8 felt 9 novel 10 prize

2 2 a 3 a 4 b 5 c 6 c 7 b 8 b 9 a

3 2 I haven't seen you ~~since~~ *for* a long time.
3 What kind of music ~~are you liking~~ *do you like*?
4 I ~~haven't been still~~ *still haven't been* to the London Eye.
5 How long ~~do you know~~ *have you known* your best friend?
6 I've been here ~~for~~ *since* last week.
7 How much exercise ~~you are~~ *are you* doing at the moment?
8 My mother and father ~~yet~~ haven't come back home *yet*.
9 More and more people ~~have~~ *are* getting broadband connections to the Internet.

② Ways of talking

1 **a** 2 have, known, met 3 Did, see, haven't been
4 Have, finished, took 5 Did, speak, haven't seen
6 Have, bought, got 7 did, learn, have never driven
8 haven't given, sent

b 2 did you move 3 did you see 4 did you live
5 did you start 6 have you been

c 1 know, have known, knew 2 has worked, works, worked 3 lived, lives, has lived
4 have broken, broke, break

d 3 have 4 to 5 ✓ 6 have 7 ✓
8 to 9 for 10 ✓ 11 did 12 since
13 have 14 a

e 2 Philip has already left school, has just left school.
3 We didn't have time to clean up last night, before we left.
4 Actually, I saw that film two days ago, on Sunday.
5 They've never seen snow, They've seen snow already.
6 I haven't heard from Mike since the party, for a few days.
7 We had an old black Beetle when I was little, for about ten years.

(f) 2 Jessica has had her mobile phone for a week.
3 William has just called.
4 When did you buy that bag?
5 Your friends arrived an hour ago.
6 Your birthday cards have been here since yesterday.
7 I haven't seen you since your party.

2 TAPESCRIPT
1 How <u>long</u> have you <u>had</u> it?
2 <u>When</u> did you <u>move</u>?
3 <u>What</u> <u>film</u> did you see?
4 How <u>long</u> did you <u>live</u> there? How <u>long</u> did you live <u>there</u>?
5 <u>When</u> did you start <u>working</u> there? <u>When</u> did you start working <u>there</u>?
6 How <u>long</u> have you been <u>here</u>? How <u>long</u> have you <u>been</u> here?

3 **(a)** 2 e   3 a   4 j   5 f   6 b   7 d   8 c
9 h   10 g

(b) 1 tell   2 say   3 tell   4 tell   5 telling
6 told

(c) 2 going to say sorry   3 say that again
4 telling the truth   5 say thank you
6 tell him a story   7 say goodbye
8 going to tell you off

4 **(a)** 1 c   2 e   3 a   4 d   5 b

(b) 2 How's things?   3 Anyway   4 I've got to be
5 seeing

(c) 1 a I b F
2 a I b F
3 a F b I
4 a F b I
5 a I b F

5 [no answers]

6 **(a)** 1 b   2 d   3 c   4 a

(b) 1 broken up   2 turned up   3 look us up
4 meet up

7 **(b)** Joanne answers all of Lauren's questions, but the underlined phrases are not appropriate / too formal.

(c) a 3   b 5   c 1   d 4   e 6   f 2

Unit check

1 2 arms   3 back   4 nod   5 make   6 telling
7 look   8 warm   9 eye   10 forward

2 2 c   3 b   4 c   5 a   6 c   7 a   8 c   9 c

3 2 I haven't finished reading it ~~just~~ *yet*.
3 ~~I've seen~~ *saw* that film yesterday.
4 Where ~~were~~ *have* you been?
5 He's had that computer ~~since~~ *for* ten years.
6 I ~~live~~ *have lived* here for six months – and I love it!

7 Have you ~~yet~~ had a shower *yet*?
8 The coffee shop ~~has closed~~ *closed* two hours ago.
9 I ~~never taken~~ *have never taken* photos with a digital camera.

3 ## A true friend

1 **(a)** 2 When we got to school there was …
3 While they were fighting we escaped …
4 I thought it was good while I was watching it …
5 People were crying when the film finished.
6 I knew I had done something silly when everyone started laughing.

(b) 2 came, were having   3 opened, were dancing
4 found, was cleaning   5 were waiting, started
6 was teaching, heard   7 called, were taking

(c) 2 came   3 called   4 ran   5 started   6 called   7 seemed
8 was calling   9 wasn't responding   10 was still ringing

(d) 2 Godzilla ran and sat next to the phone as soon as it started ringing. *or* As soon as the phone started ringing, Godzilla ran and sat next to it.
3 The hall light came on as she was parking her car. *or* As she was parking the car, the hall light came on.
4 The dog started barking as soon as I got to the gate. *or* As soon as I got to the gate, the dog started barking.
5 Sometimes an animal starts behaving strangely, then something happens to its owner.
6 Many animals are waiting at the door as their owners are still travelling home.

2 **(b)** TAPESCRIPT/ANSWERS
Godzilla the cat has a special relationship with her owner, David White. In the past, David often went away to work, and his parents came to the house in Oxfordshire, England, to look after the cat. When David called home, Godzilla ran and sat next to the phone as soon as it started ringing, his parents said. 'When other people called, the cat wasn't interested. But somehow she seemed to know that David was calling.' David is convinced he has a special bond with his cat. The calls were always at different times of the day, and Godzilla wasn't responding to David's voice because she got to the phone while it was still ringing.

3 **(a)** 1 b   2 c   3 d   4 a

(b) 1 closed, realised, had left   2 had, had met
3 didn't know, had said, cried   4 got, had started
5 didn't work, had forgotten   6 saw, had, finished

(c) 3 had   4 been   5 ✓   6 have   7 having
8 being   9 ✓   10 did   11 were

4 **(a)** 2 d   3 f   4 e   5 b   6 a

(b) 1 c   2 e   3 a   4 f   5 b   Unused phrase: d

5 **(a)** 2 b   3 a   4 b   5 c   6 a   7 b

b 1 T 2 F 3 F 4 F 5 N 6 T

6 **a** C

b TAPESCRIPT/ANSWERS
Speaker 1 = opinion E
When I was a child, my parents moved around a lot, so I went to quite a few different schools. Consequently, I had to make friends again every year in a new place. It sounds bad, but actually I didn't really have a problem with it. It was always hard to say goodbye to your best friend, as I did a number of times, but when you realise you'll always make more friends it's not so bad.

Speaker 2 = opinion B
I didn't like my best friend at all the first time I met her. I thought she was really unfriendly, and a bit superior. It was only after I met her again that I realised I'd been too quick to judge her. It's funny, but I'm like that with other things, too. I can hate a song the first time I hear it, but then after a while I really love it. I think sometimes you shouldn't judge a person on the first meeting, because there are all kinds of reasons that they might not appear as they really are.

Speaker 3 = opinion A
I hardly ever see my best friend, in fact, because we live in different countries. We don't even call or email each other that often, but it doesn't matter. He'll always be my best friend because we've been through so much together. I know that, if I ever have a serious problem in my life, he'll be there for me, and I hope he thinks the same about me. Of course, it's good to have friends you see every day, so you can share everything, but it doesn't have to be like that.

Speaker 4 = opinion D
I suppose I'm not the kind of person who needs to have a 'best' friend. I mean, I've got a lot of people I call 'friends', but no one person that's more special than anyone else. I think if you have a group of people you can do things with, then that's fine. Everyone makes changes in their lives, people go different ways, and if you just have your 'best' friend – well, then what happens (when/if) you lose him or her?

Speaker 5 = opinion F
I can't imagine life without my best friend. We grew up together, and we've always stood by each other when things weren't so good. Of course, we've had our problems – I remember we once fell out for a couple of weeks for some stupid reason, probably to do with some boy we both fancied – but I think it's normal to argue with a friend. Everybody needs one person who has shared everything in your life, you know, who knows everything about you.

Unit check

1 2 had 3 While 4 stood 5 letting 6 get 7 loyalty
8 out 9 friends 10 up

2 2 c 3 b 4 c 5 a 6 a 7 b 8 b 9 b

3 2 My brother and I ~~wasn't~~ *weren't* going out until you called.
3 I hadn't ~~meet~~ *met* your friend before last night. He's very nice.
4 We were so late that the show ~~already started~~ *had already started.*
5 We got here ~~as soon~~ *as soon as* we could.
6 I realised that I ~~left~~ *had left* my money at home.
7 ~~Were~~ *Had* you already been here before last year?
8 It was sunny and the birds were ~~sung~~ *singing.*
9 I hurt my leg while I ~~had played~~ *was playing* football.

4 A working life

1 **a** 2 been doing 3 started 4 seen 5 had
6 been doing 7 been snowing

b 2 painted 3 called 4 gone 5 been taking
6 been painting 7 been calling 8 taken

c 1 eaten 2 have you been waiting 3 have you been doing 4 's gone 5 Have you finished
6 haven't been sleeping

d 2 have you had 3 have you been doing
4 have you been saving 5 have you known
6 have you been downloading

2 **a** b shouldn't c ought not d should
e better f ought g better

b 2 b 3 f 4 e 5 d 6 a 7 c

3 **b** TAPESCRIPT/ANSWERS
born, fourteen, awards, recorded, fall, ought, talk, all, forms, forty, four, orders

4 **a** *Across*
1 qualifications 3 salary 4 trainee
8 experience 9 part-time 11 employer
Down
2 full-time 5 employee 6 unemployed
8 resign 10 apply

b 2 applied 3 employer 4 employees
5 salary

c 2 unemployed 3 resign 4 trainee 5 part-time

5 **a** 1 b 2 f 3 e 4 c 5 a **Unused sentence:** d

b 2 surprised 3 songs 4 in the middle
5 were expensive 6 didn't like very much
7 children's

TAPESCRIPT

Interviewer So, first of all, how was the show?

Abby Brilliant. I didn't think it was going to be so good, but it was probably one of the best live concerts I've seen.

Interviewer Who did you enjoy watching the most?

Abby Well, Westlife are always great, and of course it was a local show for them, being in Dublin. But actually the best performance was Girls Aloud. I was surprised how good they were. Their dance routines are getting much better since *Pop Idol*, and they've got some good songs. I really like *Mars Attack* and *Boogie Down Love*.

Interviewer And how was the quality of the sound in the theatre?

Abby Oh, fantastic. We weren't near the front, but we were right in the middle, so we got great sound.

Interviewer What about the cost of the tickets? Didn't you find it a little expensive?

Abby Yeah, €35 is a lot for me, actually. But there were quite a lot of bands on, so I suppose it was value for money, although I didn't like Luke Thomas very much. Sorry, Luke! And they did give a lot of money away to charity – they made €250,000, I think they said, for Childline, which is a children's charity. So you don't mind paying a bit more when it's for a good cause.

6 (**a**) 1 ten 2 ticket 3 £20 or £30 4 clear
5 fourteen 6 two or three 7 three hours

TAPESCRIPT

A few days ago I went to a really good concert at the M.E.N. in Manchester. There were ten different singers and bands, would you believe! They gave some of the ticket money to a charity for the disabled, which was great. It was quite expensive, though – some tickets were £30, but I paid twenty because I wasn't near the front. It didn't start very well, because the sound wasn't very clear, but it got better. The light show was great! I felt pretty old there, though. I mean, I'm only 16, but the average age of the crowd was probably about 14. There was only time for most bands to do two or three songs, and sometimes it got a bit boring waiting for them to change over. The big stars were Blue, and they came on last. The whole concert was about three hours long. Not bad, eh? And my favourite act? Craig David – he was fab. He's a brilliant singer, and his dancing was pretty cool. Some of the singers I didn't like very much, but all in all it was really good.

(**b**) 1 d 2 b 3 a 4 c

Unit check

1 2 should 3 for 4 qualifications 5 work / working
6 trainee 7 part-time 8 experience
9 employee 10 been

2 2 c 3 c 4 a 5 b 6 a 7 c 8 b 9 a

---

3 2 Our TV ~~hasn't working~~ *hasn't been working* very well recently.
3 Hi, Mum! Can you believe I've ~~been lost~~ *lost* my keys again?
4 Do you think I ~~had sell~~ *had better sell* my computer?
5 My friends ~~hasn't~~ *haven't* been emailing me. I wonder what's wrong?
6 At last! We've been ~~tried~~ *trying* to reach you all morning.
7 You're not well. You ~~ought take~~ *ought to take* some time off.
8 Have you ~~cried~~ *been crying*? Your make-up looks funny.
9 You ~~should better~~ *had better* not tell anyone – it's a secret.

5 Travel

1 (**a**) 2 're going to play 3 'm going to sneeze
4 's going to be sick 5 're going to play football
6 's going to do his homework
7 's going to crash 8 're going to break it

(**b**) 2 's having a meeting with Jake
3 's driving back to Manchester
4 's playing squash with Andy
5 Thursday morning he's flying to Madrid
6 Thursday evening he's having dinner with Carlos and Conchita
7 Friday afternoon he's going back to Manchester
8 Friday evening he's taking Julie to the cinema

(**c**) 2 Will, get 3 won't rain 4 won't find
5 won't have 6 will like 7 won't like
8 will find

(**d**) 2 A 3 P 4 A 5 P 6 I

(**e**) 2 We're visiting my grandparents on Saturday.
3 My dad won't give me money to buy a new computer.
4 I'm seeing the doctor tomorrow morning.
5 Planes will fly from London to Australia in ten hours in the future.
6 My friend Mike is going to leave school next year.

2 (**a**) TAPESCRIPT/ANSWERS
1 They're ⟨going to⟩ have a party.
2 They want me to go, but I'm not going to.
3 My dad's ⟨going to⟩ be really angry!
4 Are you ⟨going to⟩ watch the match tonight?
5 I don't want to watch it. Are you going to ?
6 We're ⟨going to⟩ have a test tomorrow.

3 (**a**) 1 cruise 2 timetable 3 boarding card
4 customs 5 baggage 6 platform
7 flight 8 departure lounge

(**b**) 1 in 2 at 3 in 4 on 5 at 6 at
7 to 8 off

4 (**a**) 1 D 2 E 5 F 6 C 7 B Unused summary: 4

(b) 1 c   2 b   3 d   4 a   5 b

5 1 takes off   2 go back   3 headed for
4 touched down

6 **(a)** A 6   B 3   C 5   D 1   E 2   F 4

(b) 1 N   2 F   3 T   4 N   5 T   6 F

Unit check

1 2 got into   3 took off   4 solo   5 flight
6 touched down   7 customs   8 won   9 hero
10 welcome

2 2 c   3 b   4 c   5 a   6 c   7 a   8 a   9 b

3 2 I'll ~~to do~~ *do* my homework tonight.
3 I ~~seeing~~ *'m going to see* the doctor tomorrow morning.
4 I think it's ~~going snow~~ *going to snow* this afternoon.
5 My parents and I ~~am~~ *are* going to fly to Paris tomorrow.
6 The traffic's very bad – we ~~not will~~ *won't* arrive on time.
7 What are you ~~go~~ *going* to study at university?
8 What time ~~do~~ *are* you leaving tomorrow morning?
9 We ~~having~~ *are having* a party on Friday – do you want
to come?

6 Live forever!

1 **(a)** 2 'm likely to   3 're likely to   4 isn't likely to
5 'm not likely to   6 're likely to

(b) 2 My parents will be unhappy with my results.
3 My brother is likely to arrive late tomorrow.
4 The match on Saturday won't be very good.
5 I might go to the cinema this evening.
6 I'm likely to pass next week's test.
7 They aren't likely to be at home tomorrow.
8 There probably won't be much to eat at the party.
9 We might not visit our grandparents next
weekend.

(c) 2 I might pass the exams.
3 He might not arrive on time.
4 I'll probably be late.
5 My mother isn't likely to lend me any money.
6 My sister probably won't buy that car.
7 They are likely to be at the party.

2 **(a)** 2 phones, will ask   3 won't open, push   4 leave,
will be   5 isn't careful, will hurt   6 won't come,
don't want   7 stop, will get   8 won't bite, leave

(b) 2 If John invites me to the party, I will go.
3 I will beat Sally unless I play badly.
4 I will be very upset if he loses my camera.
5 Unless you go now, the shops will be closed.
6 If my friend comes round, we will play computer
games.

3 **(a)** 1 as soon as   2 until   3 when   4 unless
5 as soon as   6 until   7 When   8 If

(b) 1 as soon as   2 Unless   3 until   4 if   5 until
6 unless   7 as soon as   8 If

4 **(a)** 1 earning   2 arguing   3 worrying   4 revising
5 thinking   6 getting

(b) 1 getting ready for school
2 earning money for yourself
3 thinking about what to wear
4 revising for exams
5 worrying about your problems
6 arguing with people

(c) 1 about   2 about   3 for   4 for   5 with
6 for

5 [no answers]

6 **(a)** 1 the fact is   2 between you and me
3 I know what you mean   4 believe it or not

(b) 1 between you and me   2 believe it or not
3 the fact is   4 I know what you mean

7 [no answers]

8 **(a)** why you are suitable for the post
your level of English
what you will gain from working with children
what you will gain from working in the UK

(b) André does not mention the level of his English.

(c) 1 If I get one of the jobs, …
2 … they are likely to improve …
3 … will learn …
4 Thank you for considering …

Unit check

1 2 If   3 might   4 probably   5 for   6 until
7 with   8 about   9 likely   10 unless

2 2 c   3 a   4 a   5 c   6 b   7 c   8 b   9 c

3 2 He's ~~likely be~~ *likely to be* late.
3 The teacher ~~not might~~ *might not* like it.
4 I'll tell you the results ~~as soon~~ *as soon as* I know them.
5 I'll tell them when they ~~will arrive~~ *arrive*.
6 He ~~not will be~~ *won't be* happy when he finds out.
7 The test is ~~likely to not~~ *not likely to* be very difficult.
8 I've got to stay here ~~unless~~ *until* five o'clock tonight.
9 Unless they ~~don't invite~~ *invite* me to the party, I won't go.

7 Campaigning for survival

1 **a** 2 d 3 a 4 d 5 b 6 a

b 2 A language called Hindi is spoken in many parts of India.
3 The 2004 Olympic Games were held in Athens.
4 Boeing 747 planes are called Jumbos.
5 Most American films are made in Hollywood.
6 The 2002 football World Cup was won by Brazil.
7 John Lennon was killed in December 1980.
8 The *Titanic* was sunk by an iceberg.
9 Gorillas are found in forests in Africa.
10 Buildings are designed by architects.

2 **a** 2 You can have your photos developed.
3 You can have your ears pierced.
4 You can have your computer repaired.
5 You can have your eyes tested.
6 You can have your clothes dry-cleaned.

b 2 They're having their photograph taken.
3 He's having his car repaired.
4 She's having a garage built.
5 He's having his hair cut.
6 They are having a computer delivered.

3 **a** TAPESCRIPT/ANSWERS
1 She's <u>having</u> her eyes <u>tested</u>.
2 They're <u>having</u> their <u>photograph</u> taken.
3 He's <u>having</u> his car re<u>paired</u>.
4 She's <u>having</u> a <u>garage</u> <u>built</u>.
5 He's <u>having</u> his hair cut.
6 They're <u>having</u> a <u>computer</u> de<u>livered</u>.

4 **a** 1 good 2 fun 3 effort 4 best 5 progress
6 money 7 sense 8 mess

b 2 did 3 doesn't make 4 makes 5 did
6 make 7 have made 8 make

5 **a** 1 has been built 2 have been sold
3 have been killed 4 have been made
5 haven't been invited 6 has been made

b 1 The woman has been robbed.
2 Three houses have been knocked down.
3 Their pizzas have not been delivered yet.
4 The bank robbers have been caught.
5 That car has not been cleaned for weeks.
6 The fire has been put out.

6 **a** 2 will be protected 3 will not be increased
4 will be given 5 will be put 6 will not be closed 7 will be helped 8 will be reduced

b 1 will be built 2 won't be finished
3 Will, be heated 4 will be supervised
5 won't be allowed 6 Will, be given

7 **a** Bowen is talking to Inspector Eliot. 5 sets of fingerprints were found.

b 1 b 2 d 3 d 4 a 5 d 6 b 7 a

c 1 She was a cleaning lady.
2 Forley saw Catherine Crowther.
3 In a drawer in his desk.
4 The Wilvers and Mrs Brook.

d Students' own answers

8 1 b 2 b 3 c 4 a 5 c

TAPESCRIPT
1 OK everyone – listen please! Listen! Now, from now on you're free to look around the town, do some shopping, have tea – whatever you want. OK? But please be back here – here! – at a quarter past eight, all right? Eight fifteen. That's because the bus will leave here at exactly half past – we won't wait for anyone who's late. So if you're here at eight fifteen, then you'll be safe because there'll be fifteen minutes before we leave. Got that? OK – off you go, and have fun!

2 Well, Sally, let's look at your maths results from this term. Erm … OK, you got 58%. Well, that's not too bad, I suppose – and let's remember that last term you only got – what was it? – oh yes, 47%, so you've made some progress. But really this still isn't quite good enough, is it? I mean, 58% is OK, but with a bit more hard work and concentration you could do better than that, I'm sure. So you need to do something about it, OK?

3 Mike Hey Andy – how are you doing?
Andy OK thanks, Mike.
Mike Hang on – there's something different about you. What is it?
Andy Maybe it's this!
Mike Oh yeah – wow, that's neat! When did you have it done?
Andy Yesterday. I've always wanted to have an earring – and now I've got one!
Mike Did it hurt at all?
Andy Nah – you don't feel anything at all, you know? Piercing's no problem at all.

4 Good evening, and here is tonight's news. The number of casualties in the earthquake that hit southern Russia this morning has grown – it is now believed that approximately four thousand people have been killed, but rescue workers say that this number is likely to increase as the rubble is removed from buildings that have been destroyed. Many of the people killed were office workers …

5 Woman Hello? Is that Home Pizza?
Man Yes madam – can I help you?
Woman Yes – I'd like to have a pizza delivered, please. Ham and mushroom, family size.
Man Certainly, madam. What's the address, please?
Woman 18 Hampton Gardens.
Man OK. That'll be £6.25.
Woman Do I have to pay for delivery?
Man No, madam. And in fact, if your pizza isn't delivered in the next 30 minutes, you won't have to pay anything.
Woman Great – thanks, goodbye.

Unit check

1 2 taken 3 was 4 developed 5 made 6 made
7 have 8 effort 9 had 10 were

2 2 a 3 a 4 b 5 a 6 c 7 b 8 a 9 b

3 2 I'm going to the hairdresser's to ~~cut my hair~~ *have my hair cut*.
3 Pandas ~~found~~ *are found* in the forests in China.
4 I took my car to the garage and had ~~repaired it~~ *it repaired*.
5 You can't buy this car because it's ~~be~~ *been* sold already.
6 I took my film to a shop and ~~developed it~~ *had it developed*.
7 Three cars ~~was~~ *were* stolen in our street last night.
8 The new pool won't ~~build~~ *be built* until next year.
9 Yesterday, two criminals ~~have been~~ *were* arrested.

(8) Reality TV

1 **a** 2 The travellers weren't allowed to enter the country.
3 Our parents never let us play outside.
4 The teacher didn't let us leave early.
5 They made us switch off our mobile phones.
6 The children were made to do a test.

b 2 You aren't allowed to walk on the grass.
3 You are allowed to cycle.
4 You aren't allowed to use your mobile phone.
5 You are allowed to use the computer for 30 minutes. *or* You aren't allowed to use the computer for more than 30 minutes.
6 You are allowed to take photos, but you aren't allowed to use flash.

c 2 The teacher made us stay longer at school yesterday.
3 I don't let my sister borrow my things.
4 My father didn't let me borrow his car.
5 You aren't allowed to smoke here.
6 We were made to tidy our rooms last Saturday.

2 **a** 1 [→] series 1 [↓] sitcoms 2 contestant 3 episode
4 presenter 5 audience 6 figures 7 quiz
8 viewer 9 celebrities

b 2 contestants 3 presenter 4 allowed 5 viewers
6 winner 7 successful

3 TAPESCRIPT/ANSWERS
1 how (✓)
2 know
3 now (✓)
4 mouse (✓)
5 loud (✓)
6 shout (✓)
7 slow
8 house (✓)
9 found (✓)
10 snow

4 **a** 1 must bring 2 can stay 3 have to go 4 don't have to stay 5 mustn't go 6 can't bring

b 2 mustn't 3 can / 're allowed to 4 must / have to
5 should/must 6 don't have to

5 **a** 2 boiling 3 fantastic 4 freezing 5 enormous
6 starving 7 exhausted

b 2 really/very, really/absolutely
3 really/very, really/absolutely
4 really/very, really/absolutely
5 really/very, really/absolutely
6 really/very

6 1 on TV 2 on time 3 on the phone 4 on strike
5 on holiday 6 on offer

7 **a** 3 he 4 the 5 did 6 (✓) 7 the 8 can
9 with 10 (✓) 11 not

b 1 F 2 N 3 F 4 T 5 T 6 N

c 1 c 2 d 3 e 4 a 5 b 6 f

TAPESCRIPT

Dave There's a song called *Somebody's Watching Me*, by a guy called Rockwell. It's kind of old, but really good – and the video is really weird!

Paul So – what happens?

Dave Well, it starts off with Rockwell – he's a black guy, right, from the States – and he picks up a newspaper but it's all written in oriental writing, Japanese or something.

Paul Uh huh.

Dave And then you get a scene of inside his kitchen – it's, like, an ordinary kitchen, but there's this big black bird, a raven or something, flying around inside it.

Paul Ugh.

Dave Right! I told you it was weird! Anyway, so the next thing you see is Rockwell in the shower – only he's wearing shorts, so I guess he thinks someone's watching him.

Paul Like the title of the song?

Dave Yeah. So – oh, what happens next? Erm ... oh yeah, then he goes into his living room and he switches on the TV – and he can see himself on the TV! So he thinks that this is much too strange, and he gets scared and runs outside – but his garden has become a graveyard at night, he's looking at all these tombstones and things!

Paul Then what does he do?

Dave Well, I can't remember everything, but I do remember he hears a bell ring, and someone shouts 'Mailman' so he goes out to look at his mailbox .. and ..

Paul And?

Dave Nah, I'd better not tell you – you'll have to find the video and watch it for yourself!

Paul Oh Dave – come on, I'm not a baby ...

d 1 e 2 a 3 f

8 **a** [no answers]

b 1 on the market   2 a good reason   3 been going
4 very believable   5 no matter

Unit check

1 2 contestants   3 made   4 had   5 freezing   6 presenter
7 enormous   8 allowed   9 winner   10 fun

2 2 a   3 b   4 c   5 a   6 c   7 c   8 b   9 c

3 2 You ~~isn't~~ *aren't* allowed to come in without asking.
3 We wanted to go out, but our parents didn't ~~make~~ *let* us.
4 Sorry, madam – you can't ~~to park~~ *park* your car here.
5 The teacher let us ~~to leave~~ *leave* early yesterday.
6 I was made ~~wear~~ *to wear* a uniform.
7 I'm not deaf – you ~~have to~~ *don't have to* shout!
8 This is a no-smoking area – you ~~can~~ *can't* smoke in here.
9 We're late – we ~~mustn't~~ *must* hurry up!

9 Good and evil

1 **a** Verbs with gerund: enjoy, detest, mind, imagine, suggest, feel like, practise
Verbs with infinitive: promise, ask, offer, afford, learn, hope, choose

b 2 to be   3 having   4 making   5 to give   6 living
7 to build

c 2 playing   3 to fight   4 to help   5 to help
6 writing   7 to kill   8 reading

d 2 I hope to see you again soon.   3 My teacher asked to see me after the lesson.   4 He detests being called Timothy.   5 I can't imagine him getting angry.
6 You'll have to learn to be more patient.

e 2 feel like going   3 afford to buy   4 miss living
5 promised to give   6 to practise driving
7 mind getting up   8 decided to study

2 **a** preparation, imagination
preference, difference
enjoyment, agreement, entertainment
kindness
protection, reaction
popularity, possibility

b 2 enjoy   3 protection   4 imagination   5 agree
6 entertainment

3 **a** TAPESCRIPT/ANSWERS
1 pre<u>pare</u>   prepa<u>ra</u>tion
2 <u>pre</u>fer   <u>pre</u>ference
3 en<u>joy</u>   en<u>joy</u>ment
4 <u>la</u>zy   <u>la</u>ziness
5 pro<u>tect</u>   pro<u>tec</u>tion
6 <u>pop</u>ular   popu<u>la</u>rity

4 **a** 1 b   2 d   3 c   4 a

---

b 2 e   3 d   4 a   5 b

c 2 meeting
3 to drive, driving
4 eating
5 to buy
6 to go, going
7 to tell
8 to work, working

5 1 F   2 F   3 T   4 T   5 T

6 1 hanging out with   2 look up to   3 felt left out by
4 hooked up with

7 **a** TAPESCRIPT/ANSWERS
Critic   The human race has always been extremely interested in the dark side of life and the monsters that live there. This is a healthy thing because without evil there is, of course, no such thing as good. But what worries me is how our perception of these monsters and of evil has changed.
Presenter   And how has it changed?
Critic   Well, first we need to have a look at some of the classic monsters from the past and in my opinion the golden age of the monster was in the late 19th century and early part of the 20th century.
Presenter   The age of Frankenstein, Dr Jekyll and Mr Hyde, Jack the Ripper …
Critic   Exactly. Now what was so interesting about these monsters is that there was a reason for their existence. They were symbols of what could happen if we did wrong. Frankenstein's monster and Mr Hyde, for example, were the products of men trying to play God. There was a message there for us.
Presenter   So what's gone wrong?
Critic   Well modern monsters have no motivation. They're just very two dimensional.
Presenter   For example.
Critic   Well let's look at some of the most popular cinematic monsters of the last 20 years, Freddie from *Nightmare on Elm Street*, Jason from *Friday 13th* and Michael Myers from Halloween. What we basically have are three killing machines. Now, of course, there are stories about how they became such blood-thirsty monsters but no-one really remembers any of the reasons. What audiences
are interested in is how many people will die and how violent their deaths will be.
Presenter   So you're saying there's no message.
Critic   Exactly. We don't learn anything from all this violence. All it does is make us scared to go to sleep at night.

b 1 of life   2 as good   3 19th century, 20th century
4 play God   5 Modern monsters   6 killing machines
7 people will die   8 sleep at night

Unit check

1   2 hooked   3 left   4 shy   5 hang   6 getting
     7 vandalism   8 doing   9 to do   10 popularity

2   2 b   3 b   4 c   5 a   6 a   7 a   8 a   9 c

3   2 He asked ~~to me go~~ *me to go* to the party.
     3 I stopped ~~to work~~ *working* as a teacher last year.
     4 She's decided ~~studying~~ *to study* German in Berlin for
       a year.
     5 Did you remember ~~saying~~ *to say* 'Happy Birthday' or
       did you forget?
     6 I promise ~~tell~~ *to tell* you as soon as I know.
     7 I want to learn ~~playing~~ *to play* the guitar.
     8 We can't afford ~~going~~ *to go* on holiday this year.
     9 I suggest ~~to leave~~ *leaving* an hour earlier.

10 Getting into trouble

1   **(a)**   1 f   2 c   3 a   4 e   5 d   6 b

     (b)   3 took   4 wouldn't be   5 asked   6 would say   7 gave
          8 would spend   9 told   10 would want   11 kept
          12 would feel

     (c)   2 Imagine you saw two men fighting in the street.
          3 Suppose you forgot to revise for a really important
             test.
          4 Say you found 500 Euros in the cinema.
          5 What if you borrowed your friend's stereo and you
             broke it?

     (d)   (possible answers)
          2 I would call the police on my mobile.
          3 I would fail the test.
          4 I would tell somebody about it.
          5 I would say sorry and offer to have it repaired.

2   **(a)**   2 burglary   3 joyriding   4 pick-pocketing
          5 arson   6 shoplifting

     (b)   1 caught   2 into, crime   3 wrong, law

     (c)   (possible answers)
          2 Steve should do community service and be put
             on probation.
          3 Helen should pay a fine and be sent to prison.

3   **(a)**   2 could   3 had   4 didn't   5 wasn't   6 loved
          7 didn't   8 knew

     (b)   (possible answers)
          2 He wishes his parents understood him.
          3 If only his little brother didn't annoy him all the
             time.
          4 He wishes his computer wasn't broken.
          5 If only he had enough money to buy a new bike.
          6 He wishes he could find his house keys.
          7 If only he wasn't too shy to talk to girls.

(c)   (possible answers)
     2 If only I was free.   3 I wish I didn't work here.
     4 If only I had a car.   5 I wish I could play football.
     6 If only I spoke Chinese.   7 I wish I was a rock star.
     8 If only I could go skiing.   9 I wish I was a bit taller.

4   TAPESCRIPT
     1 I <u>wish</u> I was somewhere else.
     2 If <u>only</u> he loved me.
     3 I <u>wish</u> I didn't have so many problems.
     4 If <u>only</u> I could go to the party.
     5 I <u>wish</u> it was Saturday.
     6 If <u>only</u> she understood.

5   **(a)**   2 and besides   3 that's a good point
          4 you never know

     (b)   1 the way I see it   2 You never know   3 and besides
          4 That's a good point

6   2 turn   3 broke   4 slow

7   [no answers]

8   **(a)**   2 A   3 C   4 B

     (b)   1 A   2 D   3 B   4 C

Unit check

1   2 down   3 imagine   4 could   5 would   6 away
     7 can   8 caught   9 into   10 put

2   2 a   3 a   4 b   5 c   6 a   7 c   8 a   9 c

3   2 If I lived by the sea, I~~ll~~ *'d* go surfing every day.
     3 He wishes he ~~is~~ *was* taller.
     4 If she ~~is~~ *was* an animal, she'd be a horse.
     5 What would you ~~do, if~~ *do if* you failed your exams?
     6 If only ~~I'm not~~ *I wasn't* so tired.
     7 If I ~~did meet~~ *met* Tom Cruise, I'd ask him for an autograph.
     8 She wishes she ~~works~~ *worked* for a different boss.
     9 I wouldn't do it if you ~~pay~~ *paid* me.

11 Two sides to every story

1   **(a)**   2 bought   3 don't feel like   4 didn't go
          5 feel like   6 didn't buy

     (b)   2 Although   3 even though   4 Although
          5 in spite of

     (c)   2 We could understand him, in spite of his strong
             accent.
          3 Although I didn't feel very hungry, I ate two pieces
             of cake.
          4 The main course was delicious. However, the
             dessert was a bit disappointing.
          5 Despite not being very tall, he plays basketball very
             well.

2 TAPESCRIPT
1 Nobody knows except Joe.
2 Don't drive so slowly in the snow.
3 Even though she didn't go, I enjoyed the show.
4 Although she won't tell me, I already know.

3 **(a)** 2 over 3 up 4 away 5 over 6 up 7 on
8 back 9 out

(b) 2 come up with 3 think it over 4 make up my
mind 5 sleep on 6 talk it over 7 go away
8 come back 9 sort it out

4 **(a)** 2 f 3 b 4 a 5 c 6 e

(b) 2 She can't be happy. 3 They might not speak
English. 4 You must like olives! 5 They might
know. 6 He can't live near here.

(c) 1 might 2 might 3 can't 4 might 5 can't
6 must

(d) (possible answers)
2 must be tired 3 can't be very good 4 must be
boring / can't be very exciting 5 must be famous
6 must be lonely / can't have any friends

5 **(a)** Harry found a whistle and he blew it.

(b) 1 B 2 C 3 C 4 C Unused phrase: A

6 1 C 2 E 3 G 4 D 5 F 6 B

Unit check

1 2 Although 3 result 4 Moreover 5 go away
6 coming back 7 came up 8 official 9 minds
10 ignored

2 2 a 3 b 4 b 5 b 6 b 7 a 8 a 9 a

3 2 I don't believe you. That ~~can't to be~~ *can't be* true.
3 I've been working all day. ~~Although~~ *However*, I don't
feel tired.
4 I passed the exam, despite ~~I didn't study~~ *not studying*
for it.
5 She ~~must~~ *can't* be his wife. He's not married.
6 He still loves her, ~~however~~ *although / even though* she's
horrible to him.
7 It's snowing. It's ~~might~~ *must* be cold outside.
8 In spite of ~~knowing not~~ *not knowing* any of the songs,
I enjoyed the show.
9 She's ~~not~~ *is* a very good artist although she's never had
any lessons.

(12) Mysterious places

1 **(a)** 1 he is 2 is he 3 they're 4 are they 5 he's
6 is he 7 we're 8 are we

(b) 2 where they are 3 why they are all laughing
4 why she is so angry 5 how old she is
6 where they are from

(c) 2 ? 3 ? 4 ? 5 [.] 6 [.] 7 ? 8 ?

(d) 2 do they live 3 the film starts 4 does the film
start 5 she spoke to 6 did she speak to
7 it is to London 8 is it to London

(e) 2 Do I need a visa?
3 Do you know where they went?
4 Where did they go?
5 Do you happen to know if she left a message?
6 Did she leave a message?
7 Do you know when they will be back?
8 When will they be back?

2 **(a)** 2 lost 3 didn't phone 4 haven't 5 angry
6 don't eat

(b) 2 could have been 3 might be 4 could have built
5 don't believe 6 can't have built 7 must weigh
8 must have been

(c) 2 can't have left 3 might have run 4 can't have
finished 5 must have been 6 might have seen

(d) (possible answers)
2 have won the lottery 3 have been joking
4 have had a number 1 hit 5 have missed her bus
6 have loved her much 7 have forgotten to ask
anybody 8 have been driving too fast

3 TAPESCRIPT/ANSWERS
1 They must have been disappointed.
2 She can't have left already.
3 I could have helped you.
4 She might have gone home.
5 We must have forgotten to tell him.
6 She couldn't have seen us.

4 **(a)** 2 d 3 f 4 b 5 e 6 a

(b) 2 tied in 3 called off 4 passed away 5 went out

5 **(a)** 1 went 2 where 3 to 4 Although 5 most
6 in 7 all 8 has 9 enough

(b) 2 Q 3 SH 4 B 5 B 6 Q

TAPESCRIPT
Speaker 1: The Smash Hits T4 Poll Winners Party is
not the most serious of music award ceremonies
but it is certainly one of the noisiest. Up to 11,000
screaming fans attend the party to see their
favourite pop artists receive their awards. The
awards, which are voted for by fans, include most
attractive male and female artists and best
haircut.
Speaker 2: The Mercury Music Prize is considered
one of the most serious awards in the record
industry. Twelve judges nominate twelve 'best
albums of the year.' On the night of the ceremony,
they make their final choice and announce the
winner. The prize is often controversial because
the judges prefer originality over success or
popularity.

Speaker 3: The Q awards are well respected, particularly in the independent music industry. Some of the awards are chosen by readers of the magazine and viewers of QTV. Other awards are chosen by judges. The most important award is 'The best act in the world' and past winners have included Oasis, Coldplay and Radiohead.

Speaker 4: The Brits are perhaps the most famous of all the award ceremonies. They are considered the Oscars of the British music industry. Of the fifteen different categories, four are voted for by the public. These include 'best pop act', 'best British video', 'best British single' and 'best British newcomer'.

6 1 off 2 against 3 on 4 about 5 up

7 **(b)** 1 was falling 2 saw 3 was shivering 4 had been killed 5 screamed 6 was shaking 7 had saved 8 had gone 9 walking

Unit check

1 2 between 3 most 4 might 5 neither 6 must 7 message 8 we are 9 wonder 10 have

2 2 c 3 a 4 c 5 c 6 a 7 a 8 b 9 b

3 2 Can you tell me when ~~is~~ the next train to Liverpool *is*?
3 I can't find it anywhere. She ~~can't~~ *must* have taken it with her.
4 They might ~~had~~ *have* been speaking Polish.
5 Nobody's sure what ~~did really happened~~ *really happened*.
6 I don't understand why ~~would he~~ *he would* say a thing like that.
7 She had six children and no husband. Life ~~must~~ *can't* have been easy for her.
8 I don't know what ~~can we~~ *we can* do.
9 Do you happen to know when ~~will he~~ *he will* get home?

⑬ Love

1 **(a)** 2 I'll go to the cinema with you on Saturday.
3 I have to get up early in the morning to catch the train.
4 There's been an earthquake in China.
5 I'm sorry I can't get home earlier.
6 I'm going to France in the morning.
7 I have to leave before eight o'clock.
8 I can't type very fast.

(b) 2 said Tony was 3 said he had not stolen
4 explained that he couldn't go 5 told us she had not learned anything 6 he was going to marry Cathy
7 said he didn't want to 8 would give me

2 **(a)** 2 Jane asked if we would get to the concert on time.
3 Carol asked me if I could install the game for her.
4 My little sister asked why she couldn't stay up longer.

5 The driver wanted to know where the hospital was.
6 He asked me if I had been to Canada.

(b) 2 don't think 3 Why's that 4 it was awful
5 was brilliant 6 doesn't mean 7 I'll go

(c) 2 hadn't 3 didn't 4 wanted 5 had seen
6 had said it was 7 found 8 had seen
9 had been 10 knew 11 didn't mean
12 was probably 13 would go

3 **(a)** 2 Donna 3 Jenny 4 Kevin 5 Robert 6 Jenny

(b) (possible answers)
1 slim 2 wavy, double 3 ponytail, tattoo 4 bushy, cropped, moustache, wrinkles

4 2 c 3 d 4 b 5 a 6 a

5 **(a)** 2 wanted 3 said 4 would 5 offered
6 suggested 7 said 8 weren't 9 told
10 might 11 asked 12 said 13 was
14 apologised 15 refused

(b) 2 Pete begged me to lend him my DVD player.
3 Cathy apologised to her dad for forgetting his birthday.
4 My mother agreed to make pizza for supper.
5 She explained that she was late because of the traffic.
6 She refused to do it.
7 Tom persuaded Alan to watch the football match with him.
8 Lucy suggested playing tennis.

6 **(a)** 1 similarities 2 difference 3 paid 4 reception
5 traditional 6 dancing 7 happiness

(b) 1 F 2 F 3 T 4 T 5 F 6 F 7 T

7 **(a)** TAPESCRIPT
1 What's your favourite colour?
2 How are you enjoying the meal?
3 When will you be back?
4 Do you often watch TV?

(b) TAPESCRIPT
1 He asked me what my favourite colour was.
2 We asked them how they were enjoying the meal.
3 He asked her when she'd be back.
4 They asked me if I often watched TV.

8 1 going out 2 married, divorced, getting back
3 falling in love 4 engaged, married

9 1 a 2 b 3 c 4 b 5 c

Unit check

1 2 hair 3 ponytail 4 cropped 5 ambitious
6 bad-tempered 7 sympathetic 8 determined
9 fit 10 tattoo

2 2 a 3 b 4 c 5 a 6 c 7 a 8 c 9 a

3 2 It seems Cathy is ~~falling love~~ *falling in love* with Nick.
3 Is it true that your sister and her husband have broken ~~down~~ *up*?
4 Nick persuaded me ~~coming~~ *to come* to his party.
5 Jane told Martin ~~going~~ *to go* out.
6 I asked her ~~come~~ *to come* to my party.
7 She asked me what ~~was~~ my favourite food *was*.
8 I promised that I would ~~be not~~ *not be* late again.
9 She said that she ~~not had~~ *had not* stolen the money.

14 Anger

1 **a** 1 d 2 c 3 a 4 b

b 2 would, have said, had shown 3 would have saved, had gone 4 wouldn't have bought, hadn't given 5 had passed, would have driven 6 would have heard, hadn't shouted 7 hadn't run after, wouldn't have fallen 8 would, have phoned, hadn't been

c 1 c 2 g 3 f 4 d 5 a 6 e 7 b
(suggested answer)
If Daniel hadn't gone to the concert, he wouldn't have stood next to Annie in the queue. If he hadn't stood next to her, he wouldn't have started talking to her. If he hadn't spoken to her at the concert, they wouldn't have gone dancing together. If they hadn't gone dancing together, they wouldn't have fallen in love. If they hadn't fallen in love, they wouldn't have got married.

2 2 I wish I hadn't broken the vase.
3 If only I hadn't kicked the ball.
4 I wish I hadn't played with my pen.
5 If only I hadn't driven so fast.
6 I wish I hadn't bought a sports car.

3 **a** 2 a 3 b 4 f 5 c 6 e

b 2 She should have taken a jumper with her.
3 He shouldn't have taken the risk.
4 They should have bought something earlier.
5 They should have called the police.
6 He should have worn better shoes.

4 **b** TAPESCRIPT/ANSWERS
2 I (shouldn't have) listened to her.
3 I gave it back to her, but I shouldn't have.
4 We (should have) bought it.
5 They didn't tell us, but they should have.
6 You (should have) written to me.

5 2 c 3 d 4 d 5 d 6 d 7 b 8 a 9 a

6 1 the thing is 2 What I mean is 3 There's something I want to say 4 in that case

7 2 by 3 person 4 missed 5 had 6 about 7 which/that 8 to 9 them

8 **a** The situation was embarrassing because they thought the TV was broken when in fact they had not switched it on.

Unit check

1 2 temper 3 regretting 4 hot-headed 5 difficult 6 keep 7 furious/cross 8 cross/furious 9 tantrum 10 work

2 2 c 3 b 4 b 5 c 6 c 7 a 8 a 9 c

3 2 If they had asked me, I would *not* have ~~not~~ told them.
3 If only I ~~known~~ *had known* about the problem before!
4 I'm tired. I wish I hadn't ~~work~~ *worked* so much.
5 We ~~should told~~ *should have told* her before she phoned.
6 We should have left before it ~~gets~~ *got* dark.
7 I wish she had ~~be~~ *been* here, then we could have discussed it.
8 They had a big argument and fell ~~up~~ *out*.
9 Please don't worry, I'm sure we can work something ~~in~~ *out*.

15 Fear

1 **a** 2 who is still very popular
3 whose name I have forgotten
4 where her family have a restaurant
5 which was why I couldn't go to school
6 which I read five times
7 which is not far from San Francisco
8 which I know I wrote down

b 2 who 3 which 4 whose 5 where 6 who 7 who 8 where

c 2 I love scuba diving in the Indian Ocean, where you can still find a lot of attractive fish.
3 Next month Stephanie will move to London, where her partner has a flat.
   Next month Stephanie, whose partner has a flat in London, will move there.
4 Alex, whose sister studies with me, is getting married next year.
5 Barbara, who works as a secretary for Jo & Co, has won the lottery.
6 My new computer, which I got for a very good price, is fantastic.

2 **a** 3 ✓ 4 ✓ 5 I live in Green Street, where there are two new cinemas. 6 Thank you for your email, which I read last night. 7 My dad works in *Tops* restaurant, which is famous for its seafood. 8 ✓

b TAPESCRIPT/ANSWERS
1 Paris, which is visited by millions of tourists every year, is famous for its art.
2 That's the place that I was talking about.
3 Let's meet at the shop where your dad works.
4 Is that the girl who wrote you a love letter?
5 I live in Green Street, where there are two new cinemas.

6 Thank you for your email, which I read last night.

7 My dad works in *Tops* restaurant, which is famous for its seafood.

8 He is the man whose daughter won in the lottery.

3 2 impatient 3 informal 4 logical 5 impolite
6 unhelpful 7 inexpensive 8 regular 9 impossible

4 (**a**) 2 the 3 a 4 – 5 the 6 the 7 – 8 –

(**b**) 3 ✓ 4 ✓ 5 ✓ 6 the 7 ✓ 8 ✓ 9 ✓ 10 a

5 1 sit out 2 sit through 3 sitting for 4 sits back

6 (**a**) 1 a 2 d 3 d 4 b 5 a 6 c 7 d 8 a

(**b**) 1 Jacky
2 a She was killed in a street in Italy.
2 b To have an adventure and start a new life in a foreign country
3 A tile fell off a roof and hit her on the head.
4 He was 27.

7 2 happy ending
3 can laugh about it
4 they know it's a film
5 they teach them about good and evil
6 learns how to deal with his own fears
7 dangerous for very young children

TAPESCRIPT

Interviewer Dr Smith, as a psychologist, why would you say people love frightening stories?

Dr Smith Well, there are various answers. One is that frightening stories can be entertaining. We love telling stories, and if you have a story to tell that is somehow frightening then other people are usually very interested in it. Now, most of these stories have a happy ending. So the listener feels some of the fear that the story teller felt in the situation but in the end the listener is happy because the story ends positively. Often there is also comic relief – we can laugh about how the story ends.

Interviewer Can frightening stories harm people?

Dr Smith I don't really think so, as long as the person who reads or listens to the story is a healthy adult person. When you and I watch a horror film, for example, we know it's a film, even when we watch the most horrible scenes. You might be scared during some of the scenes, or even have a bad dream afterwards, but that's it. You know it was a story and you watched it for entertainment, nothing more.

Interviewer How about young children? Could frightening stories have a negative effect on their development?

Dr Smith Well, many fairy tales are frightening. They are full of evil people, and witches and ghosts. But these fairy tales are important for children. They teach them that the world is about good and evil, and that the evil is part of our lives. A child who listens to such stories also learns how to deal with his own fears. Horror films are a different story. Some of them are certainly dangerous for very young children. We believe that …

Unit check

1 2 who 3 sat out 4 which 5 impolite 6 leave
7 illegal 8 seems

2 2 b 3 c 4 c 5 a 6 b 7 c 8 a 9 a

3 2 She is in ~~Paris where~~ *Paris, where* she is studying Medicine.
3 Shall we have a look on ~~Internet~~ *the Internet*?
4 His father is ~~policeman~~ *a policeman*.
5 I love animals, especially ~~the dogs~~ *dogs*.
6 He sat ~~through~~ *back* to watch the film.
7 Can you see that man ~~which~~ *who* is trying to cross the street?
8 Colin Campbell, ~~that~~ *who* wrote *The Lady in White*, is a very good writer.
9 The Queen sat ~~out~~ *for* nine hours while the artist painted her picture.

16 Happiness

1 2 a 3 e 4 d 5 f 6 c
Pictures: a2, b4, c5, d1, e6

2 (**a**) 2 used to laugh 3 used to speak 4 Did, use to wear
5 used to play 6 didn't use to eat

(**b**) 1 speak 2 getting 3 drinking 4 care 5 live
6 run 7 living 8 be, buying

3 2 d 3 c 4 a 5 c 6 a 7 c 8 a 9 d

4 (**a**) 2 bumped into 3 sorted, out 4 takes after
5 put up with 6 make, up 7 break down
8 call, up

(**b**) 2 He ran away from her.
3 We get on well with each other. / We get on with each other well.
4 We look forward to our holidays.
5 We can put him up for the night.

5 (**a**) TAPESCRIPT/ANSWERS
2 a Pick your coat up.
2 b She picked (up) her pen.
3 a I've given (up) sweets.
3 b I've given them up.
4 a The plane took off.
4 b He took (off) his shoes.

6 (**a**) 2 a 3 b 4 c 5 e

(**b**) 1 be up and about 2 go on and on
3 're on the up and up 4 in and out 5 up and down

7 (**a**) 3 age 4 did 5 been 6 the (DJ)
7 ✓ 8 ✓ 9 was 10 ✓ 11 could 12 ✓
13 ✓ 14 a 15 ✓ 16 Dido's 17 she

(**b**) 1 T 2 F 3 T 4 F

(**c**) 1 C 2 A 3 A 4 A

TAPESCRIPT

Carolyn Hey, Kevin, have you seen the video for *Thank You*?

Kevin You mean Dido's? Sure.

Carolyn Yeah, it's great, but …

Kevin What do you mean 'but'? I thought you were a Dido fan, Carolyn.

Carolyn Hang on a minute, I am. But you know what, I checked out this website recently where they talk about mistakes in videos, and I found something that someone posted on mistakes in the *Thank You* video.

Kevin Really? What are they?

Carolyn Well, I haven't checked it out, but they say that there is this hairdryer in the bathroom, and Dido takes it and goes into the kitchen with it, right?

Kevin Yeah, I remember that.

Carolyn Well, and she puts it somewhere in the background. As the video continues, the hairdryer disappears and then later appears again.

Kevin Oh, really?

Carolyn Yes, and they also claim that towards the end of the video she takes this umbrella, which is white, and in the next scene it's black!

Kevin I can't believe it. Let's check it out immediately.

Carolyn Yeah, OK!

8 **(a)** 1 f   2 a   3 e   4 c   5 b   **Unused statement:** d

Unit check

1 2 used to   3 strange   4 sorry   5 puts up with
6 look up to   7 takes after   8 going on and on
9 stupid   10 feel

2 2 b   3 c   4 b   5 b   6 a   7 b   8 c   9 b

3 2 He had no friends and so he felt very ~~lone~~ *lonely*.
3 We used to ~~going~~ *go* to discos a lot, but now we're too old!
4 I'm not used to ~~be eating~~ *eating* so much.
5 I ~~picked~~ *picked up* a bit of Spanish when I lived in Madrid.
6 There's no way I'm going to ~~put with this up~~ *put up with this*!
7 I really take ~~from~~ *after* my father, we look almost the same.
8 I think she ~~up made~~ *made up* that story.
9 She didn't feel ~~need~~ *the need* to explain what she was doing.

Acknowledgements

The publishers are grateful to Pentacor**big** for: text design and layouts

Annie Cornford: Workbook key